The Secret Artist

THE SECRET ARTIST

A Close Reading of Sigmund Freud

LESLEY CHAMBERLAIN

SEVEN STORIES PRESS

New York / London / Toronto / Sydney

Copyright © 2000 by Lesley Chamberlain

First North American edition published September 2001.
First published by Quartet Books (U.K.) in 2000.

Seven Stories Press
140 Watts Street
New York, NY 10013
www.sevenstories.com

In Canada:
Hushion House, 36 Northline Road, Toronto, Ontario M4B 3E2

In Australia: Tower Books, 9/19 Rodborough Road, Frenchs Forest NSW 2086

Library of Congress Cataloging-in-Publication Data

Chamberlain, Lesley.
    The secret artist : a close reading of Sigmund Freud / Lesley
Chamberlain.—A Seven Stories Press 1st ed.
        p. cm.
    Includes bibliographical references and index.
    ISBN 1-58322-260-X
        1. Freud, Sigmund, 1856–1939. 2. Psychoanalysts—Austria—Biography.
3. Psychoanalysis—History. 4. Psychoanalysis and art. I. Title.

BF109.F74 C37 2001
150.19'52'092—dc21
[B]

                                                          2001041070

9 8 7 6 5 4 3 2 1

College professors may order examination copies of Seven Stories Press titles for
a free six-month trial period. To order, visit www.sevenstories.com/textbook, or
fax on school letterhead to (212) 226-1411.

Phototypeset by FiSH Books, London

Printed in the U.S.A.

In order to raise an accusation against the whole nature of the world, you dismal philosophical blindworms speak of the *terrible character* of human passions. As if wherever there have been passions there had also been terribleness! As if this kind of terribleness was bound to persist in the world!—Through a neglect of the *small* facts, through lack of self-observation and observation of those who are to be brought up, it is you yourselves who first allowed the passions to develop into such monsters that you are overcome by fear at the word "passion"! It was up to you, and is up to us, to *take from* the passions their terrible character and thus prevent their becoming devastating torrents.—One should not inflate one's oversights into eternal fatalities; let us rather work honestly together on the task of transforming the passions of mankind one and all into joys.

> —Nietzsche, "The Wanderer and His Shadow" from
> *Human All Too Human* (tr. Hollingdale)

...the great and enigmatic man...in whose being one has the sense of powerful and driving passions which nevertheless express themselves in such a curiously muted way.

> —Freud, "A Childhood Memory of Leonardo da Vinci"

Acknowledgements

Professional thanks are due once again to the Society of Authors, who provided a grant from the Authors' Foundation to help me complete this book. Thanks also go to my friends Ian, Maxine, and Chip for their unwavering support, my editor Jeremy Beale, but above all my daughter and my husband for their indulgence.

Contents

The Secret Artist

Introduction

Freud is often hailed as a writer by his admirers outside psycho-analysis, and many see it as opening up new ground when he is also read creatively within that profession. But in what way is he "a writer"? These days everyone is a writer. I wonder here to what extent he is an *artist*. By "artist" I mean not just the common claim that Freud is a *good* writer. Art demands a different order of talent, one which is creative and transformative, and brings with it a vision of possible imaginative structures which the artist also goes some way towards realizing. Stylishness is only an adjunct to this more fundamental business. I argue that Freud is fundamentally an artist, but that the artistic expression of his desires and fears is repressed.[1]

Since the argument will only be complete when we have re-examined Freud's writing and his life, however, I first invite the reader to imagine, and to keep reimagining, Freud's achievement as if it had taken the form of three novels. The first two putative novels, to which I shall give the banal and already used titles *Vienna 1900* and *Love Story*, reflect Freud's recurring psychological and social interests. Family relationships, the making of the personality, the growth of the capacity for love, the desire to be successful in the world, and everything which can upset these processes and ambitions; had we read novels on such matters by a talented Viennese turn-of-the-last-century writer called Freud, we would surely remember them with affection. Then there is a third novel, with a quite different title – something like *Look What I Can Do!*, which seems to come from a much more modern and subjective world. This brilliant, idiosyncratic work we would probably more admire than love.

Why imagine these novels? The answer is this. Had Freud left us these works of literature, we would find it easier to respond immediately to the question of what kind of artist he was, and to what degree of achievement he rose. The as-if-he-had-written-it-as-a-series-of-novels strategy pictures the potential truth of the argument that follows.[2]

There is literary evidence for Freud's artistry which is not difficult to find. The richness of Freud's imagination is particularly apparent in two kinds of instances. These are when he interprets dreams, and when he writes up his famous case-studies: "The Ratman," "The Wolfman," "Dora" and "Senator Schreber." Freud had a unique and pioneering gift which allowed him to construct a fantastically meaningful semblance of reality out of word-games. He also had a classical talent for characterization and narrative. But where does his other clinical, theoretical and technical writing fit in? I would suggest that overall the content of Freud's writing is based on imaginative sympathy with the human condition, together with a capacity to create character on the page, and generate action. But clearly what Freud also has is the ability to sustain a vision which gives a human life meaning. And so I also claim Freud's actual theory for art, and treat the "scientific" form of his arguments as part of the content of his imaginative vision.

Let me then repeat the question. Is Freud an artist? To the purely literary evidence in favor of that judgement I shall then want to add two other kinds of related, less pure evidence.

The first is autobiographical and involves threading our way backwards and forwards between the writing and the life, in a way many almost up-to-date literary critics would dislike. The greatest moment in Freud's career as an artist came with his self-analysis around the age of forty, which prompted him to write his disguised psychic autobiography in *The Interpretation of Dreams*. Freud comes into sharp psychological focus as an artist, and sharp artistic focus as a craftsman, whenever we consider how he reworked his own experience into the created object he wanted to present to the public.

The second body of evidence for Freud's being a kind of artist is also personal to Freud, but approaches the question negatively, necessitating a psychoanalytical questioning of Freud himself. A vexing facet of his psychology is why he offered to the world such a degraded view of art and artists as we find in the essay "The Artist and Creative Imagination" and *The Introductory Lectures on Psychoanalysis* of 1916–7. This view not only conflates the aims and achievements of art and artists, but also tends to belittle them as no more than profitable forms of egoism.

If Freud himself was an artist, why did he judge "the artist" so negatively? Because he was hostile to the repressed artist in himself? Threatened by the example of those who dared to go openly where he did not? Whatever the untestability of such speculations, it is here that we enter the territory of "the secret artist" by applying original psychoanalytic theory to Freud himself. We can use the theory as a tool, while simultaneously bearing in mind that Freud invented it to make sense of all that he discovered during his self-analysis, and that therefore the theory is also an autobiographical statement about the kind of content he attributed to his inner life. Both theory and content centre on the tension between hidden/revealed.

An example is the way Freud understands repression. When a wish is unacceptable to us, it gets confined to our unconscious, where it continues to affect our daily lives and beliefs and behavior by a process we are at pains not to become aware of. Thus we deny it, and in a sense lie to ourselves, but with good reason, according to Freud's system. Freud's whole edifice is built upon the impossibility of perfect self-knowledge. From the theory of repression we are led to the idea that our consciousness is full of falsehoods.

I suggest that one of the "lies" Freud told himself was that he was a scientist, not an artist, and, further, that the two spheres were quite distinct. He didn't know it was a lie, because the drive behind the assertion was unconscious. From the evidence of his writing and his life I construct the following psychological situation. Freud associated the practice of art with pleasure, and also with abandoning the need for self-control. These apparently undisciplined areas of the spirit frightened him and so he repressed them in his own intense case.[3]

Repressed desires come out in disguise. But in what disguise did Freud's repressed artistic self-expression emerge into consciousness? Negatively distorted it surfaced as a neurotic distrust of artists. I call this laughable complex "pen envy." But Freud's talent was also positively disguised as the "science" of psychoanalysis.[4]

Of course there is a problem with this argument, because it has a missing centre, namely Freud's own, ultimately impenetrable psyche, which is like a dark tunnel into which we can only see by the light of Freud's own tools. But I repeat my point that the tools are a clue to at least what he thought was there, and part of the evidence. The rest we infer from Freud's life and a close reading of his work as literature.

I want to gloss the "secret" in my title, which I imagine should be *verborgen* in German. *Der verborgene Dichter.* Freud is a *secret* artist, because the desire to fulfill his artistic talent was unconscious as much to him as it has remained to his various publics; and because the ways of the unconscious are secret in the sense of hidden.[5]

To see Freud as a secret artist seems to me so much more useful than following the negative fashion of debunking him as a scientist, on which I mainly comment in my notes. It not only sets into an absorbent context the question of his "lies," but also leaves us free to appreciate what Freud's imagination did by way of humanizing the twentieth century. The truth of art is quite different from the truth which Freud's scientific critics have in mind, and in the context of art it makes no sense to demand the proof of Freud's truth claims. Either we know or suspect them from our experience of life, or we do not. As for the artist himself, he may be a realist or a fantasist, or a mixture of the two.[6]

1

BEGINNINGS

What Freud wanted and already expected as a young man was success, and his early letters and autobiographical writings radiate the confidence and ambition and talent that would make it possible; but also the complexity that would not make it easy. At seventeen he wrote to his friend Fluß:

My "concerns about the future" you take too lightly. A person who only worries about being mediocre is already secure, you say to comfort me. Secure from what, I have to ask; not secure after all and reassured that he isn't? What difference does it make, whether you are afraid of something or not? Isn't the main thing whether what we fear is true? Certainly it's true that stronger spirits are also plagued with self-doubt; does that mean that everyone who doubts his merits is a strong spirit? He may be an intellectual weakling, but a decent man, out of upbringing, habit or self-torment. I won't ask of you that, when you find yourself in a position of doubt, you analyze your feelings unmercifully, but if you do it, then you will see how little about yourself you can be sure of. The splendor of the world surely rests on this multiplicity of possibilities, only unfortunately it is no firm foundation for our self-knowledge.

The young Freud, already with a remarkable gift for expressing himself with style and originality, was driven by two problems which occupied the heart of his mature work: self-knowledge and success.[1]

How an individual can be fulfilled, by finding his place in the real world, concerned Freud throughout his life. It shaped his whole philosophy, theory and practice, of psychoanalysis. Self-knowledge, given a special depth through psychoanalytical insight into childhood, was the goal. It was the purpose of the exercise, even if the essential foundation for self-knowledge remained defective. The contents of the unconscious could never after all be entirely grasped, for every manifestation was "overdetermined," that is, legitimately subject to multiple interpretation. But, considering Freud as a writer, we should notice that, whereas the goal of self-knowledge could have had many philosophical precedents from Plato on, Freud's psychoanalytical process built most evidently on the *dramatic* precedent in Aristotle's theory of tragedy. Aristotle thought that, through a mimetic sequence enacted before his eyes and ears, the viewer of a Greek tragedy might reach the heights of emotional involvement but then, at the command of the dramatist, leave the theatre purged of all strong emotion, ready to resume his place in society as a more balanced and useful character.

Freud liked to use the un-German verb *agieren*, from the Latin *agere*, which translated the Greek *drama*, for that central process in psychoanalysis whereby the patient acted out desires and attitudes towards the analyst which had long been buried in the unconscious. In fact in the practice of psychoanalysis it would be immensely problematic to replace a tragedy on stage with the person of the analyst. But the derivation of the central process of psychoanalysis from an Ancient Greek aesthetic model remained for Freud the route to self-knowledge. The process was essentially dramatic and it essentially involved the artistically inspired suspension of disbelief along the way to self-improvement. It appealed to the man I shall call the "deep" Freud by giving him a vehicle for his compassion, and it made the main thrust of his project therapeutic.[2]

But there were several other Freuds, with different qualities, who invite a different characterization of the work. Indeed, to suspect otherwise would be simple-minded, as those severe critics who accuse Freud of fraud seem to be. That they expect a self-proclaimed man of science to be any more monolinear than a man of letters, or indeed any more "moral" in a sense they can obviously understand, is hardly worth an answer. What can be said rather is that Freud was a complex man, whose various and contradictory aspects became woven into the substance of his work, leading to the very puzzle over classification that we face today. He possessed a great deal of self-knowledge, and was no stranger therefore to self-recrimination, and both *these* drives went into the work, with the implicit question mark: isn't it like this for all of us? Isn't there almost a compulsion to deceive ourselves? Here already the problem of that missing firm foundation for self-knowledge is given a slightly different turn.[3]

Freud's eventually successful life brought compromises, the kind of compromises and paranoiac self-protective behavior in which his *ad hominem* critics have reveled in recent years. But Freud was always highly critical of his own ambitiousness, which must count as an important aspect of his character. At one point in the predominantly autobiographical *The Interpretation of Dreams*, for instance, having described a friend's desire that the sick man blocking his professional path would soon die, he observes:

Naturally I had a similar wish a few years earlier to take up a post that had become free, and I felt it far more keenly; wherever there is a hierarchy in the world and the chance of advancement there is scope for the suppression of unadmirable wishes. Shakespeare's Prince Hal cannot resist the temptation even at his sick father's bedside of trying on the crown.[4]

The tough, worldly aspect to Freud, which involved covering his nastier tracks where he could, and keeping his eye firmly on his goal, was a very important part of his makeup. Furthermore, because soul-healing was his daily business, Freud could seem quite offhand about his patients' suffering. But this is not to set up a hard and fast contrast with the positive aspect of Freud's compassion and with his philosophical seriousness. For, firstly, the "deep" tradition of self-knowledge might turn out to be just what could stop a man or woman being successful in the world. Surely it was realistic to identify success with wealth, professional esteem, and the kind of love which includes full sexual happiness. Our happiness *does* hinge on these goals.[5]

The difficulty for Freud the medical practitioner was in getting patients to see this rather simple social reality, after they had been hindered for so long by so many private fears and culturally manufactured ideals. Dare to be superficial! might have been his message. But to the degree that patients were ill they had difficulty deriving any satisfaction from socially given reality, while to the degree that they failed to become reconciled with their real circumstances they fell ill. These were Freud's *deep* concerns as a therapist. The burden of socialized Western man *circa* 1900 was what Freud wanted to alleviate, if only to a small degree. He wanted to bring more superficiality into the world.

The first hindrance to his own success that Freud came up against while still a child was his Jewishness. When a soothsayer prophesied that the clever twelve-year-old boy, his mother's "golden Sigi," might become a government minister, it was pointed out that this would be an all the more exceptional achievement for a Jew. The young Freud had meanwhile already intuited the added difficulty he would face in the world when he witnessed loutish Gentiles knocking his father's hat off in the street, and his father doing nothing about it. By the time he got to university, aged seventeen, the extent of Jewish discomfort in the late-nineteenth-century European empires was quite clear to him.

The university, which I entered in 1873, immediately brought me some keen disappointments. Above all I had the sense that I was supposed to regard myself as inferior and not a fully-fledged member of society [*nicht volkszugehörig*] because I was a Jew.[6]

This expressly autobiographical passage goes on to say that Freud rejected the first aspect of his damnation and didn't care too much about the second. Rather he turned it to his advantage, learning early on what independence of mind was, and how to stand in opposition, having been excommunicated from the "compact majority." But standing in opposition, being an outsider, always affects human character. Ridding himself of the stigma of his Jewishness involved Freud in many psychological contortions, filled his dreams, and added an edge of resentment and extra keenness to his desire for success.

As he matured Freud had broad interests and was in no hurry to narrow them. He prolonged his studies to seven years and several times changed direction in medicine. Overwhelmed by his own intellectual potential he had to remind himself to sharpen his focus with a quote from Goethe's *Faust*, to the effect that each of us has a very specific talent at which to excel. Later he would reproach himself for casting the net of his reading passions too wide, for a professional man really ought to concentrate on his own field. But when Freud finally opted to concentrate on nervous diseases, among the subjects he was happy to leave behind, he said, was philosophy.

Here is a real parting of the ways to be examined, even given the fact that philosophy was not so far removed from psychology in Freud's day. Freud claimed in retrospect that he disliked "systems," and his very constitution made an affiliation with philosophy impossible. But at the beginning of his most productive and innovative writing, he had contradicted this view in a letter to his friend Wilhelm Flieβ. There he suggested that, reaching the age of forty, he realized he had merely gone the long way round to achieve what he wanted in and from philosophy.[7]

The psychological background to this rejection was that Freud was as fond of repudiations as Nietzsche, who also liked to throw out statements about what he was and was not. In the case of both writers, they seemed to want to remind us of the uncertain name of their projects. But in Freud's case there was also a distinct element of self-deception.[8]

11

That Freud practiced philosophy by another name emerges early in his career, when he learns about the new and uncertain treatment of hysteria by hypnosis and is fired to think about the intricate workings of the unconscious.

The year was 1885, and Freud, aged twenty-nine, already lecturer in neuropathology at the Vienna Physiological Institute, arrived in Paris on a grant to study with Jean-Martin Charcot. Charcot believed that the physical symptoms manifested in cases of hysteria had ideogenic causes, which is to say they were truly "in the mind." This view, disputed now, was a vital influence on psychoanalysis, because what Charcot went on to show was that symptoms caused by ideas could also be temporarily cured by ideas. Freud saw demonstrations before his own eyes.[9]

In John Huston's wonderfully humane and intense film of Freud's early career, Charcot performs miracles which inspire Freud and herald his greater work to come. In an almost religious atmosphere, the relationship between the two men is shaped to recall John the Baptist and Jesus Christ. Charcot's dramatic demonstrations of an ideogenic cure probably didn't convey themselves to Freud as miracles, but they must have reminded him once again of the Greek tragic stage, and how real human passions can be invoked by artificial means, and then dispatched to curative effect.[10]

Freud had reservations about hypnosis, because he felt the mentally distressed patient should not be asleep, but be actively involved in the cure. A follower of Socrates in this respect, who had no interest in short cuts to self-understanding and self-healing, Freud also considered that the cure should last, whereas the hypnotic cure was only effective while the patient remained asleep.

Still Freud agreed with Charcot that there seemed to be invisible causes of certain physical afflictions and the words Charcot used when his audiences protested against what they found distasteful: "*La théorie c'est bon, mais ça n'empêche pas d'exister!*" impressed him for the rest of his life. He took away from Paris a view of "the genuineness and legitimacy of hysterical phenomena," and out of that new feeling for the invisible causes of physical afflictions the concept of the Freudian unconscious was born.[11]

Some interesting philosophy helps to explain the nature of the system which Freud gradually built up to treat the problem of hysteria. For a year in Vienna, some years before he took up the scholarship to France, Freud had been a student of the philosopher and psychologist Franz Brentano. Brentano, whose main interests lay in classifying the foundations of empirical knowledge, once did an experiment on our sense of the intensity of our perceptions. He managed to reverse the assumption that of two sources of light the one nearer to us will always seem stronger.[12] In another experiment using light and the spectrum, Brentano also observed that there are plainly things in the world which we know, but don't know we know. Take for instance our apprehension of mauve light, in which we do not appreciate the presence of blue and red until we are told. In fact this was where Brentano, as an empiricist and a materialist, began to run up against problems in accounting for all knowledge empirically, just as Hume did before him, and this problem area would be thoroughly interesting to Freud.[13]

Freud heard Charcot introduce the nineteenth-century soul doctor's problem of processes which exist in the human makeup but which the medical profession didn't want to know. The offense to cultural authority and the dignity of man was too great. Charcot's work invited Freud to confront things-all-too-human which we don't know we know; things we don't dare to know, because culture doesn't allow us to know. No wonder the basis for self-knowledge is uncertain, Freud might have concluded, because we don't even admit the existence of a primary unconscious, let alone the substance of the murky truths it contains. Brentano moreover had shown by experiment how our understanding is susceptible to such gaps.

When he comes to characterize the unconscious, Freud surely draws on his own experience of the contemporary medical establishment to suggest that the unconscious is a place which stores all the unacceptable things about human nature which a hypocritical society refuses to acknowledge and therefore transforms into reasons for individual guilt and shame. This is the social origin of the unconscious. But Freud also adds in two important elements from philosophy. First, the unconscious is where the kind of psychic forces reside which, because we can feel or see their impact on behavior, we know exist, even though this can't be shown. We can't know those forces in themselves, because, unlike red and blue, they can't be isolated from the composite which gives them their half-hidden expression. Secondly, the unconscious is a place, or a mechanism, for storing *intensity* as a cause of action.[14]

How to characterize the notional "place" where intensity is stored for future expression is such an important question in Freud that it is rarely asked. But here another theory of Brentano's, his famous "intentional inexistence," recommends itself. Revived from the medieval mystics, this notion represents an enquiry into the shadows in the mind. It follows the dispositions we have to believe in objects, states of affairs and so on and how these exist without necessary reference to objects and states of affairs in the real world.

> The intentional in the Scholastics . . . means a certain mode of existence, the characteristic irreal kind of being attributed to likenesses . . . the goals of an intention to do something as opposed to the being of real objects.[15]

I don't think there can be a better description of the status of the Freudian unconscious than Brentano's intentional inexistence. Just because it is a notion originally used in medieval mysticism does not mean Freud's unconscious is necessarily a mystical concept. It tries to capture a world of mental shadows which directly determines a person's perception of reality; a world of shadows whose (in)existence as intention is best captured in terms of stored force. What Freud wants to say psychologically is that there is a pattern of energy in us that wants to get free. He will go on to explain that this force will hitch a lift with any idea, socially appropriate or inappropriate, to come into being or realize its intention. Proust said something very similar in *In Search of Lost Time* about the kind of promiscuous jockeying beneath our consciousness which seems to be the prelude to certain thoughts coming to the surface and not others, so that the whole world of expression, as opposed to essence, looks accidental. One has the impression that both Freud and Proust derived something from Darwin here, and applied the large pattern of competition in nature to how they imagined competition in the unconscious to work.[16]

Freud transforms Brentano's philosophy of intentional inexistence however by making it serve a potentially therapeutic use. In order to know where the hidden intensity comes from which often spoils our lives, we can work back from the way we consciously perceive reality. What is the intentional or shadow element built in there? Where does it come from? How can we get rid of it? Freud suggests that if the process of the unconscious wish reaching expression is relatively unhindered by moral and sexual inhibitions, the intensity will flow, and the result will be, more or less, a healthy person; but the opposite will also be the case. So we must look at the taboos we create for ourselves and those which society forces upon us. Hysteria and other mental troubles for Freud partly reflect a hypocritical society exerting too much pressure on its members to behave unnaturally. But only in part, for there are dispositions to mental disease, and accidental factors, all of which play their part.

Freud's unconscious thus helps explain the human burden in terms of a mixture of mentalistic and social factors, some of which can be ameliorated, some of which can't. Combined with a purely philosophical argument about whether and how the intensity of our past impressions is stored in some part of our mind, and how those impressions can become reactivated, is a theory of social criticism, and also a therapeutic concern. The mixture of elements contributing to Freud's notion of the unconscious finally raises the question which psychoanalysis wants to answer: how to treat the casualties of social circumstance whose psychological problems the philosophy of intensity sheds light upon.

All of this helps to define what Freud was becoming. In the very way he created and defined the unconscious he was at once a philosopher, a social critic of the kind he became more and more obviously in later life, and finally a therapist chiefly focused on making his patients happier. The role, or even the proximity, of art at this point is very obscure. But it will come into focus as soon as Freud begins to work on the words and pictures through which the stored intensity in the unconscious comes to light.

Freud was a brilliant, idiosyncratic pupil of Brentano and Charcot, who used their insights to attack his root problem of how to tackle the uncertainty of self-knowledge. He came up with a theory of the tension or intensity which constantly builds up in the human body and psyche, married to a fascination with the various types of association between words and sensations, concepts and memories, which make the release of intensity possible. His thinking brought about a revolution in the way that post-Freud we are moved to consider any *intense* feelings we have in daily life and work, and wonder where they come from. Not all Freud's accounts of the unconscious origins of strong feelings are convincing; his intermediate reasoning often seems more apt than his final reasons; but what he gives us, uniquely, is a theory of intensity, coupled with a theory of meaning.

He is a deep thinker. Yet what I have just said might equally well emerge as the substance of a volume with an imaginary post-modern title: *Intensity: A Victim's Guide.* For what is success? Marriage, family, social popularity, the right job? In the abstract it is, for Freud, simply the management of intensity.[17]

The years between his graduation in 1881 and the establishment of his clinic for nervous diseases in 1886 really determined the character of much of Freud's professional and personal life to come. He derived a great deal of personal support in turn from Ernst Brücke, the head of the Vienna Physiological Institute, who had helped secure his Paris visit, then from Charcot, and afterwards from his senior contemporary in Vienna, Josef Breuer, also working on hysteria. These were all reassuring older men of the kind Freud evidently needed to rely on and turn to for help and advice. But professional and personal uncertainty still plagued him, chiefly because he lacked money and status, and, as he felt, he had a harder time of things professionally because he was a Jew. He had to borrow several times from friends, and on Brücke's advice moved from the physiology laboratory into general hospital work as the necessary prelude to private practice.[18] When he was under great pressure to succeed, Freud made one of the great mistakes of his career, over the use of cocaine. In 1884 he first wrongly recommended the barely known substance as a medical treatment then failed to pursue his research patiently enough to pin down cocaine's real use as a local anaesthetic. According to his commissioned 1925 autobiography, Freud rushed to finish the paper, so as to take up the opportunity to see his fiancée after a long absence. His colleague Carl Koller stepped into his shoes and hit on cocaine's specific usefulness as a numbing agent. After this débâcle the trip to France could not have come at a better time.[19]

Freud wrote: "I can say in retrospect that it was my fiancée's fault that I didn't become famous already in those early years . . . but I cannot hold against her my oversight of that time." But that rider sounds doubly disingenuous, for he was trying to pass the buck, and also the mistake was more than an oversight. Six years later Freud's older colleague and friend Ernst Fleischl von Marxow unwittingly hastened his death by injecting himself with cocaine on Freud's advice.[20]

But, to take a stand again against Freud's hostile critics today, no one should imagine that Freud, for all his doubts about the reliability of self-knowledge, led an unexamined life. Here *The Interpretation of Dreams* is a rich, under-used source for the burdens he carried with him from his early years. Two dreams in particular, "Irma's Injection" and "The Botanic Monograph," dwell on Freud's intense desire for psychoanalysis to succeed, despite his fears and doubts.[21]

Specifically Freud dreamt the dream of "Irma's Injection" on 23/24 July 1895. Irma was a young woman well known to the Freuds socially and also Freud's patient: the social connection redoubled the need for the treatment to be successful. But Freud inwardly questioned his technique in treating hysteria, and doctor and patient broke off for the summer without reaching a satisfactory resolution. When Otto, a colleague and mutual friend, reported to Freud that Irma was not better, Freud was irritated and took Otto's comment as a reproof, reinforcing the doubts of Irma's family that psychoanalysis could never be of benefit to their daughter. Keeping his irritation to himself, however, Freud that evening wrote up Irma's case to put before a respected second colleague, Dr. M. He reviewed the whole business in a dream that night.[22]

In the dream, the Freuds give a party. Irma is one of the guests. Freud reproaches her for not accepting his advice, whereupon she draws his attention to her alarming physical symptoms. He fears he has missed an organic illness. There are white patches on her throat and scabs in her nose, and he hurriedly summons Dr. M for a second opinion. The senior colleague appears not looking like his usual self, and there seems to be a need for Otto and another medical friend Leopold to add their expertise. All three now examine Irma. They diagnose an infection, but the fault is not Freud's. It seems that Otto gave her an injection, some time before, of a substance which should not have been used without caution, thinks the dreaming Freud; moreover, probably the needle was not clean; thus the blame for everything wrong with Irma is shifted on to the annoying Otto.

As the interpretation of what is really meant proceeds, Freud understands that the dream has a clear message: first of all he has more responsibility for a patient than simply to confront him or her with his view of their trouble and say take it or leave it. But the dream also picks up his constant anxieties as to whether psychoanalysis can succeed and how great is the danger of overlooking some physical cause of disease. Freud had a certain young man in mind who had gone on holiday to Egypt apparently cured, but who was now dead.

In fact, Freud made many mistakes. Not only did he blunder over cocaine, with fatal consequences, as both Irma and the Botanic Monograph dream remind him, he also nearly killed a patient by administering too much Sulfonal. Coming back to Irma herself, and the decision in the dream to send for Dr. M to take a second look at her, Freud comments at this point in his interpretation: "It seems as if I were looking to highlight every occasion when I could reproach myself for insufficient medical conscientiousness."[23]

Freud's worries about the cocaine episode alone reappear four times, and twice in lengthy detail, in the course of the whole *Traumdeutung*. The anxiety over the Sulfonal poisoning recurs just a few pages after "Irma's Injection," attached to the name of Freud's own daughter. Freud writes: "I touch again upon the story of the unfortunate Mathilde...I am evidently collecting here examples for my conscience, but also for the opposite." Interpreting "The Botanic Monograph" dream, Freud links his capacity for error and lack of conscientiousness with other professional weaknesses, such as his excessively broad interests and haste to engage new subjects. Moreover, the dream installs him as the actual author of the valuable and successful paper on $C_{17}H_{21}O_4N$, the alkaloid derived from *Erythroxylon coca*, not the one he did write, "Über Coca," showing not only that he has all these professional weaknesses, but that he continues to be envious of more successful colleagues like Coller.

The themes of success, ambition, secret doubt and envy come boldly to the fore in Freud's dreams to enlighten some of the most difficult episodes in his life. The Vienna Physiological Institute where Freud worked from 1876–82 under Brücke, for instance, turns into a den of murderous rivalry. Meanwhile Freud carries forward his unconscious susceptibility to ruthless competitiveness and envy into the most important relationship of his life with another, again older, man, Wilhelm Fließ. The friendship began in 1887 and lasted in an attenuated state until 1904.

Fließ was a Berlin ear, nose and throat specialist with an interest in neurology who agreed with Freud on the importance of sexuality in mental and spiritual health. His preoccupation with the nose and the sinuses as organs capable of secondary sexual expression seems to have led Freud thoroughly astray. Freud and Fließ caused their patient Emma Eckstein terrible pain, after Fließ operated on her nose and left a thick swab of gauze inside.[24] Fließ's theory of the nose was evidently also behind Freud's interpretation of Dora's catarrh as a substitute for thoughts about vaginal secretions, and indeed as a representation of the repressed desire to masturbate. Fließ also had a passion for the significance of numbers, which fired Freud's interpretative imagination. But most important for the relationship between the two men was Fließ's theory of bisexuality, where he would have liked his reputation to rest. Some time before 1900, Fließ explained the gist of this idea to Freud, namely that feminine men are attracted to masculine women, and vice versa, and that we all comprise a mixture of both sexes.

About the same time, and not later than 1899, when the first edition of *The Interpretation of Dreams* was published, Freud had the following dream which he didn't name, nor draw attention to for its own sake, but used as an illustration of what the relative clarity of certain elements in dreams can mean. He also first proposed it and then withdrew it as a rare example of a dream coming so undisguisedly close to life that it might be called "fantasizing during sleep" to mark it off from those much more elaborately distorted products of the night which he usually addresses. I call it the "Perfect Theory Dream."

I remember having a dream which when I woke up appeared to me to be particularly well put together, clear and without gaps, so that even while still intoxicated by sleep I proposed to admit a new category of dreaming, which was not subject to the mechanisms of condensation and displacement, but which might be called "fantasizing during sleep." Closer inspection revealed that this rare dream manifested the same rents and leaps in its fabric as any other; so I dropped the category of dream fantasizing once more. I still don't know whether I did the right thing. The reduced content of the dream was that I expounded to my friend a difficult theory of bisexuality that had taken years to research, and the power of the dream to fulfill wishes was responsible for making this theory (which wasn't itself communicated in the dream) seem clear and without gaps *to us.*

Thus what I regarded as a judgement of the completed dream was part of the dream content, and indeed the most important part...[25] [my italics, LC]

The extraordinary thing about this dream is in the first instance the way it foreshadows the crisis which was to befall the two friends. In 1900, Freud and Fließ had a violent row over Fließ's lack of confidence in Freud's work, although they continued to correspond. Then in 1903 another Viennese writer, Otto Weininger, caused a sensation when he published a book called *Sex and Character*, in which he set out a theory of bisexuality. A devastated Fließ couldn't believe in a coincidence: Freud must have told Weininger or there had been an indirect line of contact via one of Freud's analysands, Hermann Swoboda. Freud denied it and the two exchanged no more letters after July 1904. But the accusation turned out to be true. In 1906 Freud admitted that Weininger had come across the bisexuality theory through his discussions with Swoboda, and also that Weininger had visited Freud and shown him his manuscript. But Freud insisted the blame lay with Weininger, who had conveniently since committed suicide, for not acknowledging his intellectual debts.

Peter Gay, Freud's most sympathetic recent biographer, writes:

Freud found the controversy an unsettling experience. His offense was less his indiscretion in discussing bisexuality with Swoboda than his failure to be candid with Fließ about Weininger's visit... He had counseled Weininger not to publish it. Still, when it came to Fließ's share in Freud's discoveries, Freud displayed an impressive capacity for repressing inconvenient memories.[26]

But what really was going on in Freud's mind *vis-à-vis* Fließ? The Perfect Theory Dream, *dreamt before any of this happened*, is the dream of a man divided between loyalty and envy. Freud begins by telling us that he had a perfect dream (A) of a perfect theory, which amounted to a new category of dreaming (B). The clarity of the dream (A) makes (B) seem faultless, brilliant, a new category of dream. Yet on closer inspection (B) seems just as faulty as other theories and Freud discards it. On the other hand, when the dream is once again considered, (A) now seems "in its reduced content" to have been a theory about bisexuality (B₁) about which Freud was telling his friend, clearly Fließ.

(B) and (B₁) are both products of the wish fulfillment underlying dream (A). That is to say, dream (A) is about having a new theory, while it is the unconscious wish behind (A) which insists that (B) appear perfect. But another part of the dreaming Freud's wish is evidently that he and Fließ *together* recognize the perfection of the bisexuality theory B₁. In other words Freud has a mixed unconscious wish, both to appropriate the perfect theory, and yet to share it.

But then Freud drops (B) on the grounds that it is just as faulty as any other theory. It was only over thirty years later, at the age of seventy-four, that he added to the passage quoted above the sentence: "I still don't know today whether I did the right thing." (*Ich weiß heute nicht, ob mit Recht.*) Was he worrying over whether he did the right thing in dropping the bisexuality theory? Surely not. He readily absorbed it into his work, in a way for which, as Gay suggests, he never gave Fließ the credit. It might be that what Freud was actually worrying about was the need to make a public statement over dropping the Seduction Theory, which he rejected in the autumn of 1897, having shared for several years with Fließ his excitement over its greatness and the promise of "a certain wealth, complete independence [and] travels" it held out. Such a reading is possible because Freud tells us dreams displace and distort the causal relations they allude to in life, and readily substitute one person or object for another and mix up antagonist and victim. His personal dreams are autobiographical statements in code, to which he provides a fairly good key. But even if we reject this theory, we can still hear Freud's confession that he has done *something* wrong. Gay draws the conclusion from the facts of Freud's correspondence that he went on feeling hurt over the Fließ affair to the end of his life. Possibly the Perfect Theory Dream contains a double self-recrimination.[27]

In *The Psychopathology of Everyday Life*, published just over a year after the dreambook, in 1901, Freud had provisionally written up the matter of his jealousy over the bisexuality theory in quite a different professional tone, as if he had really learned something about himself; indeed, as if self-knowledge were a question of a calm and rational approach to life, and relatively easy:

> In the summer of 1901 I once remarked to a friend with whom I was then actively engaged in exchanging ideas on scientific questions: "These neurotic problems can be solved only if we decide fundamentally to accept an original bi-sexuality in every individual." To which he replied: "I told you that two and a half years ago while we were taking an evening walk in Br—. At that time you wouldn't listen to it."
>
> It is truly painful to be requested to renounce one's originality like this. I could neither recall such a conversation nor my friend's revelation . . . Since this incident I have grown more tolerant . . . It is scarcely accidental that a random selection of examples of forgetting can only be explained by dwelling on such painful themes as finding fault with one's wife, examining a friendship that has turned into the opposite, reflecting on a mistake in medical diagnosis or being rebuffed by one's peers, or borrowing someone else's ideas . . . The tendency to forget what is disagreeable seems to me to be a quite universal one . . . [28]

The passage gives the impression that Freud is in control, whereas what we have teased out of the Perfect Theory Dream shows he was not.

For a start that dream, unnamed and buried well down the book, shows by the very way it is written and featured, how Freud is torn between revealing and concealing the truth he suspects about himself. Yes indeed, he seems to want to tell us, I wanted to change places with Fließ, I was jealous, and I wanted him to admire my brilliant theory, rather than the other way round; and yet consciously I wanted to stand alongside Fließ, for Fließ was my friend. We worked together and I respected his judgement. But how much does Freud even want to tell us this, when the evidence is presented as such a puzzle? It is one of the great curiosities about Freud's work that dreams both help him avoid facing what he knows, and become central to his doctrine of revelation.

Freud makes the point just a page before the Perfect Theory Dream that the most intense feelings are often censored out of our dreams, and that intensity of feeling may end up corresponding to the amount of effort the dream puts into its vivid and coherent presentation. Since we know already that this was a dazzlingly clear dream, then evidently the feelings behind it blazed white hot too, and perhaps it might also be called the "Perfect Love Dream," and also the "Perfect Regret Dream," about how out of the great collaboration between Freud and Fließ a step forward for mankind might have ensued, instead of enmity.

Freud's dreams often substitute one person for another, in such a way as to make the competitive dreamer, usually Freud himself, victorious. In another dream about Fließ the process of substitution is as complex as the emotions behind it. An acquaintance of Freud's enters the coffee house complaining bitterly that he has been attacked by Goethe in an essay "On Nature." In reality Fließ had been attacked for his numerology theory. Freud had complained and broken off his links with a medical journal whose editor had recently published the damning review. In the dream Freud actually takes Fließ's place as the writer under attack. The dream twists things round to suggest that they stand as brothers-in-arms.

> I can say to myself: Just as happened to your friend, so you will fare with the critics, you've already had some experience of it, and so I can replace the "he" in the dream thoughts with a "we." Yes, you're right, we two are the fools.[29]

But, making a further twist, the dream then suggests that *neither Fließ nor Freud* are to be called mad for *their* new thinking, only all those critics who denounce them.

There is, as has long been suspected, a great deal of irrationality in Freud himself, which becomes the material he works on, and which is deeply entangled with the nature of the theories he puts forward. We must expect those theories to contain aspects of his personality, though not for that reason discard them. What I have just been demonstrating, for instance, is what great resources Freud had for self-deception, and how ready he was, consciously and unconsciously, to conceal things from and deceive others on the surface of things, while finding a quiet way out that would satisfy his own conscience. In particular the claim that he was doing science looks like just one more device unconsciously aimed at the concealment of his real enterprise, autobiography. The interests of science gave him the justification for near-perfect control over what should become known about himself publicly, while at the same time the theories he invented allowed him to unload the burden and create or produce something out of himself.

The burden was sexual and psychological, it was Jewish and it was also political. In one confessional fantasy a Jewish colleague who has failed to gain promotion is transformed by Freud's dream into an incompetent figure, so that Freud can reassure himself it is not Jewishness that stands in his own way. In another dream he deeply begrudges the long time he takes to get anywhere in his career, compared with what surely would have been the case had he been a Gentile. Freud also worries how to bring up his Jewish children without a homeland, and his hostile feelings towards the social injustices of the Austro-Hungarian Empire come out in dreams which depict Freud as a revolutionary, at least in spirit.[30]

The Interpretation of Dreams is however the confession of a self-avowed political liberal. It objects to a society which fosters public sexual hypocrisy and it despises a social structure which cramps some lives while privileging others. Not only fierce and perverted sexual wishes, but feelings of resentment at inequality, jibes against an overly revered God and Church, resentment at the anti-Semitism dominating all walks of Viennese society and the loud complaints of body and psyche against a constricting and dishonest morality all come to the surface of Freud's mind and to the reader's attention across the spectrum of his writing, but especially in his dreams.

His Revolutionary Dream, he tells us, sprang directly from a real experience. He was waiting on a railway platform in Vienna to go on holiday when he saw Count Thun, a high-ranking politician of the day, arrive in an open carriage despite the rain. The Count without explanation brushed aside an official who, failing to recognize him, had asked to see his ticket. Quietly disgusted at the repeated spectacle of individual arrogance and privileges for the few in Habsburg Austria, Freud stood around waiting to see who else would come along and demand a free first-class compartment because of who he knew, and got ready to make a similar fuss on his own behalf. He started singing a cheeky tune from *The Marriage of Figaro* and "all kinds of impudent and revolutionary thoughts [went] through my head." Recalling with amusement how the newspapers called Count Thun "Count Nichtsthun" (Do Something/Do Nothing), Freud felt gloriously unenvious of this unpleasant aristocrat, since after all it was Freud, about to go on holiday, who was "Count Do-Nothing." But then a figure whom he recognized came along, a man who superintended medical examinations on behalf of the state, and whose relationship with the latter was so cosy his nickname was Mr. State Bedmate.[31]

Sure enough Mr. State Bedmate demands his due: a first-class compartment for half-price. Freud has to pay the full price for his, which is not even the full cause of his anger, for the accommodation he gets is anyway inferior, without a lavatory in the whole carriage. After complaining unsuccessfully to the guard, Freud threatens to bore a hole in the floor to cater for his needs, but middle-class respect for property stops him, and eventually he falls asleep.

Some hours later, the need to empty his bladder wakens him from a long and complex dream in which a Count Thun or Taaffe is addressing a crowd, including a large group of students. Then the setting changes to the university lecture hall, then official-looking offices and corridors, possibly government offices, where the dreamer's way is barred by an old woman. Yet she seems to think he has right of way, and offers to accompany him. He dodges her company and thinks he's very clever to do so. Then the dream moves to travelling out of town. Freud is in a carriage and asks the driver to take him to the station. At the station he chooses a destination expressly where the royal court will not be in residence.

Details in this dream confirm that it is a fantasy set in the revolutionary year 1848, which brought Austrian liberal sentiment to the fore. There is a link to Zola's novels with a revolutionary content, *Germinal* and *La Terre*, while both Thun and Taaffe appear as reactionary figures who stand for the end of Austrian Liberalism in Freud's day, fifty years later. Thun is the scion of an ancient Bohemian feudal family, who favors the free exercise of Czech nationality and language. The Imperial and aristocratic forces Thun represents combine a kind of contained nationality with political autocracy. By contrast the Austrian liberals to whom Freud belongs are in matters of language and culture German nationalists.

The second dream scene – in the corridors of officialdom – Freud refuses to interpret in detail, "for reasons of censorship." There is an allusion to the contemporary Austrian Social Democrat Viktor Adler and the sense that Freud is following in his footsteps, playing the role of a top man in the earlier revolutionary period. In any case, he comes up against, but outwits, the censorship.

The third scene Freud later realizes has to do with his brother, and their recent travelling together. The interpretation via the person of the coachman leads him to see in the dream a repudiation of the power of inheritance. As he sums up: "It's nonsense to be proud of one's ancestors."[32]

The deeper Freud penetrates the dream the more he finds sexual material from his childhood. But what he finds overall is most interesting to us, all the more as it is tucked away in a footnote:

> The entire content of this dream, with its rebelliousness, its *lèse-majesté*, and its scoffing at high authority, goes back to a revolt against the father. The prince is the father of the land, and the father is the oldest, first and for the child the only authority, from whose perfect power the other social authorities derive

over the course of human cultural history (wherever "matri-archy" does not demand that this sentence be qualified).[33]

This note shows the point where Freud's content and style and his historical position converge. Freud carries the torch for a style of politically committed, witty literature in the style of Heine and Börne. He is in tune with the anti-Idealist tone of Young Germany, the liberal and anti-clerical movement with which these writers were associated. But to this political, social and cultural iconoclasm which inspired his father's generation Freud adds sexual revelation as a means to shock, and also defines as his own theories of sexuality and the unconscious which by their very nature must challenge received authority. Within the coarse nugget of rebelliousness, moreover, is lodged a particular antagonism towards the received authority of high art and the respectability of its practitioners which Freud will only fully make public towards the end of his life.[34]

In *The Interpretation of Dreams* Freud tells us an enormous amount about Freud himself. Freud the voluptuary, Freud the would-be revolutionary, Freud the outsider and bitter victim of anti-semitism, Freud the ruthless seeker after worldly success, Freud the doctor of compassion and Freud the empirical philosopher tempted by speculation all come into focus. There is also Freud the thinker who doubts our human capacity to know ourselves with the same passion as Descartes once doubted man's knowledge of the world. Descartes turns out not to be a skeptic, but Freud certainly is. And then there is Freud the theorist, who leaves us open-mouthed. That Freud can have bona fide theories becomes however more and more problematic, because the more one reads Freud closely the more bewildering the conflation of autobiography and theory becomes. It seems as if Freud actually wanted to set before us the question: "Well, go on then, what is self-knowledge? Am I not the greatest example of it? And yet you can't even see what I'm doing, can you? I'm setting before you my limitations." In a great novel of *Vienna 1900*, featuring the sexual frustration and hypocrisy endemic in middle-class life and the anti-semitism and bureaucratic corruption threatening one ambitious and rebellious young man's social and professional success, this would have been the philosophical undertow.

2

THE ARTIST

There are many pious, incantatory tributes in Freud to the power of the word and the insight of the artist.[1] Freud unconditionally admires the content of high art, and the skill and perspicaciousness of writers in understanding the human soul. He often observes that artists, in German *Dichter*, intuitively know what psycho-analysis seeks to explain.[2] They articulate our perennial unconscious fears and desires. Freud pays tribute to the art of Aeschylus and Shakespeare by borrowing Oedipus and Hamlet to legitimize his theories. But Freud had a strange attitude to artists themselves, seeing them essentially as magicians who could charm their way to success. He both admired that charm and accounted for it in uninspiring terms. The admiration, based on a conflation of the artist and the power of his art, crops up in his two 1907 essays "The Artist and Creative Imagination" and "Madness and Dreams in Walter Jensen's *Gradiva*," and, most interestingly, in the *Introductory Lectures on Psychoanalysis* of 1915–17.

1 The artist is from the outset an introvert too, who is not far off neurosis. He is driven by excessively strong instinctual needs, wants to earn honor, power, wealth, fame and the love of women, but lacks the means to achieve this satisfaction. Thus like any other unsatisfied person he turns away from reality, and transfers all his interest and also his libido to the wish-figments of his fantasy life. From here the way could lead to neurosis.

2 Many things must coincide for [the artist] not to develop in this way; it is after all well known how often artists more than other people suffer from a partial block of their productive capacity through neurosis. Probably their constitutions contain a powerful capacity for sublimation and probably the repressions that make for conflict are loosely packed.

3 But the way the artist finds his way back to reality is like this. He's not the only one to lead a fantasy life. A general human consensus approves of the intermediate kingdom of fantasy, and everyone depriving himself of something in life can expect from there comfort and consolation. Only for non-artists the amount of pleasure they can get from the sources of fantasy is very limited. The relentlessness of their repressions obliges them to make do with any paltry daydreams which can make it to consciousness. When a man is a true artist he has more at his disposal.

4 In the first place he knows how to rework his daydreams so that they lose the all-too-personal quality which puts other people off; they can be enjoyed by others. He also knows how to tone them down, so that they don't easily betray those unworthy origins. In addition he possesses the puzzling capacity to shape certain material until it faithfully resembles the idea he had in his fantasy.

5 He can then attach to the representation of his unconscious fantasy such a pleasure gain [*Lustgewinn*] that at least for a while the repressions are overcome by the representation and their effect suspended [*aufgehoben*]. If he can do all that, then he makes it possible for others again to draw comfort and consolation from the pleasure sources of their own unconscious, to which they had lost access. He earns their gratitude and admiration and has now achieved *through* his fantasy what in the first instance he only achieved *in* his fantasy: honor, power and the love of women.

This rich passage sets out Freud's "official" view of art. There is no other place where the range of Freud's thoughts over the realms of art, psychological health and worldly success is so apparent.[3]

The latter three paragraphs, which I have numbered for convenience, include what happens when art and the artist wreak their magic on the audience. The charm of the work induces a state of willing disbelief. We are prepared to stay in our seats or not put the book down. Because we are under a kind of spell, the artist can put us in touch with our deepest and possibly most repugnant or frightening feelings without shocking us. He can even persuade us temporarily to contemplate, and live with, alienating revelations about humanity. Freud does not ever explain the artist's skill in formal terms, but in "The Artist and Creative Imagination" (*Der Dichter und das Phantasieren*) assumes that the difference between artistic finesse and the unappealing way "ordinary" people tell their stories and dreams is well known. What interests him is the psychology of charm.

But when the writer displays his tricks or tells us something which we are inclined to believe are his personal daydreams, we experience a high pleasure which probably flows together from many sources. How the writer does that is his most intimate secret. The technique for overcoming that repulsion [which we feel at the personal source of stories we are told, LC] no doubt has something to do with the limits arising between every individual "I" and the other. In it lies the actual *ars poetica*.[4]

The fourth paragraph quoted from the Twenty-Third Introductory Lecture takes up the psychological transaction in blunt terms. The artist acquires power through knowing how to conceal his own presence. Because he has it in his power to transmute egoism, he does not give us the impression of having dredged his material from his own depths. Avoiding evoking the discomfort in us that might arise if we felt he were telling us his own secrets, he bestows legitimacy on what he reveals, and to this disguise adds the promise of pleasure.[5]

Art of course gives a feeling of aesthetic freedom without the need for moral judgement. The artist passes on his own freedom of imagination and desire not to prejudge characters and situations. He makes us feel good about our own fantasies and helps us accept the demons inside. Under the influence of art we experience relief from the hardness and fastness of our own identity too, as we hold opposites in balance. Our imaginations are stretched, and we regain some of the freedom of childhood. In "The Writer and Creative Imagination" Freud talks of the *Lustgewinn*, the pleasure gain, when all this relief comes to pass. He puts a particular physical emphasis on the nature of the relief that art affords, so that in the end we are more inclined to think of a quantity of pressure being lifted (*aufgehoben*) than a qualitative change of outlook having come about.[6]

That Freud seems to be talking about the physiology of aesthetic reception as much as anything that might traditionally have been called spiritual is brought out further in the last paragraph which also concludes the Twenty-Third Introductory Lecture. Pleasure is the excitation of tension coupled with the expectation of release. Freud's interest in the physical power of art is so strong he almost seems to measure the reader's pulse and breathing. Whether it is the pleasure Shakespeare offers to us in unravelling the tensions built up in *King Lear*, after the beauty of the language and the human plight have hooked us, or the appeal of Sherlock Holmes being dealt a hand of apparently random facts and out of them piecing together an intriguing piece of villainy, the level of art doesn't matter. The physiology of the play of forces in the soul is what links art to all human activity. The same pattern, with more or fewer blockages in the dynamic system, reproduces itself in art as in sex, in neurosis and in jokes. It is the pattern of tension and release.

Freud argued that everything in the body, including the brain mechanisms, physically tended towards the pleasure of offloading pressure. The alternation of charge (*Besetzung*) and discharge (*Aufhebung*), is the basis of Freud's "Scientific Psychology." The first term becomes *cathexis* in Strachey's Latinized medical English and the latter looks like the *catharsis* of Aristotle's Greek. We are driven to tell jokes by this *Aufhebungslust* or the anticipated pleasure of relief. Surely no cycle of tension and release is more powerful and immediate than the sexual. But then the sexual is never far from either the neurotic or the aesthetic for Freud. His German in the 1907 essay clearly shows that the promise of pleasure which art holds out involves the idea of a seduction. The *Lustgewinn* or the *Verlockungsprämie* is both spiritual temptation and animal bait.[7]

Reading, watching plays, listening to music is arousing. Freud thinks something similar also happens in dreams, where there is a kind of anxiety lest the dream end prematurely, without delivering full satisfaction. But the excitement builds up specifically in art because the writer flirts with us, holding out possibilities of enjoyment.

> We can guess at two ways in which the technique works: the writer modifies the character of the egoistic daydream by changing things round and veiling them and infects us by means of a purely formal access of pleasure, that is by means of aesthetic pleasure which he offers us in the presentation of his fantasies. The kind of access of pleasure offered to us here is called "a premium to tempt us" [*Verlockungsprämie*] or "an anticipation of pleasure" [*Vorlust*], and it is offered to make possible the release of greater pleasure out of psychic springs which reach deeper. In my view all the aesthetic pleasure created for us by writers has the character of such "forepleasure." The actual pleasure of a work of art consists in a release of tensions which take place in our soul. Perhaps no small contribution to this success is that the writer puts us in a position henceforth to enjoy our own phantasies without the least reproach or shame.[8]

Artistic and sexual charm for Freud *begin* by being of the same nature. Writers exercise a quasi-erotic hold on us through the power of words and then lead us on to deeper pleasures of the soul. Two Freuds seem to merge in this view of art and love, the Platonic-cum-eighteenth-century German Idealist and the nineteenth-century materialist. The materialist in turn gives way to the Darwinist Freud, who makes the aesthetic process part of the basic reproductive drive. The artist is the man capable of the peacock display. He is better than most at getting a mate. Naturally we all envy the artist his power to charm, since he is nature's top dog.[9]

And yet, to return to deeper things, whether viewed materialistically or Idealistically, or in terms of evolutionary biology, allowing ourselves to be carried away by art is in no small way comparable with being open to love and this takes us back to Freud's first two points in the long passage from *The Introductory Lectures*. The artist can be neurotic, but he may not be if he has a fortunate psychological constitution, and his position will certainly be helped by his ability to express himself through art. The artist with his loosely packed soul and his ready imagination is therefore a model to all of us of psychic health. With the honor, wealth and sexual love which seem to fall to him because of his gifts, he really does hold out the prospect of a happier life.

Yet what is his gift, except to have mastered the art of disguise? The artist transforms his base thoughts and instinctual needs into something that will not frighten his audience. He compensates for secret shyness. It is all alarmingly simple.[10]

Most of us *are* happier with some measure of disguise, or at least restraint, in public life. We accustom ourselves to a social persona before we confront another naked psyche. Disguise is the business of jokes. We feel people *should* play roles rather than directly expose us to their inner thoughts and needs. Disguise gets women into bed, thinks Freud. The blatant facts of lust might otherwise put them off. But whether we are talking about men or women, in Freud's day or now, there is something right about the confidence he considers we derive from feeling "free." The perfect personal playmate and the perfect work of art have much in common for Freud. They charm us because they give us enhanced scope to be "ourselves." They do this by appearing to enlarge our inner or outer space. We want to stay with them. Artistic charm and social disguise in this sense are no mere decorations to our lives, but repeated, essential, humanizing little holidays from necessity. Especially had we lived in Vienna in 1900, the masked ways of art and charm would have given us the feeling of an extra, quasi-secret freedom existing within a carefully regulated society. It is part of the accomplishment of the balanced human personality to be able to sustain forms of disguise and, with that, to accept living with a certain tension. But neurotics often cannot disguise their inner troubles, and on the other hand are the victims of an involuntary process of disguise, whereby their troubles emerge anyway as tell-tale symptoms, giveaways to the analytic observer. The neurotic is in this way the opposite of the artist. But, as Freud began his conclusion to the Twenty-Third Introductory Lecture, the two conditions, artistic and neurotic, are also evidently very close, with neurosis looking like a near-miss. Neurosis befalls a man when his disguise isn't good enough artistically, or it isn't sufficient to do the trick psychologically.

We pick up an interesting trail when Goethe, Freud's favorite writer, enters the picture. In his address on receipt of the Goethe Prize for Literature in 1930, Freud contrasts another of his great psychological interests among the artists, Leonardo da Vinci, with Goethe. There seems to have been in Leonardo something which blocked his development, which made him uninterested in things erotic and thereby also not interested in psychology. *In diesem Punkt dürfte Goethes Wesen sich freier entfalten.* Goethe was the reverse. His development was freer. I suggest he was the model for what Freud called *eine gewisse Lockerheit der. . . Verdrängungen*, literally "a certain looseness of repressions" and which I have translated as the loosely packed soul of the artist.[11]

Goethe's ability to be at home in his skin became a psychological landmark in German literature from the moment his more problematic contemporary Schiller picked up the difference between their two personalities and set it down as two fundamental creative attitudes and approaches to the world. Driven by ethical principle and a talent for abstraction, Schiller was evidently the less happy and rounded of the two, a shortcoming which spilled over into his dramatic writing and his poetry. In *The*

Aesthetic Education of Man (1795), Schiller took the difference between Goethe and himself almost as the basis for mending civilization after the wrong outcome of the French Revolution. He observed that until men could make balanced personalities of themselves under the guidance of art, and with a developed sense of play, there could be no improvement in the political society around them. Freud seems to pick up this tradition with his portrait of Goethe as the open personality resistant to neurosis. Goethe is the prototype of the successful artist and also the successful personality at home in the world.

Freud makes the link between the world's stock of continually wretched and unproductive neurotics and Goethe in a veiled way in "The Writer and Creative Imagination":

> *So there is a type of human being whom indeed not a god, but a severe goddess − necessity − has charged with telling what they suffer and what brings them joy.* These are the nerve-ridden [*die Nervösen*], who must *also* confess their fantasies to the doctor from whom they expect delivery through psychic treatment, and we have reached the well-founded conclusion then that our patients tell us nothing other than what we could also hear from healthy people.[12]

My emphasis here draws attention to the echo of one of Goethe's most famous couplets. When the mature Goethe distanced himself from Werther, the lovelorn suicide he created in his youth, he famously confessed:

> *Und wenn der Mensch in seiner Qual verstummt, gab mir ein Gott zu sagen, wie ich leide.*

A god let me articulate my pain. Generally men suffer in silence.

Freud suggests that up to a point neurotics share the artist's gift. Neurotics' repressed thoughts *have* a way out. *Something* is expressed: they have a problem to work on, one might say (or, as one of Jung's patients reported, "Life is so gripping'). But it needs to be converted, translated, funnelled in a particular way if it is to bring about a cure, because essentially neurotics do not get things out in the *right* way.

Psychoanalysis picks up on what happens naturally in dreams, when our repressed wishes are translated automatically into entertaining stories, and tries to convert it into a deliberate therapy. It offers the patient a route out of his sick self by becoming at least a kind of artist, and also his own god, a goal which harmonizes Freud's endeavor with Plato's. All the sick soul has to do is mobilize his imagination.

Freud never taught the "free the creative artist in yourself!" message as such, but he went so far in "The Writer and Creative Imagination" as to exclaim:

> If only we could discover in ourselves or people like us an activity somehow related to creative writing [*Dichten*]![13]

That hope is the key to how psychoanalysis would ideally function.

In fact Freud suggests psychoanalysis works in apposition to the creative powers in the human being; it is a kind of an annex to the main building, from where the way to art leads by an open internal door. But Freud's enlistment of art and the artist ultimately in his pursuit of success seems necessarily to detract from art for its own sake. He has to deal hefty blows at the intrinsic value of high art in order to carry out his project.

Fifty years ago the critic Lionel Trilling, who represented the highest moral and aesthetic values for literature, issued a noble complaint on the basis of the "official" writings on art.

> ...it must seem to a literary man that Freud sees literature not from within but from without...He is always outside the process. Much as he responds to the product, he does not really imagine the process. He does not have what we call the *feel* of the thing.[14]

Freud's therapy has prompted many an artist and critic to insist that high art has an autonomy and the act of storytelling a legitimacy which takes it beyond the self-interest of the teller. The artist is driven perhaps most of all by the desire to create form out of something formless, while his or her emotional motivation may be as much to communicate with other souls as to manipulate and deceive them. The drive to make things is not the shit Freud is literally tempted to see it as, nor is the work of art only the struck match which has briefly cast light on an alien person's inner world. Art is not explained by the psychology of the artist, nor by a mechanical theory of unloading. The process is teleological in an Aristotelian sense – there is a goal and some good to be derived from getting there – but the goal and the good remain mysterious.

Freud reduces art *for his psychoanalytical purpose* to the unattractive but triumphant psychology of its maker in fact by basing his judgements on popular writing. For him the imaginations of popular writers display patterns in common with neurotics and common daydreamers. Their fantasies, night dreams and daydreams, tend to feature either sex or ambition, and proceed from unconscious subjective need. Freud highlights predictable plots in which the hero, who is the male author's *alter ego*, always wins his battle with the world, while a female writer's heroine wins love. The triumph of the disguised writing subject in glorious survival seems all the more keenly guaranteed by stories which begin with severe threats to the well-being of the protagonist: shipwreck, imprisonment or domestic unhappiness. It is Freud himself who says that such writing, which consists essentially in the writer projecting self-justifying and vengeful fantasies, is without critical acclaim, and a Leavisite definition would agree. It would suggest that a world so lacking in the complex and unpredictable morality which self-examination entails is not literature at all, but dross.

Freud does sustain a promising distinction between "writers who take over ready material, like the old epic poets and tragedians" and "those who seem freely to invent their material and are *not* most highly valued by the critics." Yet it is this latter kind of "writer" to whom he keeps turning back. *This* kind of writer's success, not Goethe's and Shakespeare's, is what he really envies. The question just keeps repeating itself: isn't it interesting that *a writer* can transmute her hostilities and anxieties into entertainment, while the rest of us, full of similar dark feelings, lack an efficient (and lucrative and estimable) psychological clearing system? Good God, there must be a way of overcoming that![15]

Freud probably does believe in the greatness of art to express human profundities in a way that psychoanalysis can never quite catch. It is a famous sentiment of his, expressed in his essay on *Gradiva*, that artists are colleagues who intuitively know what psychoanalysis seeks to explain. But Freud on the artist leaves us with a changed world: one in which lip service may be paid on a good day to a high art which is otherwise generally seen as irrelevant. In its place comes a new world of self-liberation and self-making.

In 1880 Nietzsche predicted in *Human All Too Human*:

What place still remains for art? Above all it has taught us for thousands of years to look upon life in any of its forms with interest and pleasure, and to educate our sensibilities so far that we at last cry: "Life, however it may be, is good." This teaching imparted by art to take pleasure in life and to regard human life as a piece of nature, as an object of regular evolution, without being too violently involved in it – this teaching has been absorbed into us, and it now re-emerges as an almighty require-ment of knowledge... Perhaps art has never before been comprehended so profoundly or with so much feeling as now, when the magic of death seems to play around it... The artist will soon be regarded as a glorious relic, and we shall bestow on him, as a marvellous stranger upon whose strength and beauty the happiness of former ages depended, honors such as we do not grant to others of our own kind. The best in us has perhaps been inherited from the sensibilities of earlier ages to which we hardly any longer have access by direct paths; the sun has already set, but the sky of our life still glows with its light, even though we no longer see it.[16]

(The quality of this passage from Nietzsche might be borne in mind as we move towards determining what kind of writer *Freud* was.)

Freud's longtime secretary and always the disciple with the greatest interest in art and creativity, Otto Rank, developed the self-help strain in Freud's thinking when he set out his keynote theory of the neurotic as a kind of artist.

> The neurotic is not merely someone who failed to adjust to the world, but a potential superior individual who fails at being creative. A good therapeutic result means that the patient adjusts himself and also sometimes the circumstances – which involves creativity. His task is "to create himself and then to go on and create externally."[17]

When Freud treated his patients to the talking cure, he set the patient up as a potential artist who in his talking and dreaming produced "texts" and "stories" for patient and analyst together to work on. But in so doing Freud devolved art into a new framework. He gave writing *and* poetry a new meaning in this therapeutic, self-help context. He fathered the creative writing class. He split the aesthetic atom, releasing a vast energy for individual creativity, but mainly at the sub-artistic level.[18]

Only one dangerous, difficult activity of imagination remained in the corner of the picture. One might think here of the artist who does not quite cure himself, and who does not have the ideally loosely packed personality. This is the artist who is tempted to turn to fantasy for all his satisfactions in life, as Freud suggested could be the case at the beginning of the long paragraph from the Twenty-Third Introductory Lecture. This is the case where fantasy becomes a substitute or even a legitimate alternative to self-knowledge; perhaps even a glorious acceptance of the defectiveness of self-knowledge. Only, as Freud sees it, the artist taking this route, and I shall suggest this is essentially Freud's own position as an artist, will still want to disguise his activity. Compassionate therapy based on the idea that the artist is the best model will provide a good shelter.

Freud's official thoughts on art are highly interesting for the way they lay down the foundations of the self-help tradition. But of at least equal interest, and less obviously the case at first sight, is the way they create a forum of theory to house Freud's own practice as an artist. Here is the writer who disguises the deep feelings which other people can't normally contemplate. Freud disguises these deep feelings not in what would normally be called art, but in the theory of a new science. He is also the writer disguising himself, and the writer who must by definition conceal the subjective origins of what strikes his imagination if he wants to succeed with his audience. Freud is the writer specifically disguising talk of his own sexuality. He probably wasn't born with a loosely packed psyche, but he has learned through self-analysis to undo the bolts. He has the essential artistic capacity to regress. He knows that fantasy may satisfy more than life. It may provide enough narcissistic or solitary pleasure. Finally, he knows that there may be no need to go on hammering away at the need for self-knowledge if one has enough imagination to get by in the world on pure invention.

3

SELF-DISCOVERY/SELF-REVELATION

Freud paints a self-portrait in the Twenty-Third Introductory Lecture when he refers to a type of man with excessively strong instinctual needs and ambition. We know from the correspondence with Fließ, *The Interpretation of Dreams* and *The Psychopathology* that he learned about neurosis through studying himself, and we feel that he has also taken some vital autobiographical material to construct his portrait of the artist, as if he were asking: is there a route by *this* means to unload some of the sexual burden, or, more generally, the burden of intensity? The evidence of art suggests any self-revelation will have to be disguised. And so, judging that Freud applied this principle also to writing science, we work back from the surface of his texts to try to discern the man he was.

Freud interrogated his dreams and memories and his self-awareness, and was willing to reveal a certain amount directly. Here in *The Psychopathology* for instance he is particularly aware of one part of himself playing tricks on another. Half-amused and half-ashamed, he catches himself blotting out what he doesn't want to know.

The border between intention and accident hardly seems discernible...an apparently clumsy movement may be utilized in a most refined way for sexual experience. In a friend's house I met a young girl visitor who excited in me a feeling of fondness which I had long believed extinct, thus putting me in a jovial, loquacious and complaisant mood. At the same time I endeavored to find out how this came about, as a year before this same girl made no impression on me.

As the girl's uncle, a very old man, entered the room, we both jumped to our feet to bring him a chair. She was more agile than I and also nearer...She carried it with its back to her, holding the edge of the seat with both hands. As I got there later and did not give up my claim to carrying the chair, I suddenly stood directly behind her and with both my arms was embracing her from behind, and for a moment my hands touched her lap.[1]

But much of the autobiographical material gleaned from dreams and from Freud's theoretical writings looks more problematic than this, because we can only suppose Freud's experience was such on the basis of later echoes and shadows. Readers may find my technique doubly offputting when they realize that constructing as a series of longer fragments Freud's deliberately scattered and half-concealed autobiography resembles the way Freud himself tried to piece together the psychic history of his patients from a mixture of facts, confessions, hints, symptoms, instructive lies and guess-work. On the other hand all the evidence prompts the question: was Freud not waiting for a reader to psychoanalyze him, given the trail he left? It was one of his most important points about repression, that it always left signs. There seems no reason why he should not have utilized the trick which he discovered, or invented, in order half to conceal and half to reveal his "real" self.[2]

That Freud's childhood was dominated by sexual fascination and confusion we are tempted to read back from his whole construction of the Oedipus theory, plus the facts of his particular family circumstances. The confusion stemmed mainly from the twenty-year age difference between his parents, and the fact that although he was his mother's first-born son he was his father's third. He had two adult half-brothers, Emanuel and Philipp, and a nephew John who was a year older than he was. It seems to have been true that Freud slept in his parents' bedroom till he was six months old, an episode which later helped him "understand" the Wolfman; and perhaps Freud did at the age of four see his mother naked when they stayed in a hotel room together. In any case these memories impressed themselves upon him indelibly, to the extent that he assumed all men in their infancy desired their mothers, hated their fathers and were jealous of their siblings.

Another anecdote in *The Psychopathology* wraps up an aspect of the maternal theme in a story about a child's feeling of powerlessness and insecurity. The absence of both mother and nanny in the child's life coincides with an almost painful sexual curiosity, and a new experience for a young child: being the bemused victim of clever adult words. Freud was two-and-a-half and living with his twenty-five-year-old half-brother Philipp. His mother Amalie had just given birth to Anna, a sister. The anxious boy was shouting and crying at his brother to open a cupboard because he thought his mother might be in there. Philipp opened it and Sigi saw there was nothing there, but just then his mother came into the room, looking very slim. This "memory" mingled with a second remembered scene, centered on Sigi's worry about the sudden disappearance of his nanny. When he asked where she was, Philipp, who had reported her to the police for theft, said confusingly that she was "inside." Not understanding the joke, Sigi feared that Philipp had also put his mother "inside" the cupboard, i.e. made her pregnant, since the two were far closer in age than the young Amalie was to Freud's forty-three-year-old father Jakob. Though there is clearly a degree of "secondary reworking" from adulthood here, the memory reveals rich Freudian childhood fears about the arrival of siblings; confusion about where babies come from, and about muddled sexual roles within the family; a preoccupation with inside/outside and hidden/revealed; and jealousy that any other man should have a sexual connection to his beloved mother/nanny. But particularly Freud remembered Philipp the male rival exercising power over him with clever words. To Freud's enquiry about the whereabouts of the nanny, "He answered evasively and playing with words, as was always his way...the unkind brother." "She's banged up," we might say, to bring the sexual and penal meanings closer in English.[3]

With his nephew John meanwhile Freud was very close but often at loggerheads. Wherever there was conflict in his dreams with colleagues and friends at the Vienna Physiological Institute Freud would see repeating itself the fundamental mixture of love and hate and competitiveness he felt towards John. It was John who came to mind when he found himself, as often, caught in ambivalence towards other people. But Freud also felt love/hate towards institutions such as Jewishness, and all elements of leadership and tradition, *including the power of high art*, because these in a sense embodied the power of the father.

Freud remembered a dire prediction of Jakob Freud's that his third-born would not amount to much. The eight-year-old boy had urinated, evidently into a pot, but in his parents' bedroom. The shame he was made to feel was reversed in "The Revolutionary Dream" which ends with the adult Freud accompanying a blind man on to a train. The blind man is his father, and Freud holds out a glass into which the father urinates. The ticket collector comes and goes without comment, though the father's naked member is clearly visible. The old man is dependent on Freud, as the son once was on the father, and as Freud interprets the dream, it contains a strong desire for personal vengeance, as well as the need to blaspheme against the generation of the fathers and against authority and propriety in general. I suggested in the early part of that dream that where Freud is in rebellion over having to pay full-price for a second-rate carriage, while others enjoy corrupt privileges, he tellingly threatens to express that rebellion by wetting the floor. The Revolutionary Dream reminds us how often "naughty" and "dirty" things in Freud are weapons of defiance. In his theory Freud of course attached great importance to the emotional aspect of the bodily functions, including masturbation, which he thought children reveled in. The famous analogical chain linking baby, penis and feces is a kind of glorification of the "dirt" of childhood, as he imagined it.[4]

But where I especially detect a re-creation of Freud's childhood is in his theory of the infantile character of the unconscious. Its character is mocking, deliberately perverse, with the spirit of a practical joker and also of a clown holding two fingers up to logic. Devoted to undermining appearances, it bursts in unannounced and constantly angles to get attention, disrupting the gentility of adult life by shouting rude words and displaying parts of the body that ought to be covered. Often seeming like a disturbed child, it shoulders the burden of deviance which Freud would otherwise carry alone. Thus consciously or otherwise Freud can use the science of the unconscious as a screen for his secret "naughty" thoughts.[5]

This comes out in small ways, as well as in the invention of the major tools of his trade. With such terms as *a tergo, matrem nudam* and *grumus merdae*, Freud may have been satirizing a discomfited medical profession; but he was also playing his own game with things that could both be said and not be said. Moreover, when he revealed aspects of the secret sexual lives of Senator Schreber and the Wolfman it was as if he were devising a Victorian peepshow. Freud gets huge pleasure from shocking good taste, and while the comparison with Shakespeare springs to mind, suggesting that Freud's bawdy relieves the burden of seriousness he otherwise leaves with us, we mainly feel the infantile joker at work. In his essay "The Unconscious," for example, Freud suggests that a man squeezing spots in the bathroom mirror is expressing his real desire to masturbate. Freud had a serious scientific interest in the structural affinity between the two activities but the text suggests the pleasure in breaking social taboos by both talking about and *illustrating* masturbation was just as great. The spot bursts out, the man shoots out, Freud comes out with very naughty things, which makes three ejaculations in all, and all of them enjoyed in public.[6]

The Freudian unconscious makes the persistence of deviant sexual thoughts into adulthood normal and in a way we should be grateful for what in politics would be a policy to emancipate the disadvantaged fringe of society. Still most of us aren't quite happy that the man in the dirty raincoat is king of Freud's netherworld, a power which fills the world with voyeurs for every hidden orifice and where high-minded Victorian public men secretly obsessed with repletion and evacuation view penny-in-the-slot pornography at the end of an art-nouveau pier which we would otherwise want to admire as a step forward for civilization. Even Freud, in a dream called the "Latrine Dream," considering the "science" he has created, hopes he can save his children from all of this psychic shit in which he sees the world enmired.

> A piece of raised ground, and on this a latrine in the open air, a very long bench, at the end of which is a large latrine hole. The whole rear edge is thickly covered with little piles of shit in all sizes and states of freshness. Behind the bench a bush. I urinate on the bench; a long stream of urine washes everything clean, the pats of shit dissolve easily and fall down the hole. As if at the end something still remained.[7]

In the Latrine Dream, Freud notes that the hill and the bush look like Aussee, where he has sent his children, away from Vienna, whereas the bench (minus the hole) resembles a present from a clinging female patient, and is a general reminder of how Freud's patients respect him, and how he must carry on working even when he loses heart. The piles of excrement stand for Italy, not known for its fine facilities, but where he loves to escape and rest, and would ideally go on holiday. The obvious interpretation is that Freud finds his work messy and longs to escape. His impossible task makes him think of Hercules mucking out the Augean Stables. Shit, endless shit: look into the average human psyche and you will find shit, which even the most patient therapeutic efforts can't quite clear away. But the shit also begins with Freud himself, in the years of self-analysis which led up to *The Interpretation of Dreams* (1899) and *The Psychopathology* (1901).

Freud's adult sexuality is equally a tale of torment and naughtiness, burdened by the morality of the fathers, which suggests he was at least right in his own case to see the essential patterns of the psyche as determined in infancy. Crucially the adult Freud had to delay his marriage to Martha Bernays for more than four years, owing to lack of money and firm prospects, so that he was twenty-nine before he enjoyed a conjugal life and probably any relations with a woman at all. Dreams reflecting this waiting time distill Freud's frustration and resentment. When Martha says no to sex he wants to go to a prostitute, but the spirit of his father stops him. Later he wants to mete out this punishment period of four-plus years on anyone expecting a cure from psychoanalysis.

Since the theory thus formed affects the general public and the status of Freud's science, it seems strange that his critics have not taken more notice of this particular installment of self-revelation. Freud dreams that he receives a bill dated 1851. Since that is impossible, being five years before he was born, this "absurd Hospital Bill Dream," as he terms it, evidently involves his dead father. Several ideas then emerge as to what the dream might mean. One is the dismay and dwindling faith with which an older colleague, the Professor of Psychiatry at Vienna University, Theodor Meynert, has been watching Freud's analysis of a patient going into its fifth year. Freud has stored up this gesture of lack of confidence. The second theme concerns the delayed circumstances of Freud's marriage. The two themes come together when the dream turns Freud's father into Meynert in order to suggest that had Freud been the son of a professional man and a Gentile he would have got on faster and married sooner, and that financial dependency which allowed Meynert to be his judge and keeper would not have come about, nor by implication the sexual frustration of those five years.

> The most blatant and disturbing absurdity of the dream lies in its treatment of the date 1851, which seems to me no different from 1856, *as if the difference of five years meant nothing.* Yet exactly that should be brought out of the dream thought and given expression. *Four to five years*, that is the length of time during which I was subsidized by the colleague I mentioned at the beginning, but also the time which I made my fiancée wait for marriage, and through a coincidence willingly exploited by the dream thought also the time I make my closest patients wait to reach a complete cure.[8]

What we take away from this personal revelation is that because Freud had to wait four to five years to marry Martha, his unconscious linked that period of suffering with the eventual achievement of success and happiness. When experience later suggested that a successful psychoanalysis must take four to five years, Freud thought he was making a *bone fide* decision to impose that rule in the name of science, and recommended abstinence during analysis in the same scientific good faith. But what he sees now is that his unconscious had usurped his capacity for judgement and simply expressed what it wanted. Freud doesn't adumbrate the impulse here, but we should note that the involvement of the unconscious often reveals a desire for revenge, which for Freud is one of the strongest components of the submerged personality. The desire for vengeance is directed at the world at large: "If I had to suffer sexual misery so long, then so must you." The reader is entitled to wonder: can *this* be science? And the answer is clearly no, or not much of it.[9]

Freud's prenuptial torment surely also lay behind the temptation to see the problems of nearly all his patients as exacerbated by masturbation. Of course they wanted to keep quiet about it, because just like him it was a terrible secret for them to have. His patients resisted. "You would think that!" retorted Dora. Another young man however seemed to indict himself when he replied to a straight question: "O, na, nie!" which also means in German, "Oh, no, never!" On the other hand Freud's largely ignored concept of the *passing* neurosis, the *Aktualneurose*, reminds us of his essential sanity as a therapist who learned from his own experience. The *Aktualneurose* presents symptoms which resemble those of psychoneurosis, but disappear as soon as a normal sex life is enjoyed. Most of us would be grateful to Freud for such a diagnosis, which says, essentially, that being in erotic trouble from time to time is normal.[10]

When he was seventy-six Freud found a suitable illustration of the intense sexuality that troubled him all his life in the story of Prometheus. In Freud's fierce reinterpretation of Hesiod's tale, a bird comes every day and plucks at the liver of the chained hero, who has stolen fire from the gods. Normally it might be thought Prometheus had made his sacrifice in the cause of human progress. But Freud thinks Prometheus is being punished for living in abstinence, a consequence of *how* this hero stole the fire. The punishment theory hinges on the liver being the seat of pleasure, according to the medieval world view. Freud, seeing that the bird keeps pecking at the liver, surmises that the bird is the penis constantly thrusting its way forward. We understand that Prometheus is the original victim of "Civilization and its Discontents."[11]

Marx saw in Prometheus the triumph of material reality and also a model of redistribution, for Prometheus stole what only the élite gods enjoyed and made it available to the mass of humanity. But Freud's hero offers quite a different, mixed tale of success. All very well to steal fire by carrying it off in a hollow tube, but isn't that tube a worrying equivalent for the penis *qua* urinary tract? And doesn't the exhaustive use of the penis in this function preclude its use as a pleasure tool? Pleasure is what the rebellious god has renounced, in stealing the fire. He has ended his fellow gods' Dionysian existence and instead given them, and the world which projects them, morality.

Prometheus sets limits to natural excess, while storing endless fire within, and in this duality Freud sees reflected the double function of the penis and the whole plight of civilized Judaeo-Christian humanity. The heroic extinguishing of the fire enacts the process of sublimation. At the same time the male sexual fire continually renews itself and cannot be extinguished. Freud's reinterpretation of the myth of Prometheus once again reminds us how closely he interweaves coping with (his) sexuality with the success of civilization.

Success! Survival! Freud's whole system focuses on these aims with a mixture of encouragement and dismay, for conflict and difficulty lurk everywhere, without and within. The individual is in conflict with society, but also with himself. That is why success is so hard, and why the psyche wriggles and disguises itself until it can come to rest in a strong position, even if that strength is in the compromise form of neurotic compensation or fantasy.

In Freud's case some of the classic devices of neurotic compensation which the critic and the doctor would recognize actually occur in his own letters, and seem to do so unbeknown to him. These volitional processes take place in Freud in an unconscious into which he can peer with only imperfect understanding. But he has a good idea what is happening in others, namely that "resistance" is coming into play. Resistance means that unconsciously we shift our psychic weight so as to avoid losing our balance. We can't face knowing something. Freud quotes Nietzsche:

I did that, says my memory. I can't have done that, says my pride and remains immovable. In the end memory gives in.[12]

Projection for instance, which we may call an imaginative figure, or better still a psychological turn or trope, Freud defines as the most primitive defense the mind can muster. Turning around whatever is oppressing the subject from within, projection gives the subject the impression of a hectic, hostile outside world bearing down on her from which she must detach herself. But this seems exactly what Freud himself does when he bullies patients into being the carriers of feelings he finds unacceptable in himself, and then battles with their denials, which potentially block his own release. The unconscious intention is to get rid of *his* inner world by making it *theirs*.

Or, in moments of *introjection*, Freud absorbed feelings which he found repellent, and sent them back out into the world as his own view of others, in order to neutralize their incoming power to hurt him. His famously expressed hope that psychoanalysis would not be seen as a Jewish movement was only one of several striking pronouncements by which he tried to become a Jew-hater, in order to neutralize the anti-Semitic malice of his Viennese environment. His last book, *Moses and Monotheism*, seemed designed to deal a final emotional blow to the Jews by removing the Jewishness of Moses.[13]

Freud practiced unconsciously a classic "splitting" strategy to separate himself from Jews and Jewishness as a cause. This was painfully evident when his former colleague Alfred Adler died suddenly. He wrote to Arnold Zweig, an avowed Zionist:

> I don't understand your sympathy for Adler. For a Jew-boy out of a Viennese suburb a death in Aberdeen is an unheard-of career in itself and a proof of how far he had got on. The world really rewarded him richly for his service in having contradicted psychoanalysis.[14]

Adler was a psychoanalytical heretic, but he did not deserve such nastiness in the ordinary run of things. Compare this speaking ill of the dead though with a complaint Freud made five years earlier apparently on more rational grounds to Zweig, a Zionist who had fled from Hitler to the future Jewish homeland:

> this tragi-crazy land...Palestine has built nothing except religions, holy delusions, audacious attempts to conquer the external world of appearances with the inner world of desires...and we descend from that.[15]

Many would say that far from being distinct from this apparently Jewish intellectual vice, Freud's whole system is just such an attempt to conquer the external world of appearances with the inner world of desires. This is the case even though in its therapeutic aspect Freud's-*ism* tries to establish the primacy of the outer world. Freud's unconscious maneuvering, in the way it comes out in psychological tropes, thus points to a real conflict at the heart of his work. The therapeutic Freud teaches us to reconcile our inner world with the outer, socially given world if we want psychic health. But there is, as I shall show, at the same time a second Freud, given over almost entirely to fantasy as an alternative means to "health," which makes this allegation against the Jews all the more psychologically piquant.

A form of introjected anti-Semitism meanwhile lies behind a striking simile in the Ratman case. Freud likens the relationship between the unconscious and consciousness to the usurer and his client. The unconscious is ever ready to call in with interest the debt by which it has given the conscious subject a little illusory freedom. To be inferred is that the unconscious is as socially unacceptable, and as secretly necessary for the smoothing of life as the usurer, and both lenders are disliked. Here the depiction of conflict becomes the depiction of a hostile hierarchy in two parallel worlds, outer and inner. In the outside world Freud understands that as a Jew he is consigned to the murky margins; as are the insights of psychoanalysis. Meanwhile in the inner world we are all of us subject to what the unconscious demands of us. Only when we finally decode this trope by intertwining the inner and the outer, do we see that *as the usurer, or the unconscious personified, or the inventor of the unconscious*, three equivalent roles, Freud is in a superb position to exact revenge on anti-Semitic society.[16]

The notion of being treated like dirt meanwhile suggests that Freud has deliberately, though not consciously, rooted his science in dirtiness as an act of vengeance. Freud did not consciously regard himself as malign and dirty, yet it gave him an edge to ally himself with a power – the unconscious – which dealt in a conventionally "filthy" human currency. This would be also a general psychoanalytic explanation of why Freud devoted himself to creating a science of sexuality, another taboo in his day. Moreover, it brings to mind once again Freud's infantile readiness to see anything to do with bottoms as the chance to defend himself and offend others. Nietzsche spoke of making gold out of other men's dirt, when he contemplated his "transvaluation of all values" in 1888, and Freud, who alludes to this quotation, seems to have been engaged in the same process, wanting to survive with triumph, and not as a victim, in the face of the hostility of the world.[17]

How problematic it must have been for Freud consciously to view the chaos of his inner life in the end we can only surmise. Seeing a problem through our unconscious is more like thinking about it when we are drunk, says Proust. We either can't give it the right weight or it just floats, waiting for later interpretation to put the emotion and the value back into it. This is how one might think of the dream in which Ernst Brücke ordered Freud to dissect his own lower body for laboratory use, and of that Latrine Dream in which, thinking of his work in Vienna, Freud imagines having to wash away piles of shit with his own urine. The interpretation later establishes Freud as a serious and conscientious doctor, all too aware of his responsibilities to save a new generation from neurotic illness. But still he has his obsessions. Significantly, the only line Freud ever quotes from the greatest attack on anti-Semitism in classical German literature, Lessing's *Nathan der Weise*, is one where the Jew laments: "Not all are free who mock their chains." Chains are one's personality, and Freud was tightly wrapped in those that had come into being through social pressures. What he could adjust more easily were the bolts within.[18]

That he was obsessive and disproportionately furious with those who broke away from his rule was one of the hallmarks of the early psychoanalytic movement as it grew up around him. To take one rule we have already seen to be irrationally based, Freud insisted that psychoanalysis had to last four-plus years, and denounced Rank as a confidence trickster for claiming he could heal patients in four months. The irrationality of Freud's position seems all the clearer when we remember the fascination with the mythical dimensions of numbers which he shared with Fließ. Perhaps this was one way of continuing that passionate relationship with the last father substitute. Freud unconsciously kept the magic "four years" in his science as a memento and of course was hostile to anyone who tried to take it away. The degree of irrationality involved in holding a certain position translated into the degree of hostility with which challenges to it were met. This remained the case even when the challenge was mounted by facts. After all, many of Freud's patients ran away, including Dora, and even the case-study analyzes were relatively short. When Freud fell into hostile relations with others, he looked away from what he should have seen, namely his own acts of self-repetition and vengeance. He called Rank a confidence trickster, but who exactly was the confidence trickster? To avoid confrontation with the truth Freud split this fallible part of himself off and called it Rank.[19]

He left ever more signs of the mess in his unconscious by having Rank claim "success in *four* months." Why "four"? Rank's analyzes were brief, a matter of months and weeks, but I can find no definitive mention of "four" in either his theory as set out by his excellent biographer or in the notes of Rank's patients. A prominent Rankian patient rather had a dream about "*tre*mens' (= tres mens(es) = three months), as the time when he would be strong again. No, clearly with "four" Freud was holding on to what was his own even in what Rank had made off with. The "four" was something Freud had invented and/or cherished and no one had the right to change it.[20]

Another elaborate defense of the rightness of his own theories, which were mostly a repetition of his own inner life, came with Freud's diagnosis of the Wolfman's problems. Against Jung's heresy, Freud was determined to show the sexual etiology of neuroses in childhood and so the case interpretation proceeded along those lines, whatever the real, probably hereditary, truth of the Wolfman's illness. Again, when some years earlier Freud had become aware of his latent homosexuality with regard to Fließ, he still had to come out the victor by insisting how he, among the many afflicted, was a rare example of a soul cured.[21]

With Adler and Rank and Jung, and also with his other close disciple Ferenczi, Freud goes through conflict after conflict. He repeatedly re-enacts his childhood by moving from closeness and dependence to violent repudiation. The love/hate relationship with John, and a reversal of the struggle he had with his father's authority, ensures that in Freud's middle age his battles are as fierce as ever they were in the nursery.

My warm friendships as well as my enmities with people of my own age go back to my childhood relationship with my nephew John, who was a year older, and in a superior position. I learned early on to be on my guard. We lived together indivisibly and loved each other, though in between, according to what other people said, we fought and complained about each other. All my friends are in a certain sense incarnations of this first figure . . . In my emotional life I always needed an intimate friend and a hateful enemy. I could create these over and over and quite often the ideal from my childhood brought it about that friend and enemy coincided in one person...[22]

Freud loves and leaves. On the other hand each rebellion, even when he is the father and it is a hurt withdrawal, he interprets as a step towards his own success and originality, for hatred oils the machinery of progress. Freud's Oedipal instinct, by which a man unconsciously wants to murder his father and take his place, comes out of the same psychological stable as the theory of parricide in *Totem and Taboo*. The father is tradition. He is the old order which has to be overcome if the son is to progress at all. The desire to kill the father becomes the dialectic of progress, motivated by ambition and envy.[23]

Freud, thus dedicated to a power struggle from birth, needs to feel attractive, and sometimes the intimacy of psychoanalysis, and the position of power in which it places the analyst, looks unconsciously designed to reward this need in its inventor, who confessed he thought he lacked personal charm. He is so attractive the Wolfman wants to sodomize him, while the alluring eighteen-year-old Dora yearns for a taste of his smoky breath.[24]

Isn't this Freud terrifying and overwhelming? His direct confessions have been censored and are safe, but the tortuous interpretations of dreams which he does not always complete, and the oblique parallels and signs we pick up for ourselves, suggest a case of moderate paranoia. Like Senator Schreber, to whom he also devotes a case-study, Freud invents himself a world to survive, which means coming out on top, being one of the cured.

The case of Schreber is interesting, because it suggests Freud's whole thinking is like a set of symptoms he shares with that paranoid retiree from decent society. Schreber writes an account of a wholly sexualized vision of the world, in which he feels compelled to change his sex to please God. He believes that erotic beams link a man with God, but that human beings run the risk of overwhelming the deity, eclipsing his return beams and thus denying themselves the love they need. This colorful cosmos imagined by a frequently hospitalized paranoid schizophrenic interchanges male and female sexuality, and posits sexual bliss as the final, though fatal, human goal. But it shares many aspects of Freud's more soberly stated libido theory. Its very existence also supports Freud's notion of a *metapsychology* which strictly speaking applies to his own thought too. States of mind alone lie at the root of philosophies, religions and myths, and psychoneuroses are thus in their origins and projections close, if aberrant, relations of great cultural achievements. Schreber's case in fact encourages Freud to pinpoint a general paranoid bent in the human, which seems true, and stands as a caution to the world about the destiny of imagination.[25]

A critic once suggested that Freud's system was itself only a caricature of an ego philosophy. That doesn't seem the right way to put it quite, unless one believes there is something hard and fastly good about an ego philosophy, which presumably focuses entirely on how the balanced personality can flourish in a real world. But the word "caricature" has the right feel to it, because that is the nature of the unconscious: mocking, undermining, somewhere between elfin and Mephistophelian. The very existence of the unconscious contains a double warning that we should both befriend and contain the irrational excess that lurks in the human. Metapsychology in this way seems, like a much later thinker's *deconstruction*, to be a desperate measure both to escape repressive cultural norms and to limit the aberrant and perverse elements in human nature, and the unstable standards, which have been centrally uncovered. Look, Freud seems to say, as far as philosophical truth is concerned there are only life-stories and a few comments in the margin that can be made to the reader. Don't be misled into thinking cosmic facts of life have been established. What I can tell you about though is the pleasure of imagination: the way the human race sustains itself through illusions and dreams.[26]

In the end Freud does write semi-confessions, which we might best see as part of an autobiography of the body, such as Nietzsche wrote in *Ecce Homo*. Such confessions displace the usual priority of the spiritual over the bodily or material, and move the body and its daily life centre stage. The body has its psychopathology, but we shouldn't be afraid of a technical word which covers such humdrum things as biting one's tongue or losing one's keys. Freud's theory of unconscious motivation for everyday events actually helps him move towards a goal of physical familiarity, or *Heimlichkeit*. He would ideally replace superstitions about "uncanny" happenings in life with a science of unconscious motivation. Freud was concerned on all our behalf with becoming less *alienated* from himself and saw understanding the life of the body as the way forward. How repressed desires manifest themselves in the colour and the stuff and the evil of life I learned "from my own body," he told the audience of hundreds that gathered in Vienna during 1915–17 to find out what psychoanalysis was.[27]

Nietzsche asked in *Die fröhliche Wissenschaft*: has not the whole of Western philosophy been a misunderstanding of the body?[28] Freud, who felt in his deepest being that there was this thing called the unconscious which stored up old wishes and which was vengeful, lustful, evasive, devious, combative and selfish largely on behalf of the body's wants, produced the most detailed affirmative answer to this question in history. He wrote of how "emotional states" interfere with the work of the critical thinker.

> His critical insight then is not an independent function to be respected as such, but the lackey of whatever is his emotional state at the time. It does whatever his resistance orders. If something appears not right to him he can bring a keen mind to repelling it and seem very critical; but if something suits him, he can on the other hand show himself to be very gullible. Perhaps we're all much the same; only the analysand shows this dependence of the intellect on the emotional life all the more clearly because in analysis we put him under so much pressure.[29]

But this was only a sober way of insisting that the intensity of the bodily life, present and *past*, had to be accounted for in scientific activity. The rational project alone would leave men and women in torment.

In fact, the confessional activity often does seem to be a duty done in the name of science, and to be a strain for Freud. When he compared himself to Goethe, who famously avowed that his life's work was "only fragments of a great confession," his feelings about the subject became more apparent. The allusions allowed Freud to link his own work to Goethe's. "Yes, we are both engaged in confession." At the same time Freud *consciously* observed that Goethe's essential quality was his capacity to *disguise* his own life in his art.

> Goethe was not only a great confessor as a poet, but also despite the fullness of his autobiographical writings a careful concealer. We can't help thinking of those words of Mephisto's:
>> *Das Beste, was du wissen kannst,*
>> *Darfst du den Buben doch nicht sagen.*

"The best things you can know you're certainly not going to tell those devils."[30] This was the sentiment Freud really took to heart. He quoted his favorite couplet twice in *The Interpretation of Dreams* alone, and again in correspondence with Fließ, and finally years later, in 1930, on receipt of the Goethe Prize. In the first context when he drew Goethe into his enterprise he moved from the way dreams disguise what we can't face directly to the need for social disguise in the interests of politeness; he also alluded to the maneuvers of a political writer to avoid censorship while expressing his criticisms of the state. But on the second occasion, he reflected on his own difficulties in making a science out of his study of himself. He strikes an emotional note:

> I think of the effort it costs me just to make public the work on the dream, in which I have had to make so many revelations about myself. "The best things you can know you're certainly not going to tell those devils.'

The fundamental split in Freud, between concealing and revealing opens wide here. Freud sees that concealment is integral to the artist's job, and veritably the artist's right, but it is not the job or the right of the analyst-autobiographer in his role as model analysand. And that presents a problem, for Freud is consciously keen to protect the identity of his pen. What you know you can't say, if you want to be successful. The extraordinary and original and inventive mind you are you can't overtly display if you want to be successful in Viennese society. But it remains true that you are an artist like Goethe, who can write a whole world out of himself. That, Dr. Freud, is your fate.[31]

These are worldly and social reasons why Freud held the best back, and concealed writing his autobiography. They stem from his pursuit of success. But there were also quite straightforward reasons why Freud did not call himself a writer or an artist, which would have made an autobiographical endeavor seem quite normal. Freud was a philosopher interested in memory and motivation and how language links up with perception. He was also a medical doctor devoted to the treatment of neurotic symptoms. Together these questions occupied most of his attention. Moreover, they did not blend well with a writer's personal confession. On the other hand the scientific theory he was attempting to lay down could only be culled from the edges of his personal experience, in this case of paranoia:

It is a striking and generally to be recognized feature in the behavior of paranoiacs that they attach the greatest significance to the trivial details in the behavior of others. Details which are usually overlooked by others they interpret and utilize as the basis of far-reaching conclusions. For example, the last paranoiac seen by me concluded that there was a general understanding among people of his environment, because at his departure from the railway station they made a certain motion with one hand. Another noticed how people walked on the street, how they brandished their walking sticks, and the like. (Proceeding from other points of view, the interpretation of the trivial and the accidental by the patient has been designated as "delusions of reference.")

The category of the accidental, requiring no motivation, which the normal person lets pass as a part of his own psychic activities and faulty actions, is thus rejected by the paranoiac in the application to the psychic manifestations of others. All that he observes in others is full of meaning, is explainable. But how does he come to look at it in this manner? Probably here, as in so many other cases, he projects into the mental life of others what exists in his own unconscious activity. Many things obtrude themselves on consciousness in paranoia which in normal and neurotic persons can only be demonstrated through psychoanalysis as existing in their unconscious. In a certain sense the paranoiac is justified here. He perceives something that escapes the normal person, he sees clearer than one of normal intellectual capacity, but his knowledge becomes worthless when he displaces the content of what he sees on to others...

But the partial justification which we concede to paranoia in respect of its view of chance actions makes it easier for us to understand how paranoiacs become convinced of their interpretations. There is some truth in it. Mistakes which can't be described as pathological acquire the sense of conviction which accompanies them in the same way. This feeling is justified for a certain part of the erroneous thought process or for the source it emanates from, and is then extended by us to other connections.

Exactly what to rule in, and what out, Freud finds almost impossible to decide, as he wavers between the empirical method which he knows is correct for science, and the intuition which is his genius.[32]

In his scientific thinking he is always aware of the danger of subjectivity. This does not cancel his wish that the scientific mind might produce a less tainted picture of the real. But the hope is already a lament:

Only for the most select and most balanced minds does it seem possible to guard the perceived picture of external reality against the distortion to which it is otherwise subjected in its transit through the psychic individuality of the one perceiving it.[33]

What happens technically is that

> An inner perception is suppressed, and as its substitute its content reappears, having undergone a certain distortion, as a perception by consciousness from outside...this happens not only with paranoia but a regular proportion of our attitude to the outside world is attributable to it.

It is virtually impossible for any individual not to project his inner patterns on to the world.[34]

The force of Freud's personality, and the degree to which he has analyzed it, thus confirm his skepticism and *suggest obvious limits to the possibility of successful therapy*. The following paragraph in a letter to Jung seems like an extraordinary admission, which critics of Freud's "scientific" credentials should comment on, and at least commend for its honesty:

> I have very little time, and to draw on books and reports is not at all the same as drawing on the richness of one's own experience. Besides, my interest is diminished by the conviction that I am already in possession of the truth I am trying to prove. Such truths, of course are of no use to anyone else. I can see, from the difficulties I encounter in this work that I was not cut out for inductive investigation, that my whole makeup is intuitive, and that in setting out to establish the purely empirical science of psychoanalysis I subjected myself to an extraordinary discipline...[35]

Yet once the subjective element is delimited Freud has no difficulty moving ahead, and with integrity. He positively demands the foundation of a new human science at the head of all the humanities to give a new ground to self-knowledge, and this brings him back to the theory of metapsychology which first struck him in the late 1890s and was boosted by his experience of Schreber a few years later.

As a matter of fact, I believe that a large portion of the mythological conception of the world which reaches far into the most modern religions is *nothing but psychology projected into the outer world.* The dim perception (the endopsychic perception, as it were) of psychic factors and relations of the unconscious was taken as a model in the construction of a *transcendental reality*, which is destined to be changed again by science into *psychology of the unconscious.* It is difficult to express it in other terms: the analogy with paranoia must come to our aid here. We venture to explain in this way the myths of paradise and the fall of man, of God, of good and evil, of immortality, and the like – that is, to transform *metaphysics* into *meta-psychology.* The gap between the paranoiac's displacement and that of superstition is narrower than appears at first sight. When human beings began to think, they were obviously compelled to explain the outer world in an anthropomorphic sense by a multitude of personalities in their own image; the accidents which they explained superstitiously were thus actions and expressions of persons. In that regard they behaved just like paranoiacs, who draw conclusions from insignificant signs which others give them, and like all normal persons who justly take the unintentional actions of their fellow-beings as a basis for the estimation of their characters. Only in our modern philosophical, but by no means finished view of life does superstition seem so much out of place; in the view of life of prescientific times and nations it was justified and consistent.[36]

To ask the intelligent world to accommodate a primary volitional unconscious looks like a plea on Freud's part to acknowledge a creative/destructive power in the human being dangerously detached from any necessary external reality. It is a brilliant thesis, of which I am convinced Freud felt the whole truth through the power of fantasy operating in himself. Freud thought that fantasy was destructive in so far as it rode roughshod over reality, but creative in that fantasy was driven by libidinous desire, which meant that it expressed not only the passing goal of sexual pleasure, but a grand passion felt by each of us to be both physically and mentally at home in the world. In all this I would like to call Freud a dedicated scientist of the imagination as it works in the world. He was a serious thinker, who turned his findings from self-examination to the common good.

Still I think there was something deeply significant about his rejection of himself as an artist, because of what emerged from his unconscious to accompany that conscious rejection. He lashed out with envy, as we detected in the Twenty-Third Introductory Lecture, and produced a kind of caricature of high art, to which he was otherwise quite sensitive. I call this response to art which accompanied something nasty in Freud's unconscious "pen envy," partly to respond to a caricature with a caricature, and partly to underscore fundamental links between Freud's attitude to himself as a possible artist and, on the one hand his attitude to the tradition of the fathers, on the other his sexuality. I shall look at the sexual link first.[37]

A story from his life which might have the title "The Doctor and the Artists" was relayed by his biographer Ernest Jones. During Freud's overlong engagement he had two rivals for his future wife's hand, both of them artists. Freud as we know was already living in a state of prolonged anxiety, but in his view Martha's cousin Max Mayer, a musician, and even more so Fritz Wahle, a painter, posed a particular threat to his future happiness because their professions were

> disquieting facts in themselves. Freud had views about their capacity to please ladies and indeed had once been told that Fritz in particular had the reputation of being able to coax any woman away from another man.

In 1882, Jones continued, when Freud was twenty-six, a letter from Martha to Fritz "drove [Freud] into a frantic state in which he wandered through the streets for hours at night." Finally he borrowed money to travel from one end of the German-speaking world to the other, Vienna to Hamburg, to see his sweetheart and set his mind at rest.

Jones conjures up a Victorian melodrama, but a quote he takes from Freud suggests the underlying reality:

> I think there is a general enmity between artists and those engaged in the details of scientific work. We know that they possess in their art a master key to open with ease all female hearts, whereas we stand helpless at the strange design of the lock and have first to torment ourselves to discover a suitable key to it.[38]

So, Freud is sexually jealous of a whole improbable category of men who are good at foreplay! Isn't that just what he was telling us in "The Artist and Creative Imagination," with the notion of "forepleasure," and in the Twenty-Third Introductory Lecture, with the prize of "power, esteem and the love of women," that the artist is good at getting a mate, unlike Freud? That women open up to him? To take us to the hub of the problem, Freud concludes his comments quoted above by saying that the artistic personality has no reason for keeping itself under control. The problem is Freud's and is shared by all neurotic patients. To be attractive, to be open to sexual opportunity and to love requires a personality not held under unnatural control. But Freud, with his intense and tricky personality, depends on self-control to survive, while neurotics have internalized this defense mechanism long ago.

Another memory linking Freud's attitude to the artist and his sexual fears about himself seems to be of Philipp the unkind wordspinner. Philipp rivaled Freud's love of his mother and his nanny. He seemed to have spirited them away, and to have done so by virtue of some sexual power which he disguised with clever words, at the same time as he laughed at the boy's confusion and unhappiness. What more appropriate role then for this boy to grow up with than the desire to unmask the spellbinding strategies of the wordsmith.

One of the byways Freud goes down is to become a "scientific" literary critic and thus create a vehicle for his envy and suspicion towards the power of art.[39]

	Disguised as	*Revealed as*
Art	contents — "what it appears to be about"	the psychological content of the work/the artist's untransformed input
Neurosis	symptoms	a trauma in infancy; repressed wish
Dreams	manifest dream	latent dream (a repressed wish)
Slips	unwilled failure to act as intended	repressed wish
Jokes	humor	repressed wish

I set out here the skeleton of Freud's art and social criticism. Between 1899 and 1907 Freud devotes himself to the theory of disguise and revelation, because these forms lie at the heart of what he wants to say about the struggle of the individual to survive in culture. Neurosis is a form of disguise, so is art, so are jokes. Disguise is what culture out there and neurosis within have in common. Tense and creative, and highly ordered, they teeter on the edge of a collapse which would reveal what they are hiding. Taking this scheme into the world of dreams, and imagining there a dream factory whose job is to conceal in dreams what the analyst would reveal through interpretation, Freud crowns his extraordinary critical work by picking up where Aristotle left off in *On Rhetoric*. He classifies the tropes of imagination, and in *Jokes and Their Relation to the Unconscious* perhaps covers ground that Aristotle did in his lost volume on comedy.

I suggest Freud fears that exceptionally *he* will not be captivating as a writer. He certainly admits to this fear as a writing psychoanalyst. He fears he will not win but lose love because of what he has to say about himself, even if he can disguise it. A dream contrasting Goethe's harmonious and Freud's bestial view of nature echoes this fear. The series of statements which Freud makes about the artist culminates in the idea that writers fare well in the world because of the way they attract love. All of them, says the outsider, but not me.[40]

One feels the unconscious tension here because Freud *is* a writer. Freud splits himself off from writers, *Dichter*, just as he does in a remarkable paragraph in his speech of thanks for the Goethe Prize. There is an immediate irony that Freud is being awarded this prize for *literature*, which we see and surely Freud saw. The secretary of the prize depicts the nature of Freud's achievement in subtle tones. "Freud's strict scientific method" and also his "bold interpretation of the metaphors of the poets" are what we are gathered here to celebrate.

This was Freud's response:

> Our attitude to our fathers and teachers is once and for all an ambivalent one, for our respect for them regularly conceals a component of hostile rejection. This is a psychological disaster [*ein psychologisches Verhängnis*], it cannot be changed without violent suppression of the truth, and it must perpetuate itself in our relationship to the great men whose lives we want to study.[41]

Freud was rewarded for his contribution to the established humanities, even as he declared himself their enemy. "A component of hostile rejection...must perpetuate itself in our relationship...to great men."

This is the anthropology of pen envy. The envious late-born artistic individual turns on the part of the patrimony that matters most to him, extracts from it what he sees as the creative process and then sets up the curative business of psychoanalysis to rival not what artistic skill can do in terms of artifacts of lasting value, but to borrow the model of what the artist is, in order to help more people succeed in the world.

Envy is deeply engrained in Freud's system. Freud speaks in a letter to Fließ, albeit with an exclamation mark, of "innermost (impersonal!) envy."[42]

Fifty years ago the Catholic thinker Jacques Maritain wrote:

> I think that at the bottom of Freudian metaphysics there is what Max Scheler has called "resentment": the resentment, Freud

himself has explained, of a soul insulted and humiliated since childhood, a resentment, as it seems, against human nature itself; a resentment, above all, against all those things – rational, moral and religious forms and regulations – which according to him, in pretending to subdue the world of instinct in the name of an ideal, only add to men's misfortune and provoke psychic disorders.[43]

Maritain goes on to say that "Freud bears a special grudge against cultural sexual morality," but the same could be said for his attitude to high art, with its mixture of cultural authority to incite resentment and psychological insight to incite jealousy. One would want to psychoanalyze in this respect Freud's treatment of his son Martin's poetry-writing as a disease.[44]

For Freud envy is present in our every reaction to authority and public stature. We respect the differences that keep "great" people apart from us while simultaneously wishing we could replace them. We tell ourselves that essentially they are not special, and do not deserve their place. This might seem to be a specific reaction to hierarchical Viennese society *circa* 1900 and more widely to reflect the revolutionary politics that would break out across Europe in the next twenty years. Of course there are parallels between the Bolshevik and the Freudian spirit.[45]

But according to Freud, envy is not just the product of a wrongly constituted society, as it must be for Marx. It is our existential fate, our *Verhängnis*. We love, but we are also relieved to see the final departure of the loved one. Hypocrisy, insincerity and envy gather together under the Freudian umbrella of primary ambivalence. With pen envy I am applying these general attitudes of Freud's for the first time to the patrimony of high art.

So is Freud an artist, a non-artist or an anti-artist? The interesting thing is how often, having to face the possibility of his artistic talent, he takes cover behind *science*. He neurotically exaggerates doing science, and introjects the totem of its authority, so that instead of being in opposition to this authority, he can say: "I am the authority." "Being a scientist" in turn helps him suppress the intensity and fluency and playfulness which come to the fore in his writing when he lets go.[46] The end of the Twenty-Third Introductory Lecture even suggests through the counter-example of the susceptible artist that the scientist will *not* be led astray by the pursuit of popular success, which was *half* of what Freud wanted, to be resolute. He wanted success, but it had to be great success, through new insight into the secrets of nature; meanwhile, psychologically, he needed a discipline to keep him under control, and/or a reason for self-discipline.

> Artists are tied to the condition of targeting intellectual and aesthetic pleasure as well as particular emotional effects, and so they can't present the material of reality unchanged, but must isolate little bits of it, get rid of connections that get in the way, modify the whole, and fill in whatever is missing. These are the privileges of so-called poetic license. They can only show cursory interest in the origin and development of the states of the soul they depict as ready-made. And so it becomes inevitable that science, with clumsier hands and with less of a pleasure gain, occupies itself with the same material, in the poetic reworking of which people have been taking pleasure for thousands of years. These observations may serve to justify a strictly scientific treatment of the love life of mankind. Science is just about the most perfect renunciation of the pleasure principle that is possible for our psychic work.[47]

I suggest that unconsciously Freud developed *his* science to keep his deviant self under control and that the strategy succeeded. Psychoanalysis gave him a map and a key to the unconscious which otherwise threatened to disrupt his life at every turn. It turned his intensity, his disruptiveness, his infantile obsession with the lower half of the body into a brilliant theory of how a primary unconscious is at work in *all* of us, undermining our conscious and sensible and benevolent intentions. Life can't do away with the unconscious, and society only at high risk ignores its presence. But science can contain all this deviance. I put it to Freud that he made this discovery and told it as a story: *Vienna 1900*.[48]

Freud himself was artist, non-artist and anti-artist. His large and complex and intense character was woven of endless self-revelations and self-concealments. Not Plato and Goethe, as his follower Marie Bonaparte suggested, but probably Rousseau and Tolstoy are his nearest relatives as creative personalities. He recalls them perhaps in the first two novels I imagine him to have written, but more certainly in the way he agonized over the difficulty of being himself, and how he wrestled to write that self down. Rousseau, Tolstoy and Plato were all so afflicted. The philosopher Sebastian Gardner has suggested Freud's whole system is devoted to "the motivated failure of self-knowledge" and one might also say this about the personal writings of Tolstoy and Rousseau. Freud appears in this light to be the most self-searching autobiographer of the twentieth century, simultaneously sincere and "sincere."[49]

Sincere/'sincere" as an alternating way of writing resembles the game which Freud one day found his grandson playing, and which struck him with psychological significance. At a time when the boy's mother was often gone from the house, and he didn't appear to miss her, he played the *fort/da* game. It was as if he were pushing his mother away so that he could enjoy the repeated pleasure of her return. And so Freud, in his individuality and bodily solitude, plays gone again/back again with the reader, as he half-reveals something he either cannot face or hesitates to make public. A formidable theme running through his work is therefore the dialectical interworking of public/private, as it is in Rousseau and Tolstoy; and it is often another way of saying revealed/concealed.[50]

Rousseau wrote *Confessions* and Tolstoy wrote his *Confession*. Freud's *Interpretation of Dreams* is his "confession" too. What motivates these three great confessions over three centuries, from one end of Europe to the other, is in all three cases a sexuality which threatens to overwhelm the subject if he is left alone with it. Like Freud, Rousseau is obsessed with the unnaturalness and yet the reality of the urge to find pleasure alone, whereas Tolstoy is prey to such inordinate appetites that he tries repeatedly to pledge himself to monasticism. In middle age Tolstoy is so disgusted by his own sexuality that he calls upon the human race to abstain from sexual intercourse forthwith, and supports his vision with the stories "Father Sergei" and "The Kreuzer Sonata." Tormented by a diabolical representative of the fair sex, Father Sergei cuts off his "thumb" in his efforts to resist carnal temptation, while in "The Kreuzer Sonata" a man who is evidently Tolstoy's *alter ego* becomes tormented with jealousy at the idea of his wife's adultery with a young musician, and finally kills her. The theme strikingly recalls Freud's irrational fear of the sexual prowess of artists, while the whole murky world of the husband's feelings, which do not in the least stem from love, but rather more from his estrangement from love, might have been disclosed in a Freudian account of a man's unconscious.[51]

Against this repeated picture of inner darkness and torment, encouraged by religious scruples, what Rousseau and Tolstoy and Freud all clamor for is bright, open nature as an antidote to their internally manufactured poison. If only there were some way of exorcizing the demon. Rousseau proposes long walks in the country and plain food, Tolstoy likewise deifies bucolic simplicity, so long as it is grounded in hard physical work. Freud even manages to sound like Rousseau when he complains that culture wrongly brands our early experience of sexuality dirty, so that we remain uncomfortable with ourselves ever after. Uncomfortable, not at home, haunted: here again is the shadow of what is *unheimlich*, the power of which Freud's autobiography of the body set out to dispel.

> Strong forces from a later period of life have modeled our capacity to remember things from childhood, probably the same forces which are responsible for our having alienated ourselves so far away from our childhood years.[52]

Freud mostly fantasizes over a natural paradise never lost at the mother's breast. He adds to it a theory of sublimation, the most civilized and civilizing way in which the energy orphaned by this original erotic loss can be married to a good secondary purpose in adult life. But he remains one with his predecessors in that all three writers insist the loss of naturalness is not just personal. They strongly blame society for the distortion of nature they feel in themselves and see around them. Tolstoy sees this in the Frenchified Russian upper class, Rousseau sees it in towns, in progress, and in the very nature of writing even, as opposed to learning in an oral tradition from the fathers, while Freud sees it in the hypocritical life led by the Viennese bourgeoisie. As their writing approaches the genre of pamphleteering, both Tolstoy and Freud campaign for greater public sexual enlightenment, while Rousseau sets out an ideal education, which would not corrupt a man, in his didactic novel *Émile*.

A longer study would bring out the fascinating parallels in the lives and work of these three great European writers across three centuries. Freud is the most urban figure among them and the most abstract thinker, and politically the most conservative. Here I shall end the comparison by focusing on just a small matter of similarity between Tolstoy and Freud. It concerns how they behaved in family life, where they continued to be haunted by a desire for authenticity.

> It is undoubtedly due to painful experiences in life that I am unable to manifest sympathy where this manifestation must necessarily appear exaggerated, for the small amount of my feeling does not admit the corresponding expression. Since I have learned that I often mistook the pretended sympathy of others for real, I am in rebellion against the conventions of expressing sympathy, the social expediency of which I naturally acknowledge.[53]

Where Freud speaks directly of himself, he often recalls Tolstoy, the paranoid *père de famille*, who, when he repaired to his study, produced lucid prose to explain how his real self fell away from the standards established by social convention and family expectation.

For both Tolstoy and Freud there is shock at what they discover about themselves. Pettiness and paranoia and vulnerability dominate their characters, and their sexual hunger is unspeakably present day and night. But there is also comfort that this is the human truth of things which they, the fearless ones, will spell out in a hypocritical world.

Freud in a sense invents the unconscious to ground this truth, to give it a home, to make it the general condition. It is a kind of self-portrait from within. He looks at his personality from the wrong side, like a piece of knitting with all the joins and loose threads showing, and laughs and shakes his head at the spectacle. He tells us that even where we are unaware of it we are lusting after our parents or plotting to murder them and that these ugly and passionate desires are stored in the unconscious, ready to re-emerge by some other means of expression at any time, whatever our reasonable exterior may suggest. Sex underlies and belies the sanity and calm of men and women everywhere. To dynamize the metaphor, because Freud's system of personality is dynamic, sex – and envy – and this is an overall formidable drive to mastery and pleasure like Schopenhauer's *Wille* – is always threatening to break through to the surface.

But Freud's doctrine is not ultimately one of Original Sin, for unlike Rousseau or Tolstoy he understood and forgave himself, and this encouraged him to write and think and analyze; and to give psychoanalysis to humanity as a gift like a great and self-contradictory work of art. This is the product of his self-enquiry, and he issues it with a reminder to us readers that we too should not be too severe with our physical selves, indeed we should be "less good" and listen to our needs and our dreams, if we want to be in touch with who we are. Jung saw what they had uncovered as evil, but Freud saw evil elsewhere, and soldiered on.[54]

4

MAN OF THE SOUL

Otto Rank paid Freud the compliment of calling him a medically proven artist. So did the British writer and pioneer sexologist Havelock Ellis, with the observation that Freud's vision rested on a fundamentally artistic insight into his own soul. This latter assertion Freud even set up for publication, but then apparently showed anger that it should ever have been mooted. Others, undismayed by the apparent predominance of disfiguring hydraulics, have long seen poetic beauty in Freud's physics of desire, which finds a new, neo-Romantic way of locating man in nature. Still others have appreciated the tableaux of the unconscious as reproducing the bloody world of Greek tragedy.[1]

Perhaps together the eleven German volumes selected from Freud which have served me in making this book comprise the finest writer's notebook of the century. They show Freud absorbed by his observations of human character and behavior, and by language. Aware of his gift for human observation, in *The Psychopathology of Everyday Life* he compared it with that of King Solomon who could understand the animals. In *The Psychopathology* and in *The Joke and Its Relation to the Unconscious,* the works which with *Dreams* comprise his most personal and intense productive period from 1899 to 1905, Freud displays a fine ear for dialogue, a love of the rounded tale, and humor. Freud's interests developed in remarkable parallel with early structuralist poetics. His love of language seems to have come out of his native gift, though the cradle was rocked by Brentano, some of whose other disciples went on to found a new poetic linguistics.[2]

> So the word is a complex idea made up of pictures brought its way, or to put it another way, it corresponds to an intricate process of associations, which the various elements of visual, acoustic and kinaesthetic origins embark upon together.

But nothing leaves a greater impact on the reader than Freud's new vision of the human, so daring in his day. Endlessly intriguing vistas open up showing possible disguises for fear, shame, and uncertainty in social and private behavior.[3]

An interesting observation in the dreambook, that neurotics want to play all the roles, suggests a possible psychopathology for how it might be for Freud the writer to *appear* to empathize with characters outside himself. But I think Freud did have the capacity to identify with others as a form of compassion. The following paragraph from the essay "Cultivated Sexual Morals and Modern Discontent" (1908) contains a whole novel in outline, sympathetic to an unknown married woman:

> I don't know whether the type of anaesthetic woman occurs also in the uncultured classes, but I presume it likely. In any case it is positively bred by education, and these women, who conceive without pleasure, then show little readiness to have more children, often with pain. In this way the preparation for marriage renders the very aims of marriage in vain; when the woman's hesitations, due to her upbringing, are overcome and the full capacity to love awakens in her, as she reaches the pinnacle of her womanly existence, her relationship with her husband has already been spoilt long ago; what remains to her as a reward for her previous willingness to conform is the choice between unfulfilled longing, infidelity or neurosis.[4]

This outline stands some comparison with Theodore Fontane's novel *Effi Briest*, in which a young girl from a middle-class family is married off to an older man, and passes through innocence and educated resignation to late self-discovery and early social ruin. Freud's desire is to rescue men and women from the sexual ignorance which threatens a whole lifetime's happiness. Had the woman in his notebook succumbed to infidelity and he to writing a novel, its content might have reminded us also of *Anna Karenina* and *Madame Bovary*. Still Freud promises something other than nineteenth-century realism with his revolutionary moral outlook. As a would-be novelist of bourgeois life in Vienna 1900 he is more like "the ironic Jew," in apposition to Thomas Mann's end-of-Bürgertum "ironic German."[5]

Technically the irony which gives Freud's writing its flavor is possible because of the existence of the unconscious. Before Freud, mind was generally considered to be a synonym for consciousness. But Freud showed that many mental processes were shaped from some centre beyond our conscious control. The unconscious is primary, and the home of primary processes, while rationality is a secondary process. Rationality is a kind of tidying up of whatever unruly material the unconscious has thrown in to supplement and disrupt immediate conscious perceptions and memories.

Freud lays out the groundwork for his vision in his essay on Jensen's *Gradiva*:

For psychic processes which behave actively and nevertheless don't reach the consciousness of the person concerned, we have no other name for the time being than, and mean nothing else with, our "unconscious." If a good many thinkers want to challenge us over the existence of such an unconscious, and call it senseless, we believe that they have never concerned themselves with the corresponding phenomena of the soul, and that they are under the spell of the routine finding that everything in the soul that becomes active and intense becomes simultaneously also conscious, and that they still have to learn what our artistic writers evidently know very well, that there are processes in the soul which, despite the fact that they are intense and exhibit energetic effects, nevertheless remain distant from consciousness.[6]

The primary unconscious running and ruining lives is, Freud says, something artists already know all about. It seems like a deep perversity running through the human, to which Freud lends the metaphor in *Dreams* of the political despot who deliberately promotes an unpopular official. Why does the ruler do that? Freud asks the question and supplies the perverse answer. Just to show that he does not have to listen to the people. This is the degree to which we are not in charge of how our inner life presents itself, even when we befriend our passions.[7]

I have some deep desire stored in my unconscious and something triggers it into active expression. There is, Freud imagines, a censorship mechanism in the unconscious which means that the desire will not emerge into consciousness as itself, but disguised. This is essentially how neurotic symptoms form. They express inadmissable wishes which we have repressed by borrowing real expressions of pain and desire from other aspects of the physical life.

Let's take as an example the case of a hysterical headache or backache. Analysis shows us that through compression and displacement this has become a compensatory satisfaction for a whole range of libidinous fantasies or memories. But this pain was once real too, and then it was a direct sexual-toxic symptom, the physical expression of libidinous excitement. We want by no means to maintain that all hysterical symptoms have a kernel like this, but the fact remains that it is particularly often the case and that all, whether normal or pathological, influences on the body through libidinous excitement are specially suited to the formation of the symptoms of hysteria. They play then the role of that grain of sand which the mollusk has coated in layers of mother of pearl. In the same way the passing signs of sexual excitement which accompany the sexual act are used by psychoneurosis as the easiest and most suitable material for the formation of symptoms.[8]

Freud here graphically portrays the unconscious as a system predatory not only upon consciousness, but upon the whole working of the body, such that it can borrow and mimic its flushes and pains to express its own deeper discontents. If mimicry captures the agility of pyschic disease, the notion of "the pearl of neurosis" suggests a kind of mental cancer which grows ever larger, blocking our available personal freedom. The pearl of neurosis encapsulates Freud's view as to how easily, by letting this predatory system run riot from within, a life can be wasted. Proust introduces a third metaphor, of a water lily drifting forever back and forth, only appearing to move forwards. It makes him think, as it did Freud, of souls in hell.[9]

Freud discusses the case of the woman who has actually left her husband but remains fixated on her marriage. Her whole existence seems to elevate and praise her husband and mourn his loss. She can't go out of the house, can't get up out of the chair, can't sign her name and can't give presents. Freud suggests that these crippled actions are dominated by the woman's unconscious desire to stop any other man having some part of her. She doesn't want to behave like this, but it is not a process she can control.[10]

That an unconscious idea can affect a person's physical condition or actions, as with this woman's temporary lameness and paralysis of the hand, is a conviction Freud took away from his experience of hypnosis. It has often been questioned. The corollary, physical conditions for which there seems to be a word cure, seems equally to belong to the realm of magic and miracles. Yet as all people of humane imagination know, attitudes of mind can affect the course of a disease; and while shock can numb us physically and emotionally, in the body's deliberate attempt to protect us from danger in an emergency, by the same token any anxiety can radically affect posture and voice and general physical strength. Further, even if we don't accept that neuroses ultimately can be traced back to unfulfilled sexual desire for a parent there is *something* the neurotic has never come to terms with, which affects her emotional and in the end her physical well-being. Neurosis *saves* us from worse injury by rendering us unfit.[11]

Freud writes of patients such as the ex-married woman above:

One has to admit that in these symptoms of compulsive neurosis, these ideas and impulses that appear, who knows where from, and show so much resistance to all the influences of an otherwise normal inner life, that they give the patient herself the impression of being superhuman visitors from another world, immortals who have mixed in with the mortal crowd, is the clearest indication of a particular sphere of the inner life cut off from the rest. An unmistakable path leads from them to the conviction of the existence of the unconscious in the soul, and for exactly that reason a clinical psychology which only recognizes a psychology of consciousness can do nothing else with them other than to see them as signs of a particular kind of degeneration. Of course, the compulsive ideas and impulses are not themselves unconscious, no more than the execution of compulsive actions escapes conscious perception. They wouldn't be symptoms if they hadn't penetrated through to consciousness. But the psychic preconditions which we deduce for them through analysis, the connections we make for them through interpretation, are unconscious, for at least until we have made the patient conscious of them through analysis ... The possibility of giving neurotic symptoms a sense through analytic interpretation is an unshakable proof for the existence – of if you will the necessity of accepting – unconscious processes in the soul.[12]

When Freud first wanted to explain fixation and neurosis to an American audience he invented the example of a man at London's Charing Cross station who instead of catching his train to work sinks to his knees before the ancient stone cross and weeps for dead Queen Eleanor. The story is a metaphor for an ill-functioning personality. Instead of going forwards this man is stuck emotionally in the past. We are all familiar with lesser examples. Freud himself was afraid of missing trains, and yet would always be caught short just as the train approached the platform and therefore unable to board. Once when I wanted to deliver a manuscript to a publisher

I couldn't find one of the most prominent addresses in London, in the Fulham Road. The neurotically generated action makes the consciously purposeful action, what we might call being sensible, impossible, though we do our best to disguise it. By postulating an active, interfering unconscious we begin to understand how behavior can be partly or wholly out of the subject's control.[13]

Ironic symptoms, betraying the presence of the unconscious in all of us, range from nearly normal behavior to overt lunacy. Freud reports that he watches out for little signs such as betray love and crime; or, in the case of the skeptical newcomer to analysis who leaves the door of the consulting room open, he sees simply individuals at odds with themselves. Sometimes the evidence is obvious. There are people who wash excessively, and people who cannot go out. The Ratman removes a stone from the road believing that it might jolt his beloved's carriage when she passes by. "Little Hans" is preoccupied with "wee-wee makers" and terrified that horses will bite him. A young woman makes absurdly complicated preparations for sleep, and regularly experiences not a wink. These symptoms are ironic and neurotic because they betray the influence of the unconscious.[14]

We recognize neurotic symptoms by their psychic *quantity*, that there is something overdone or disproportionate about this speech or action. Certain people present themselves as excessively good, or over-anxious, or excessively conscientious, or full of "an anxious and excessive tenderness, intended as a cover for hate." Freud was interested to read that the writer Emile Zola had a compulsive need to tell the truth, while in literature Hamlet, whose every act is extravagant and of mysterious origin and uncertain intent, struck him as the quintessential neurotic character.[15]

Neurotics lack choice: they are fixated, whereas more normal people are flexible. In the neurotic, certain gestures are compulsively repeated. Of a child's fear of animals (Little Hans's fear of horses) Freud writes that:

Fed on energy from the unconscious source, this fear shows itself excessively large and antagonistic in the face of all influences from the system [we call] Consciousness and by that means betrays its origins in the system [we call] the unconscious.[16]

Freud suggests that the whole surrounding psychic area becomes affected by such excesses, so that there are many small-scale repetitions of the fundamental response to a repressed unconscious wish. The repressed material occupies more and more space in the sufferer's life, as the disturbance goes untreated.[17]

In the presence of neurosis others have the sense that certain actions or ways of speaking are replacements or compensations for something else that the person wants. Dora limps and loses her voice. Anna O can't drink water. Someone else can't go near a certain place, or pronounce a certain place name. A young woman repeatedly runs into a room, takes up a particular position beside a table, calls her maid to whom she then issues some unimportant instruction, and runs out again. The Ratman catches several trains, enlists the help of strangers, and even seeks a doctor's prescription in misdirected attempts to repay what he thinks he owes. The Ratman's and the young woman's actions are clearly ersatz. To these major examples one could add the minor list of "symptomatic and chance actions" Freud considers in Chapter IX of *The Psychopathology of Everyday Life*: playing with a watchchain, fingering one's beard, doodling with a pencil, juggling coins, kneading dough, handling one's clothing. There are moments when Freud gets out his key instead of ringing the door bell of a patient with whom he feels particularly at home; times when he gets his house keys out to open the hospital laboratory, a slip he reads as indicating his desire to be at home with his preferred, less routine work.[18]

Whenever someone in the Freud family bit his tongue Freud replaced sympathy with the question: "*Why* did you do that?" for he felt that many "accidents" were unwittingly self-inflicted wounds, just as accidental damage to things, or losses, could be unconsciously motivated.[19] Coming back to the problem of defective self-knowledge, we see that countless evasions, deprivations and prohibitions are practiced by subjects on themselves. Self-reflexiveness turns in a circle, chases its tail, instead of leading to insight and self-correction. The psychoanalytic observer's experience here is akin to the theatre audience's view of dramatic irony. What is known by the character about himself is far less than we know.[20]

In the *Psychopathology*, of Freud's tales which survive translation, there is the one about the domineering wife who reports of her sick husband that he may eat, according to the doctor, anything I like, and another about the man who reluctantly takes the platform to open a meeting and finds himself declaring it closed. Dr. P asks Freud's advice over a divorcée who has taken to drink. The doctor says he is unmarried himself, and asking on behalf of a friend. But saying "he" instead of "she" suggests to Freud he is lying. The doctor bustles off, saying Freud is dangerous, but later returns to announce his faith in psychoanalysis, because Freud is evidently so perspicacious. There are also many slips of the tongue, in which a person ends up saying exactly what he consciously didn't want to say. A man trying to ignore a colleague's fart begins, "It has come to my nose," instead of, "It has come to my notice."[21]

Freud is the poet of the mistake, who gives us the depth psychology of the malapropism and the spoonerism and the *double entendre*. He loves misleading homophones, slips of speech, and typographical errors. (I have enjoyed variously seeing *analust* and *analist* appear on my screen, suggesting I am now pretty in tune with Freud.) Freud loves mistakes because they open up so much scope for humor, and he watches how what first strikes us as "funny ha ha" shades into "funny peculiar." Freudian people are peculiar. Freud is the great poet of eccentricity in Western culture.

> Compulsive neurosis finds its expression in the way patients busy themselves with thoughts which actually have no interest for them. They feel impulses which seem quite alien, and they are driven to actions which give them no pleasure to execute, but which are quite impossible for them not to carry out. The thoughts (compulsive ideas) can make no sense in themselves or

are a matter of indifference to the individual, [and] often they are thoroughly silly, [but] in every case they are the beginning of an effortful sequence of mental activity which exhausts the patient and to which he gives himself up only very unwillingly. He has to brood and speculate, as if something vital in his life were at stake. The impulses that the patient feels can equally make a childish and senseless impression, though mostly they have a shocking content, like temptations to serious crimes, so that the patient doesn't only reject them as alien, but flees from them horrified and protects himself from carrying them out with prohibitions, denials and constraints. In the way of things they never break through to execution, not a single time; the upshot is always that flight and caution are victorious. What the patient really carries out, so-called compulsive actions, are very harmless and certainly trivial things, mostly repetitions, ceremonious elaborations of activities from everyday life, and yet these necessary jobs, going to bed, washing, dressing, going out for a walk become the most wearisome tasks, hardly to be discharged . . . That's really a crazy kind of suffering. I think not even the most exuberant psychiatric imagination could have come up with a construction like that, and if one didn't see it before one's eyes every day, one would hardly make up one's mind to believe it.[22]

When the Ratman's fusses about that stone in the road that might dislodge his beloved's carriage he is comic in the way he can't make up his mind where he is going. Similarly the way he gets on and off trains, and is afraid of missing the train he is not on, or bypassing a station, makes us laugh. Freud insists such behavior is *almost* normal and a comic reinvention of adulthood rests on his suggestion, worthy of the quotation book, that "We are surely all a bit neurotic."[23]

"*Daß wir alle ein wenig nervös seien*" invites a redefinition, or perhaps the abolition of the whole idea of maturity in a way that really took hold in Freud's century. For if I turn to the popular culture around me now, tidying away the children's books my daughter read fifteen years ago, I see that characters like Mr. Forgetful, Mr. Muddle, Mr. Daydream, Mr. Uppity, Mr. Grumble, Mr. Bump, Mr. Rush, Mr. Fussy, Mr. Busy are so permeated by the Freudian vision that they effortlessly introduce our children to the comedy of compulsions and compensations. Instinctively the young reader knows such an exaggerated existence isn't quite right and even a bit naughty. I see too, when I watch television, that a hotel owner who fluctuates between infantile displays of frustration and clumsily concealed aggression is an unforgettable example of a man taken over by the Freudian unconscious. Brill's translation of what is normally called the Freudian slip is "the faulty act," which suggests why this character's name should be Basil Fawlty. His escapades, or escape-aids, have not only reduced millions of viewers to tears of laughter, but illustrate perfectly Freud's view that *consciousness is an organ of the senses which apprehends a content given from elsewhere.* The content from elsewhere undermines public appearances. It fills the mind with ambivalence where positive feeling is required.[24]

But here is also an important point for philosophy. If Descartes is the father of the modern, Freud creates the postmodern to bring back into the philosophical arena exactly what Descartes banished, namely the senses, and dreams and the errors of perception through sickness. Freud's "from elsewhere" links his concept of the unconscious with what a pre-scientific world called possession by the devil. The fact that this primary unconscious is predatory upon consciousness and upsets rational behavior makes it the best example in entertainment history of Descartes's *malin génie*, and Basil Fawlty the best example in philosophy too, for the *malin génie* represents the rationalist's worst fear that he is somehow not in charge. The shift from 1640 through Freud to the last decades of the twentieth century is the ground map of the contemporary humanities and the story culminates in a television comedy series. It's only a nice thought that three hundred and fifty years later we have learned to credit Descartes's malevolent devil with Freud's sense of humor.[25]

The devil's name is not taken in vain. Real sickness looms quite close to the border of Freud's funny territory. The Ratman is at his slapstick funniest when he is indecisive; but when he wants a doctor to write him a prescription saying this man must pay three crowns to a certain person or he won't get well we feel funniness passing into delusion and madness. The sleepless girl who banishes a noisy clock from her bedroom because it makes her aware of her clitoris is beginning to go crazy. The same goes for the woman with the impotent husband who rushes from room to room and gives the maid ridiculous orders. The screen persona of the actor Woody Allen aims to capture the essence of Freud's funniness problem. The portrait of this tedious neurotic is sentimental, and to take it too seriously risks banalizing psychoanalysis. Yet the hint of slapstick in that clumsy body is brilliant, just the right moment in cinematic history to duplicate, *echt* Freud.

Finally, Schreber the paranoid and compulsive lavatory user is not just a case to laugh at. The distinguished senator seems like a gift to the comic-sketch writer, for he is frantic lest "the privy" be engaged; he reckons colleagues are being sent to the lavatory at the very moment he feels the need, just to spite him. Of course he's funny. What's more he reminds us of someone. There's always someone "a bit paranoid" in the office like him. But this man is also irremediably ill.[26]

Freud writes down all these extraordinary stories as he revamps the old view of bedeviled character.

> *Nun ist die Luft von solchem Spuk so voll,*
> *Daß niemand weiß, wie er ihn machen soll.*

> Now teems the air with many a spectral shape,
> So thick that none can shun them or escape.

The quote set at the beginning of *Psychopathology* is from the Midnight scene in Goethe's *Faust*, and it brings home just what Freud sees when he peers behind the veil of rational motivation and into the unconscious. Freud's project is to release the spooks from the individual mind. Only he knows the human condition is ironic. There is no simple, natural state to aim for. Nor does a man have to be Faust to have spoiling demons within.[27]

One result of Freud's vision is that old certainties split, both in philosophy and psychology, releasing new energy for self-reflection. If we see Freud as metaphorically laying on therapeutic hands we may speak of his Binary Touch. The stultifying: "I am a good person," "I love my mother," "this action is wicked," gives way to the energizing, disturbing: "I am good/bad," "I love/hate my mother," "this action is good/wicked."[28]

Freudian man is in search of self-knowledge, but ontologically handicapped. He is poised between two modes of self-assessment, which belong to different realms. Here we are immediately in new territory for fiction, and also for literary criticism and philosophy. Man is a critical animal, capable of almost infinite self-regulation, but his health depends on *not* reining in the imagination which emanates from his unconscious. To be himself he must fantasize, but if he wants to present a rational self he must provide a key to the fantasy. He may take for himself the analysand's freedom to raise any subject, make any connections, according to the principle of free association. But if he continues to respect reason and social order he must also perform the task of the analyst and give a definite and contained shape and meaning to what is expressed.

All this has great importance for what we mean by "character." The revelation of the ironic can be summed up as a revelation of multiple narratives within the human "voice"; the idea that several skeins or discourses go to make up the plaited mental rope. Take only my awareness of my desire for success. I might fail in my job, and be conscious that I have in the view of others failed. Quite possibly for myself I will rationalize this failure into a kind of success, without being entirely conscious of it, while at night my dreams may be of situations where I have pity for others; where I am a good Samaritan. But if my dream is analyzed it may turn out that what I want is pity for myself. Here are four possible narratives derived from one event, seen both from outside as if through a window, and by holding up a mirror to my inner life, and together they hugely expand the traditional concept of character.

It has been said Freud simultaneously opens and holds up to personality the window and the mirror. These parallel levels of mental processing are very simple as I have invented them; Freud himself would be more complex. But they represent an important illustration and simultaneously an appeal to the reader to accept that this dynamic, interactive multiplicity, like the heterophony in Stravinsky's *Petrushka*, is what it is in Freud's view to have a mind, and, indeed, to be a person. Freud has his own striking image of our human makeup, with the personality comprising a troupe of actors, every one of whom chooses a different play for his benefit performance.[29]

The heterophony that Freud discovers for character suggests to me a program for the humanities which Freud never wrote, but which reaches down to us from his influence. It includes psychoanalysis and literature, literary criticism and philosophy. In our self-reflection there will be theory, which traces transformations, or processes, and there will also be the pictures we make of ourselves to enjoy as such. The theoretical questioning to which we submit our humanity and the creative harvest we exact from it are twin processes and together they present the optimum path to that goal of self-knowledge where we can't quite arrive. The activity is critical on the one hand, free-reined on the other, and somehow the two approaches should be coordinated. This seems to mean that the territory of art and philosophy must grow to include new areas of defective mental reflexivity (when, as it were, the artist's or the thinker's dialogue with herself breaks down), and then hyphenate their new work in perpetuity: art-critical theory, philosophy-literature. Freud evidently took those disciplines where many would see them resting now.

All this is extraordinary. There are times in Freud when we seem to be reading different centuries alongside each other. Nineteenth-century novelistic elements that would sit well in Tolstoy and Dostoevsky suddenly give way to passages with more affinity to Dadaism and Surrealism, and especially in literary terms to the Joyce of *Finnegans Wake*.

Further we have to add to the view of personality as a dynamic composite affected by different levels of consciousness and different relations to the outside world Freud's essential stress on the *economy* of the personality. In Freud's theory what complements the Aristotelian view of personality as dynamic substance is the notion of personality as an intricate economy of energy seeking *expression.*

> One can even imagine that the temperaments of all people are qualitatively the same and only differ by way of these quantitative relations.[30]

The reader may find it helpful to imagine Freud wrote a long poem called *Kräftespiel der Seele* or "The Play of Forces in the Soul." Like Freud's other work this vision seems to span both the Romanticism and the philosophical materialism of the nineteenth century and to carry its implications into the present.

In the beginning there is a wish, as there is early in life, for the love of the mother, and it is, eventually, necessarily thwarted. The wish corresponds to a charged quantity of energy. The *raison d'être* of this charged energy is to seek release. When release is blocked, the energy looks for escape routes other than the one originally planned: a nurse, or an older sister, or an aunt, may replace the mother. But an adequate outlet may be hard to find, and as natural fulfillment becomes harder and harder, the wishes get pushed back into the unconscious. The psyche is full of charged energy with nowhere to go, and this energy occupies it like toxins in a body. The charged energy finds expression in neurotic behavior, which is a distorted fulfillment of the original wish. Or it pours in a disguised form into dreams.

Freud claimed in his psychodynamics to have come powerfully under the influence of Theodor Fechner, a mid-nineteenth-century physicist with a sense of the divinity of the universe. Fechner contended that there is a one-to-one correlation between psychical and physical events, but that the modes of being contrast: externally everything is quantitative, internally all is life and soul. It follows in Freud that a simple, regular, monotonous physiological process becomes the bearer of the extraordinary diversity of human behavior and inventiveness. The system is both deterministic and accidental. The fatalism lies in the presence of certain quantities of energy; the accident is how they get expressed.

> The drives and their transformation are the last things that psychoanalysis can recognize. From there on it gives way to biological research. We feel it necessary to trace back the tendency to repress and the capacity to sublimate to the organic foundation of the character, from which the building of the soul first rises up.[31]

Psychoanalysis cannot say why a person is organically constituted as he is, but it can see the problems certain constitutions cause. In neurotic patients it is libido, the energy behind wishing and loving, and a great deal of perceiving, which stops flowing naturally; therefore all expression is somehow unnatural. The Ratman, who cannot commit himself to one woman or another, unconsciously enacts his plight by travelling backwards and forwards in a train, unable to pay his perceived debt nor not pay it. He cannot commit himself to a woman because the love he feels for his father seems to require renouncing sexual pleasure. Freud suggests that, since a crucial encounter in childhood when the father unmasked and forbade masturbation, the son has unconsciously harbored a sense of the father's "cruelty," which he both wants and doesn't want to repay, and this is causing the blockage.

Another female patient of Freud's cannot leave the house, and is fiercely jealous of her husband, suspecting him of having an affair. Actually her husband is impotent, and her sexual wishes have become diverted into a neurosis: she blames him and unconsciously fears looking for another man. Similarly the woman who keeps running from room to room, then summoning her maid to a room with a laid table, then sending her away again, is enacting her panic at her new older husband's impotence. She wants the maid to see a red stain on the sheets/tablecloth to prove that consummation has occurred. The running to and fro correspond to her husband's repeated efforts to come into her bedroom and perform successfully.[32]

The blockages which recur in these cases of psychoneurosis, which include hysteria, compulsive neurosis and paranoia, are not just simple plumbing problems. They go back to childhood and cannot easily be cured, certainly not by "easily available sex" or even the provision of a full sex life. The question remains how little direct sexual fulfillment we can cope with and still not become neurotic.

> It depends what quantity of unused libido a person can tolerate, and how much libido they can lead away from sexual matters towards the goals of sublimation. The final goal of the activity of the soul, which may be described as a striving to gain pleasure and avoid pain, presents itself from an economic point of view as the task of subduing the excitement-seeking quantities (whatever exists simply to be stimulated) which are at work in the apparatus of the soul, and avoiding the blockage which causes them pain.[33]

The relative happiness of our fate would seem then to depend on a mixture of our organic endowment, perhaps something as palpable as metabolism, and our imagination. It is the interplay of these two that Freud calls the *Kräftespiel der Seele*, the play of forces in the soul, and which I have borrowed for the title of a long poem I imagine Freud to have written.

Freud was at his most technical in the mid 1890s, when he wrote excitedly to Flieβ of *eine Art Ökenomik del Nervenkraft*, a kind of economy of nervous energy. Freud's letters from that time are full of technical tables trying to pin down the modalities of mental illness and the crucial periods of human development for future mental problems. At the same time the correspondence is richly peopled. Freud speaks of many more patients and their strange cases than he does in his finished works for he is not concerned to present only those cases where the analysis has proceeded meaningfully. In fact, many patients "run away," leaving the analyst to hold on to them only with a very tentative new psychology, which would forge the link between their physical life, mental illness and imagination.[34]

In autumn 1895, a few months after he spoke to Flieβ of the economy of nerve energy in the soul, Freud was thinking about these things in a train coming back from Italy. Life kept interrupting. He had to look askance at a fellow Jew whose behavior seemed racially typical and socially eccentric to Freud, who insisted on assimilation. He had to steal his seat back from this man, later they argued a little over whether the window should be open, and finally Freud endured having his generous packed lunch admired by this difficult fellow passenger. (The man told Freud he had not "come from home" as he assumed the cosseted Freud to have done. In fact this man and his inner disturbance is a perfect illustration of what Freud many years later will mean by *unheimlich*.) But finally there was peace and Freud had energy for work. His first intention had been to read, but the light was failing, so he sat and drafted what he would soon discard, but which historians of psychoanalysis would recover on his behalf, *Outline for a Scientific Psychology*.[35]

Twenty years ago the philosopher Richard Wollheim rested his case for Freud as a scientist on this needlessly complicated document. To more recent critics Freud's quantitative psychoenergetics have brought to mind the absurdities of Heath Robinson, and on the side of absurd beauty, M.C. Escher. Freud has been condemned as the bearer of "a highly creative imagination" who has left behind him "a work of ingenious fiction."[36] But what seems to escape Freud's scientific critics here is the old affinity between philosophy and poetry. Freud is closer to the pre-Socratic philosophers who tried to explain the world as fire, or water, or matter and spaces. The poetry of the *Kräftespiel* strikes him as the right way to ex-press a reality in which, on analogy with the law of the constancy of matter, no energy is ever lost. He wants to account   for forces which, in Brentano's original phrase, are "intentionally (in)existent." I wish to win the Nobel Prize, I want to marry a Martian, I want a unicorn as a pet. Wishes still exist, even when their objects are unreal, that is, their fulfillment is unlikely or impossible. To cite Charcot in a new context: *La théorie c'est bon, mais ça n'empêche pas d'exister.* These wishes do exist in some sense, and as such they determine the relation between the world as it surrounds me and the impossible demands I make upon it. Their flowering may be a fantasy, but their roots are true. Freud wants to capture that relation in terms of the energy of wanting. The fate of that energy should then tell me a great deal about myself. The fact that I have such unreal wishes and intentions probably defines the extent to which I am neurotic.[37]

Another reason for not damning Freud is that the human imagination is repeatedly tempted to see as a *Kräftespiel der Seele* the way man and the world connect in a dynamic interaction of matter and spirit. Freud, by letting his Romantic imagination take wing, at the same time gives himself material to understand the psychological origins of Romantic cosmology. He can also compare his vision with that of Senator Schreber, to remind himself how close the great imaginations of the world are to the imaginations of the sick:

The human soul is contained in the nerves, which can be imagined as extraordinarily fine constructions – the finest silk threads. Some of these threads are only suited to picking up sensual perceptions, others (the nerves of understanding) take care of everything psychic, which brings about the state of affairs that every single nerve of understanding represents the whole spiritual individuality of the person...

While humans consist of nerves and bodies, God was only ever nerve. The nerves of God are however not present as they are in the human body in a limited number, but are endless or eternal. They possess all the qualities of human nerves to an enormously increased degree. In their capacity to create, that is to transform themselves into all possible things in the created world, they are called rays. Between God and the stars in the sky or the sun there is a deep affinity.

In Schreber's vision, sexual activity tops the list of the individual's obligations. God demands that Schreber cultivate his sensual desires or He will withdraw his rays. Schreber's imaginings suggest that a man who neglects his sexuality upsets the whole world order. Freud observes the coincidence with psychoanalysis which suggests that "the roots of every nervous and psychic disturbance are to be found above all in the sexual life" and concludes that:

> Schreber's "rays of God," composed of sunbeams, nerve-fibers and sperm, are none other than the interests of the libido presented as things and projected outwards and they lend his madness a striking consonance with our theory. That the world must collapse because the ego of the sick man is drawing all the rays towards itself, that later in the process of reconstructing himself he must take care lest God dissolve the ray connection with him, these and many other details of Schreber's hallucination sound almost like endopsychic perceptions of the processes which I have set out here as the basis for understanding paranoia... The future will decide whether in the theory there is more madness than I would like or in madness more truth than others find credible.[38]

The *Kräftespiel der Seele* has an essentially poetic quality appreciable in the pre-Socratics, in neo-Platonic mysticism, in Spinoza and in the German Romantic Schelling. It is poetic in its attempt to capture life or nature as a dynamic, continuous process. Or, seen in the clear light of Kantian aesthetics, the intricacy, interrelatedness and energy which these processes highlight in nature seem to us beautiful because they explain the world teleologically.[39]

But with Freud we already go further than the Romantics. We get inside this poetry and see it as a working mechanism within us. We see the "wrong" side of those psychic workings which once gave us a pantheistic world and now deliver a secular account of human nature. The active bond between nature and mind becomes concentrated in the link between body and spirit. The life informing both we understand as a spring of energy waiting to be shaped and channeled. This translates into grand pictures, but it is equally the stuff of our behavior in everyday life, where our inwardness meets the outside world. The play of forces is diverted in exemplary fashion in the so-called Freudian Slip.

A man's conscious wish (a) was to open a meeting. His unconscious wish (b) was to go home. Suddenly he found himself declaring the meeting closed. The (b) wish subverted the (a) wish. The social and psychological observation which Freud adds to this misrouting of energy is that in effect neither (a) nor (b) is wholly fulfilled because of the competitive presence of the other, and what results is "a compromise formation" behind the psychic scenes and a rather muddled performance in life.

> From this example [of a Freudian Slip] you can see what the aims of our psychology are. We want not just to describe and classify the phenomena, but to grasp them as indications of *a play of forces in the soul*, as the expression of tendencies which each have their goal, and which either work together or against each other. We are concerned with a dynamic conception of the things of the soul [my italics, LC].[40]

The *Kräftespiel der Seele* lends itself to clothing in many different metaphors. Schreber uses light rays. The ancients used gods and their counterparts in the underworld for dark forces. *Flectere si nequeo superbos Acheronta movebo.* If I can't bend the gods I will move the underworld. Freud suggests this line from Virgil, which he will later inscribe over the entire *Interpretation of Dreams*, as the motto of "symptom formation," when a stream of energy is repressed underground.

Deep desires are devious devils, with many devices for self-despatch. Alliteration is another way unconscious desires leapfrog over our defenses and get into our dreams in disguise. We don't realize what is happening. Our unconscious desires drive us to identify with certain characters, to transfer feelings from one relationship to another, to project our inner world outwards and to introject, or take into ourselves and make our own situations which we cannot face outside us.

I transfer my desire for my father on to my lover. Or perhaps, being overwhelmed by this "wrong," in the sense of inappropriate, love, I reverse it into hate and then project it into a view of the world which says I hate my father because he persecutes me. I end up love/hating all men. Or as a man I introject my desire for my father in so far as I make myself both woman and man. Such diversions seem to be ways of dealing with "wrong" desires, and would in Freud's view lead back to a desire in infancy that was never fulfilled. Perhaps my mother stood in my way of loving my father.

Freud believes in the transmigration of desires, which include both positive and negative expectations. These desires leave their original home and seek repeated new embodiment. "Dora," for instance, seems repeatedly to bring to other women both the desire for love and reassurance, and the readiness to be betrayed. Her very choices ensure the eventual negative outcome. Her mother betrayed her, her nanny let her down, and then her father's mistress Frau K did the same. Psychologically these women fit over each other like near relatives in Galton's photomontage designed to show how appearances slowly mutate in the same family. Their relation in Dora's life is that they all serve in turn as objects for the set play of forces in Dora's soul.[41]

Among the German Romantics, Schelling and Fichte depict the creative subject at home in a universe of potential forces waiting to be made actual. After him Hegel systematically explores the way the subject realizes the world through his own ideas. Yet probably the most enlightening *naturphilosophisch* parallel is between Freud and the poet and scientist whose work created the foundations for those slightly later idealist philosophies, namely, and once again, Goethe. Freud claimed that Goethe's "On Nature" changed his life while he was still at school. But a look at that short work suggests it did more for Freud than just urge him to study natural sciences. It imbued him with a dynamic and anthropomorphized Romantic view of nature. That the essay was shown after Freud's death to be more likely the work of Goethe's friend Christian Tobler does not affect this story of influence.

We live in her [nature's] midst and are strangers to her. She speaks continually to us and doesn't reveal her secrets. We act on her constantly and yet have no power over her.

She seems to have set everything by individuality and gets nothing out of individuals for herself. She keeps building and destroying, and her workshop is out of reach [. . .]

There is an eternal life, becoming and movement in her, and yet she doesn't move on. She transforms herself eternally, and there is in her no moment of stasis [. . .]

Human beings are in her and she is in them all. She engages in a friendly game with all of them and is pleased the more they get out of her. With many she plays her game in secret, so that she can play it to the end, before they notice.

Even the most unnatural things are nature [. . .] She enjoys illusion. She punishes as the sternest tyrant the man who destroys this in himself and in others, whereas the man who puts his trust in illusion and follows it, she presses to her heart like a child. We obey her laws even when we resist them; we act with her even when we want to act against her [. . .]

She has no language nor speech, but she makes tongues and hearts, through which she feels and speaks. Her crown is love [. . .]

When Goethe's authorship of "On Nature" was queried late in his own lifetime, he simply retraced the outlines of an outlook which had dominated a whole age on the cusp of the nineteenth century:

You can see the leaning [here] towards a kind of pantheism, in which it is thought that underlying the phenomena of the world is a being which is beyond our enquiry, unconditional, humorous and self-contradictory. It may be taken as a game in bitter earnest.[42]

One can see that pantheistic leaning in Freud too. Also that "conditional, humorous and self-contradictory" is exactly the nature of the Freudian unconscious.

When Goethe/Tobler talks of nature playing her game in bitter earnest, at the expense of individuals, and including even the most unnatural things, we feel we hear Freud speaking: we are all caught up in an unremitting dynamic we cannot resist. We also feel that Freud would agree that nature's goal through us, and even through our unnatural ways, is love. Only apparently dissimilar from Freud is the demand of eighteenth-century nature that we should not analyze too much. We should have the grace to leave illusions in place and so allow the world to retain its metaphysical charm.[43]

In fact, Freud felt guilt about his own modernity with respect to Goethe. For Freud's "play of forces in the soul," while still being a kind of internalized pantheism, involves a complete sexualization of nature closer to Schopenhauer's. As I suggested, the guilt surfaced in a dream. This was the dream of Goethe's Attack. To recap, Freud dreamt that a friend of his, Herr M, complained that Goethe had attacked him personally in the essay "On Nature." Everyone agreed the severity of the attack was unjustified. Moreover, since Goethe died in 1832, Herr M could only have been about eighteen at the time he imagined the attack to have taken place.[44]

But what does this mean? A key word is "eighteen." Freud had recently heard from a patient that her eighteen-year-old brother had suffered a mental collapse, during which he shouted, "Nature, Nature!" The doctors had inferred a connection to Goethe's essay and attributed the young man's breakdown to his excessive zeal in his *naturphilosophisch* studies. But Freud had doubted this interpretation and suggested that with the word nature the patient's brother could have been referring, "as the uneducated do in our society," to sex. He added that when the young man subsequently maimed his own genitals this interpretation did not seem obviously wrong.

In one respect Herr M, aged eighteen in the dream, is a substitute for Freud, for Freud too was about eighteen when he was carried away by enthusiasm for "On Nature." But following a second established line of interpretation, Freud is also standing in for Fließ, his friend who had really been attacked recently for his views on natural science. Freud had cut his links with the critical journal and deplored the reviewer's incompetence. On the other hand Freud had recently been attacked himself over the publication in 1898 of *Sexual Etiology of Psychoneuroses*. His peers had declared his findings *the opposite of* nature. Freud predicted that Breuer would say he had damaged himself. The dream begins to make sense as a vehicle for Freud's multiple autobiographical presence. A deranged young man first praises Goethe's vision of nature then mutilates his own nature. Doesn't Freud too worry about mutilating nature with his new ideas? Isn't he mad too? The dream asks such disturbing questions that when Freud wakes up he has to strengthen his resolve by remembering that it was Goethe's "incomparably beautiful essay" which first set him on his present course. What by implication torments him is that the vision he has ended up with could cause a man to hate his sexuality. The long epic poem of benign nature turns into a horror story. The gory violence of a Greek tragedy steps in.[45]

The Freudian horror story is one of blood, incest, shit, war-cries and murder. It is a descent into the primitive, which resides in every one of us. We are born with the primitive lusts of our wild ancestors dormant within us, and in our own way still dance round our totems, and shun our taboos. The child in us, as we were then and as mankind once was, and the way we are now, with our childishness pushed back into the unconscious, is an ignoble, illiterate savage, driven by hunger and equipped with cunning. Even the idealistic Plato said the parents of Eros were Need and Cunning, and Freud seems to develop this idea to the point of self-destruction. One might want to think of reason – as embodied by Enlightenment Man – as being buried by a mudslide of untrained erotic desire about this moment in history.

Since all human beings, not just neurotics, have such perverse, incestuous and death-threatening dreams, we may conclude that even those who are normal today developed along a path which led via perversions and an interest in the sexual objects of the Oedipus complex; that this is the path of normal development.

What neurotics show us but in an enlarged and cruder form is what the analysis of dreams also reveals in the case of the healthy.[46]

These are fundamental unacceptable desires in all of us, feelings of lust and murder towards our parents, and other loved ones, which we repress, sometimes at great cost to ourselves, for these culturally unacceptable feelings express themselves in neurosis wherever our "brutal egoism" is neither sublimated nor faced for what it is.[47]

"[It was] easier to place in archaic heritage his own repressed childhood memories of parental intercourse," says one critic, aware of the overwhelming autobiographical input into Freud's historical anthropology. Still there is truth in what Freud sees about the formative effect of family relations, and the consequences of repression. Moreover for a writer the archaic dimension is above all a metaphor to express his vision of how humanity responds to punishment and death, and the tradition of the fathers. Freud makes his "descent" into the lower depths in the same spirit as Virgil and Dante and the Goethe of *Faust II*.[48]

What Freud sees looks like this:

The I, relieved of all ethical constraints, knows itself to be inseparable from every sexual aspiration, including those which were condemned long ago by our aesthetic education, and those which contradict all moral demands for restraint. The will to pleasure [*das Lustbestreben*] – the libido, as we call it – chooses its objects without inhibition, and has a preference for the forbidden ones. Not only other men's wives, but above all incestuous objects, which human consensus has agreed to sanctify, his mother and sister in the case of a man, her father and brother in the case of a woman. Lusts that we think of as far from human nature reveal themselves as strong enough to provoke dreams. Hatred rages abroad. Desires for revenge against one's nearest and dearest family, parents, siblings and spouse and one's own children, and wishes for their death, are nothing uncommon.

These censored wishes seem to arise out of a true hell; no censorship seems severe enough against them after their wakeful interpretation.[49]

Three reasons suggest themselves for Freud's Dante-esque journey: to combat Idealism, to combat the simplifications that spread from a superficial application of Darwin to man in society, and to learn more about himself. They propel him into *The Inferno*, with only science and a couple of works of literature like *Oedipus Rex* and *Hamlet* as his guide.

Freud knowingly followed Schopenhauer in spurning a model of man as born virtuous. Hunger, and the assertion of blind will, are the characteristics of the newly born child who will remain all his life father to the man. But we Freudian creatures are not just carnally hungry. There is also the primal disappointment of being born into the family. We have parents whom we cannot dominate, or be dominated by, whom we cannot join with, or be joined by, in order to preserve our first transient bliss at the breast. There are also siblings, and other family members around us, who thwart our fulfillment. We take our emotional characters from the competitions, infatuations and insecurity of infancy, which arise under these circumstances. In effect in adult life each of us continues to carry, if not a bestial darkness, then a *sacro egoismo* within, an unreflected self-interest which *in extremis* would overwhelm our acquired ideals of piety, respect and restraint.

Civilization at the beginning of the twentieth century was proud of itself in a way it cannot be a hundred years on. Think then of the effect Freud was trying to achieve by stressing this barbarism lurking just beyond the borders of propriety. He said that repressed wishes made him think of a heckler locked out of the lecture room, whom, for the quality of life of all concerned, it would be better to let back in. Freud, calling for the outsider to be given a seat inside, might have been echoing Nietzsche who exhorted: "Live dangerously!" Only the present age needs different lessons. And even then Nietzsche could see high culture would suffer.[50]

So much of Freud's mission was to dispel the ignorant pride that surrounded an idealized picture of mankind as abstemious, rational, nature's best and getting ever better. Just because we are out the other side we shouldn't forget the poor individual who thought of herself, quietly, secretly, as abnormally lustful and cruel. Let's be thankful Freud came to her rescue. But the story of Freud's compassion is a horror story nevertheless, for there is a pit of worms where the human soul should be. Some have tried to mitigate the impact, but not even language exists in the unconscious, only writhing, seething, blind psychic activity. Moreover, the ruthless sexual hunger driving the human being, and the impossibility of its satisfaction except in an anarchic and bestial world, suggests that civilization will always be fraught with hidden conflict and neurotic illness.[51]

Freud became more conventional. The achievements of cultivated, rational man were too great to dismiss, even in the cause of health. He became that sage of the 1920s whom mid-century American humanism adopted as its patron saint. His whole career shows that he emerged from his voyage to the centre of the psyche with a mixed vision: man is a dual creature, primitive on the one hand, capable of great cultivation on the other. Still the primary unconscious would be too much for many more optimistic and rational thinkers to accept.

With the aid of the separate investigation of sexual and ego instincts we found the key to understanding the group of transference neuroses. We were able to trace them back to the fundamental situation, whereby the sexual drives are at odds with the drives towards self-perpetuation, or, biologically, though less precisely expressed, that the one stance of the Ego as an autonomous and separate being conflicts with the other as member of a generative line. Such a duality occurs perhaps only in human beings, for which reason, by and large, neurosis may be their superior claim over the animals. The excessively strong development of the human libido, and the development of a richly articulated inner life which perhaps makes this possible, seem to have created the conditions for such a conflict to arise. It should further be immediately clear that these are also the conditions of the great advances man has made over and above his community with the animals, such that his capacity for neurosis could be seen as the reverse side of what is otherwise his gift.[52]

Freud, opening up of the dark side of man, adds a supplement to Darwin's evolutionary psychology about how individuals and species survive. Psychoanalysis is puzzled by how sexuality undermines and menaces the biological well-being of the individual;how up to a point the brilliant inventiveness which diverts our sexuality into so many cultural channels enhances the satisfactions of the soul, while beyond a certain point the same culture makes us perverse and unable to love. So much depends on the individual capacity to accommodate tension, and intensity, and lack of direct fulfillment.

One could describe Freud's whole project in terms of an adjunct to Darwin, and a great one. It can be phrased as a question about the human soul and a tragic answer. If love, otherwise known as mating, is the great token of success, which both Freud and Nature suppose it to be, why is it so problematic for so many people? Explicitly Freud set up psychoanalysis to help the psychically weak: those barely able to survive the pressures of finding a home in society for their strange or excessive or just individual desires.[53]

Roughly this point is where the first novel I imagine Freud might have written, *Vienna 1900*, about his search for selfhood and success, ends. There is an interlude, when his long poem *Kräftespiel der Seele* introduces the love theme as a cosmic vision. Immediately after, he begins his second "novel," about love.

5

REAL LOVE

I The Obstacle Race

In 1906, not long after the publication of *Three Essays on Sexual Theory*, Freud told Jung he wished to write a love life of mankind. The book he had in mind was unprecedented. No one before had written a systematic exposition of how difficult individuals find it actually to love, and be loved. The passion of Tristan and Isolde, or of Romeo and Juliet, was desperate because politically or socially forbidden; it was never a public question whether these heart-led heroes and heroines *could* love each other.[1]

A sense of the necessary inner conditions for love began to lurk in the later nineteenth century. Emma Bovary, provincial princess of adultery, was emotionally unstable, easily infatuated and didn't quite connect with reality. Her being was self-destructive. She was the illicit bourgeoise whose plight seemed to sum up something rotten about European society, and from a spectator's distance Anna Karenina's fate could be read as a commentary upon that European way of life: Tolstoy saw it as effete and unreal. Anna was a well-integrated woman who through erotic folly lost her place in the real world; loss of that reality destroyed her.[2]

The question Freud never expressly poses but which hovers behind his work is: "Why can't there be more *real* and *fulfilled* love?" Real in that it is also possible in social reality, fulfilled in that it is sexually complete. Had Freud really been a novelist he might have expanded on two eccentric ideas he later tacked on to the *Three Essays*, that human sexual fulfillment is not designed to be perfect. Continual dissatisfaction is part of our nature, which is what makes our desire for love so different from our desire for wine. Also that the evolution of culture has trimmed the less palatable excesses from our sensuality, so we never quite get the full taste. Instead Freud worked both of these theories into a "science" which answered that nineteenth-century novelists' question. He misled us with his insistence on his work as science, because science could hardly give the reason why a woman happily in love, like Violetta, *la dame aux camélias*, would allow her lover's father to persuade her to leave. Yet his hopes that a new scientific psychology might make a beginning were not entirely misplaced.[3]

One unique book prefigured Freud's work on love, and by mixing autobiography and human survey curiously resembles in texture *The Interpretation of Dreams* and the *Psychopathology*. Stendhal's *De l'Amour* comprises anecdotes and aphorisms, stories about strangers whom we care little for, and disguised versions of the author's own story. It is not a popular classic because of the form and a text which so idiosyncratically reveals the nearside of romantic illusion. Here is love portrayed not as an ennobling and thrilling passion but as bewilderment, affliction and loss of orientation. The drama reveals the oddity of people, but also the absence of anything specially likeable about their suffering. At best Stendhal himself seems comic, and, had Freud ever read this curious work, he might have smiled at the protagonist dyeing his hair green and expecting the beloved not to recognize him trailing in her wake. Stendhal's book on love is a study in self-mismanagement and rueful failure.

Freud's case-studies and works on hysteria are concerned with just that kind of failure to communicate and to love that seemed to bedevil Stendhal. Freud took an inventory of all the hurdles to love that modern mankind has invented in his instinctive self-torment, and embraced the torment in a word: neurosis.

So, an erotic drive and a rebellion against it, a desire (not yet compulsive) and a fear striving against it (which is already compulsive), a painful emotional moment and an urge to take evasive action: the inventory of neurosis is complete.[4]

So tangled and yet so simple: these jerky words seem even to be spoken with the restricted breath of a neurotic. Not only is there not a smooth flow but fierce impulses tear at the integrity of psyche. Subject to combative and abrasive internal dynamics, in the end the afflicted person only wants to deny and to hide.

How else can it be said? Neurosis exists in the shadow of love and is the bi-product or the residue of its failure. Or neurosis is a tangling of love's roots. When the seed sprouts the shoots emerge crooked. "We know that what above all makes it easy for a neurosis to set in is [a person's] incapacity to bear any prolonged thwarting of the libido." Nature gets deformed. The *Three Essays* suggest that neurotic fear stands to libido as vinegar to wine, an image which recalls those magical transubstantiations of the human which so fascinated the psychological alchemist in Freud. But the idea that a dynamic system has got blocked is not intended as a metaphor; it describes the physiological underpinnings of the mental as Freud sees them.[5]

Only another mental tool can unblock the mental problem, and that tool is memory. Freud, using Plato's word *anamnesis*, singles out the recollection of our earliest sexual desires as the way out of neurosis. The idea is that whatever our present problems they have the earliest roots. Anxieties are stored beneath consciousness, only to emerge disguised as symptoms and dreams. The analyst via interpretation aims to get back to the underlying anxiety, with the idea that the patient who confronts her anxiety directly will recognize it for what it is and it will disappear.[6]

Freud's discovery of neurosis and the recommended cure is his most serious project, a major contribution to "the development of human culture, of which sexuality is the weak point." It is also a poetic project, the time in his career when, as I have suggested, had he been a novelist, he would have written his love story. Against this hypothetical background it must be emphasized that memory, while so important as a cure, is also, even as Freud acknowledges, an unreliable connoisseur in discerning fact from fantasy.[7]

The Freudian project translates into "overcoming repression" which means undoing the defenses (resistances) which unconsciously we erect to deal with deep frustrations. We need to befriend feelings and needs inside us of which we have become afraid. A passage from the *Introductory Lectures* suggests how the analyst can help the neurotic patient, whose love capacity is blocked. Her aim is to get the patient to loosen up and give her libido a chance. Or at least recognize it for what it is:

> Through the work of interpretation, which transposes unconscious into conscious, the I [Ego] is enlarged at the cost of the unconscious, and learns to become more conciliatory towards the libido and inclined to allow it some kind of satisfaction. *It backs away less from the bold claims of the libido thanks to those claims being partly met by sublimation.* The better an actual course of treatment fits with this ideal description, the more successful the psychoanalytic therapy will be.[8]

Seine Scheu vor den Ansprüchen der Libido, with my emphasis, is the crucial phrase in the middle sentence. Nietzsche, in the paragraph from "The Wanderer and His Shadow" used as the epigraph to this book, speaks of the philosophically blind ascribing a terrible character to the human passions out of lack of observation of themselves and of "those who are to be brought up," "*derer, welche erzogen werden sollen,*" that is, children. He enjoins us to transform our suffering into joy, *Leidenschaften* into *Freudenschaften*. This challenge Freud took up, though without Nietzsche's exalted, post-Schopenhauerian cheerfulness.[9]

To try to understand the agitated, potentially isolated modern human being, Freud extended the concept of the sexual to include intellectual work.[10] He also explained why his focus on the sexual need not cause any more panic than the philosophies of Schopenhauer or Plato:

> We have to remember that some of the contents of this work, the stress on the meaning of the sexual life for all human

achievements and the attempted enlargement of the concept of sexuality, have always provided the strongest motive for resisting psychoanalysis. In the need for ringing slogans people have gone so far as to speak of the "pansexualism" of psychoanalysis and to level the nonsensical criticism that it explains "everything" by means of sexuality. One might be astonished, if one didn't oneself not forget the confusing and forgetful effect of emotional crises. Some time ago now the philosopher Arthur Schopenhauer suggested to human beings in what degree their actions and aspirations are determined by sexual ambitions in the conventional meaning of the word, and a whole world of readers was supposed to be unable to put from its mind such a fierce warning! As to what concerns the extension of the concept of sexuality, which the analysis of children and cases of so-called perversion necessitates, all those who look down contemptuously on psychoanalysis from their higher point of view may care to remember how near the enlarged sexuality of psychoanalysis coincides with the Eros of the divine Plato.[11]

In the beginning there is always an erotic desire which is stymied: a limit to love from mother or father, and a desperate compensatory attempt to usurp the place of the same-sex parent to regain bliss. The shock of the loss of the parent-lover, and the desire to do away with our rival, can be so great that we repress the memory, confining it to the unconscious where it continues to haunt us by attaching itself to later events and generally misdirecting our behavior. We acquire symptoms and (less harmfully to our lives) we dream dreams.

Freud's teaching provoked disgust, because the Judaeo-Christian child's purity was defined in contrast to adult lusts. Freud provoked a reductive response because his own teaching was unnervingly bold and complex. He saw not the traditional separation of sexual adult and asexual child, but the continuity. In a way the child in us was still innocent, but then so was the adult, for the child could not help having parents who were the first guardians of his needs, and could not help acquiring in his vulnerability injuries that would accompany him throughout his life.[12]

Freud's autobiographical memories and dreams show how firmly his own family circumstances, above all the competition with John and Philipp left their mark. The age gap between his young mother and older father, added to his confusion. His autobiographically inspired writing on love is in this way an abrupt reversal, by devastating sexualization, of the Victorian novel of the large family. Marking another point where Freud departs from Darwin, Freud's is a kind of chaos theory of our psychological coming-into-being, we who are creatures so in need of love.[13]

Beside the complexity of family, however, Freud emphasizes the forceful denial of sexual reality by which the society of his day adds to passing private misery and longterm neurosis. Homosexuals and others with "inverted" tastes are most vulnerable; but nor do heterosexuals escape. When a marriage turns sour, thanks to the conspiracy of ignorance surrounding its arrangement, the unhappy parents inevitably pass on their wretchedness to their children. Freud is often taken to task for his underinformed and old-fashioned notion of female sexuality, as well as for his classification, with the *mores* of his time, of homosexuality as a perversion. But it would be a mistake not to see through the limitations he shared with the late nineteenth century to an essential compassion.[14]

To insist on his debt to Nietzsche, as well as his affinity with literature, we can say that Freud's psychologizing-with-a-hammer would have splintered the *Bildungsroman*, had Freud only been a writer. Instead the job of inverting the safe order of the traditional family-background-and-coming-of-age German novel fell to Thomas Mann. As for Freud, though he did not write his essay "*Der Familienroman der Neurotiker*" until 1908, he was already speaking eleven years earlier of "*der Abkunftsroman der Paranoia*," "*der Familienroman*," "*der Kinderroman*," "*Rächeromane*" and "*Entlastungsromane*," in which he envisaged people telling their life stories, or himself retelling them, in terms of the origins of paranoia, their childhood, their revenge on the family and the shedding of their inner burdens. His mind was never really on literary forms with a view to his own production, but from the time of his friendship with Fließ he envisaged and worked with narratives which traced a sexual etiology.[15]

For reasons connected with how he perceived his own life, as I suggested above, Freud's narratives deal incessantly with chaotic beginnings, and the waywardness of the infant flesh. Yet they quickly open out, in line with his broad sense of libido, to include power and ambition. Much of Freud's theory reflects the way "love" is a screen for power relations in the family, and in adult hands exploits the child's weakness and ignorance. For adults have us children in their power, and, however kind and well meaning, drag us along behind them, in their complicated lives, hitch us to the tails of their passionate arrangements and their feuds, make us scapegoats for their failings and look to us for comfort and solidarity and deliverance. Perhaps what we *first* remember from childhood is being powerless and dependent.[16]

Freud used his own childhood to illustrate how decisive are our first experiences of love and power, and guilt and shame. Even in his late twenties, sure of being his own man and wanting to be perceived as a public saviour, he still dreamt of being a lost child.[17] When he tells us how Philipp exploited his sexual ignorance and fear at losing his mother and his nanny, we feel the strength of his bewilderment; in the dream of seeing his mother naked, we have to deal with a thrill hard to place in a child of two and a half, and infer a remembered idolization and a retrospective flirtation with guilt. Before he was one year old, while still sleeping in his parents' bedroom, Freud even "remembered" a sexual encounter between his parents.[18] This fundamental "memory," which also contained a strong element of repressed homosexuality, Freud thrust on his patient, the Wolfman, and made an Ur-pattern in the psychic history of the world.[19]

I don't accept in its literalness Freud's Oedipal mythology, but there are consequences of the doctrine I want to retain. The Christian who insists on the brilliance of the resurrection as a metaphor, in order to keep alive the good effects of the faith, is in a similar position. Not the eternity of the spirit and the promise of the next life is what Freud teaches, but the truth that our emotional characters stem from the competitions, infatuations and insecurity of infancy. Freud's work on love makes us stronger because it reduces the pride and shelter we can derive from such absolute notions as Love, Goodness and our own cause. We travel, as with Dante, into hell. But we also have to unpack a little those deep prejudices which can make "personality" immovable and sometimes barely more than a screen for fear. When we realize our goodness is less than it seems, we turn into better people.

Vladimir Nabokov, anti-Freudian though he claimed to be, actually displayed a thoroughgoing Freudian humanism on love, complete with Freud's kind of irony and verbal tricks, when he wrote *Lolita*. That novel, published in 1955, exactly exposed the prejudices of a whole generation of simple-minded hypocrites idealistic about love and the innocence of the child. We don't know for sure that Freud taught Nabokov how society can create perversions, and how these may take on a certain false glamour. But we do know that Nabokov wrote about a perversion which seduced its own bearer. We also know that Humbert Humbert was in love and that one of his author's names for him was the Rousseauesque Jean-Jacques Humbert. Nabokov doesn't explore the parallel between Freud and Rousseau which we have high-lighted. The allusion to Rousseau is a satire on how the ideal of childhood innocence can become perverse in itself. But in that Nabokov is well in tune with Freud.[20]

Freud's positive project targeted the greater social and sexual success of his patients. The desire was to bring Dora and the Ratman back into the fold, not for one moment for society's sake, but to lead them towards greater personal happiness. Freud was not a model of tolerance by today's standards, and some things remained with him "perversions" where, ironically thanks to his influence, we would no longer use the term. Freud was troubled by masturbation, underinformed on women's sexuality, and too personally uneasy with homosexuality to entertain a consistently liberal view. Still he gave us a more relaxed attitude to sex, freed from values of God and the soul, and gender, and divorced from insensitive stereotypes. Under the umbrella of the positive project, he told people worried about their sexuality that we are all a mixture psychologically of male and female. Thanks to Freud, "normality" is a word around which quotation marks naturally sit.[21]

It is hardly possible to argue that Freud's project was not clear. Freud worked for the alleviation of pain and of the distortion of life caused by sexual repression, from society and from within. He elucidated the range and power of unconscious motives so that such awareness would increase our conscious choices and either give us greater control where choice is possible or greater humor and compassion where it is not; and with paranoia and narcissism he offered us some understanding of the origins of evil.[22]

Perhaps it is still unconsciously held against Freud that the kinds of problems upsetting his patients: hypochondria, sexual fantasy, fear of going out of the house, sleeplessness, nervous coughing or limping or twitching, sound self-indulgent and prompt ignoble explanations.[23] A man (or woman) who for instance always chooses a partner already spoken for Freud understands as someone who cannot love unless that love does harm to a third person. Freud calls it the complex of "the injured third person." In another kind of complex, a man repeatedly attracted to provocative and unreliable women actually needs jealousy to fuel his desire. Yet again some afflicted men and women feel they must "save" the beloved, while others cannot have a relationship without plotting revenge. The Freudian revolution consists in seeing that such constant minor digressions from a hypothetical norm are the condition of dealing with human nature in terms other than of nobility.[24]

In sum, the positive project was not born to promote an image of human freedom and dignity. It was a matter of love-next-door seen in blunt terms: the success of having a partner, the success of taking one's place in society thanks to that, and the success of procreation. Freud drew inspiration from Darwin. He replayed the struggle in cultural terms, and saw an ever higher price being put on self-mastery. In such a world the weak don't so much die out as succumb to neurosis.[25]

Freud saw it as very much part of the human condition that the individual struggles for a place in society, and competes for love. He experienced both of these competitions personally and intensely, with their concomitant jealousy and envy and the temptation built into them to try to control others and to cheat. He developed psychoanalysis to improve the chances of greater happiness in individuals who lacked social and erotic success; who were not at home with themselves and others; whose internal system had become blocked in some way which prevented efficient running of the psychic machine.

Psychoanalysis in other words was motivated by recognition of the relatively simple ways of the world. At the same time it acknowledged the enormous inner troubles which prevented individuals from following the natural, simple path that evolution apparently intended. It queried why the life stories of so many people were actually self-defeating, and in that sense unnatural. Freud's psychological vision with its neurophysiological under-pinning looks like a combination of Rousseau with peering into the brain to see, though only darkly, how to get rid of the hindrances to happiness: a neurological gnosticism perhaps.

Freud acknowledged the objection to his work as somehow trivial beside the prevalence of real misery in the world. One can almost see Pirandello's Six Characters turning up on stage as he addresses a Vienna University audience with these words:

For everything that we have brought together under the heading of "real denial" [*reale Versagung*], as life's misfortune, which entails going without love, [that is] poverty, family strife, the wrong choice of spouse, disadvantageous social circum-stances and the strictness of society's requirements, [all that is] the pressure under which a person stands. There would be abundant material there for an effective therapy, but it would have to be the kind of therapy which according to legend Kaiser Josef dispensed, the benevolent intervention of some powerful person, whose will causes human beings to bend to its purpose and difficulties to disappear. But who are we that we make such benevolence a part of our therapy? Poor ourselves and socially impotent, necessitated to scratch out a living through our medical activity, we are not even in a position to give our care to those without means, as other doctors practicing other methods of treatment can do. Our therapy takes too much time and is too tiring.

Nor can psychoanalysis do anything about inherited disposition.

Don't believe that we underestimate it; the very fact that we are therapists puts us in a position clearly to feel its power.[26]

Fifty years ago John Huston nevertheless portrayed Freud as the preacher of the gospel of love, and it is only in today's scientistic, positivist climate that there is such a vulgar preference for defeating Freud on issues taken straight out of contemporary newspapers, like child abuse and medical negligence. Whatever the connection, these matters do not explain, or explain away, Freud.

II The Real Thing

The problem with scientistic Freud criticism is that it is both too simple and too moral, in the wrong places, to give an account adequate to literature and the humanities of such an important thinker. The difficulty for both patient and analyst is exactly to know what is emotionally real.

What we find so confusing [is] the undervaluing of reality, the neglect of the difference between it and reality. We are tempted to take offense over the patient's bothering us with made-up stories.[27]

Psychoanalysis embraces a non-rational reprise of the skeptical question in philosophy: how can I know that the life I have constructed out of memories, desires and beliefs is not a fantasy? The question may be asked of oneself or of another person.

One answer is that society will erect barriers if I don't choose suitable objects for my satisfaction. This helpful, materialistic, sensible view, more appropriate in Freud's day than our own, doesn't necessarily imply acceptance of what society demands, but is consonant with that Freud who urged people against bringing up their children to be revolutionaries. He speaks in this connection of Ego-interests and self-preservation, and calls the whole bundle of compromises *material* reality.

What Freud on another occasion calls the reality-ego strives to reconcile the innate desire for pleasure with the culturally constrained need to survive. An external world comes sharply into focus at this moment of adjustment, requiring the individual to judge and act. But illness can make fastening on to an external world impossible.[28]

Freud begins his 1911 essay "Formulation of the Two Principles of Psychic Occurrence":

> For a long time we have noticed that every neurosis has the consequence, and therefore probably the tendency, to force the patient out of real life and to estrange him from reality... The neurotic turns away from reality because he finds either the whole of it or a part unbearable.

The neurotic finds refuge in fantasy, which, by degrees, makes him ill.[29]

Psychoanalysis aims to undo this fastening on fantasy. It wants to return the sufferers of hysteria, anxiety neurosis and compulsive neurosis to an engagement with real objects. The project can be undertaken in such cases of "transference neuroses." But what today we would call the disorders of schizophrenia and paranoia are prime examples of barely treatable conditions because there is no transferred "interest." These "paraphrenias" so distance the sufferer that he seems to experience life through a veil. A narcissistic neurosis has just so much in common with paraphrenic affliction that the patient, completely absorbed in herself, becomes indifferent to the world. She is less sick, but equally resistant to help.[30]

The capacity to maintain some relationship with an objective world is tantamount therefore to being able to love. The infant finds autoerotic satisfaction in his own being but as he matures he transfers his needs to objects outside himself. The crucial qualification for emotional maturity is to be able to fix on a real love object, and this is the subject of Freud's essays on narcissism, on repression, and on "drives and the fates of drives." It is also part of his commentary on the unconscious:

> While the Ego experiences the transformation from Pleasure-Ego to Real-Ego, the sexual instincts undergo those changes that lead them from initial autoeroticism through various in between stages to object love in the service of the reproductive function.

This mixture of Hegel and Darwin is the highest statement of Freudian normality and marks the positive limits of psycho-analysis. Our psychic workings achieve a kind of perfection, a crown, when love of another becomes a reality.[31]

Only so much can go wrong on the way.

> Our experiments have shown that of the promptings which determine our love lives only a proportion achieve full psychic development; this proportion is turned towards reality, is at the disposal of the conscious personality and comprises a part of it. Another part of these libidinous promptings has got arrested in its development, it is turned away from the conscious personality as it is from reality, can only extend itself in fantasy or remains entirely in the unconscious, so that it is unknown to the person's consciousness.[32]

We nearly all of us bring *some* unconscious needs to our appre-hension of the world. These set our emotional responses on definite tracks. They determine the set of our personality and what scope it has to change. Freud writes eloquently of the few exceptions in *The Psychopathology*. Reading afresh this passage which I have already quoted, it seems as if the finest lovers are the chosen few, and, like Romantic poets, distinct from the herd:

> Only for the most exquisite and balanced souls does it seem possible to preserve their picture of perceived external reality from the distortion that it otherwise undergoes as it passes through the psychic individuality of the perceiver.[33]

For the rest of us the good-enough human condition is a mixture of predetermined patterns – or deferred expectations – and openness to the new. Only analysis tries to pin down *what* the deferred expectations are, and, where much distorting material is hidden, it clearly has great work to do.

Whatever Freud's speculations about the libidinous origins of everything, it seems incontestable that feelings of not being loved and not being able to love contribute greatly to introversion, repression and neurosis. The bond with reality is fundamentally one of satisfied desire. We know the world by giving to it and receiving from it. A libido which either gets sidetracked into persistent fantasy or is channeled back into an inflated notion of the self will invariably produce a distorted view of the materially real – and one would want to add of nature too.[34]

In the 1914 *Introduction to Narcissism*, Freud proposed a comparative scheme for two main types of misrouted libido. This involved a distinction between ego-libido, the desire for self-preservation, and object-libido, the drive towards erotic gratification. Its bifurcated complexity first made the case for psychoanalysis as a supplement to evolutionary biology.

Essentially the 1914 essay takes a psychoanalytical look at man's second nature as a self-reflective creature, and sees how self-consciousness gets entangled with his primary need for satisfaction in love. If it hardly needs saying today that our sexual drives, contained in object-libido, are often at odds with the ideals we set up for ourselves as reflective persons, it was less clear in Freud's day.

This is perhaps one reason why Freud so admired Schnitzler's play *Paracelsus*, where a woman in love with the wrong man has headaches but makes no connection between the two states; where another has never lost her love for a man she knew before her marriage; and where the husband with a black and white view of fidelity has no idea of the delicate complexities of love. In a contrived, protected context, in which hypnotism works like the magic of Shakespeare's *The Winter's Tale*, Schnitzler's characters are brought to face the erotic wishes and fears they hide from themselves, and they are freed. Fortune of a kind smiles on their invention, even as Schnitzler sends us away with a sense that life may still be more difficult. To face up to a loss, for instance, may simply entail too much grief. Freud speaks of neurosis as the modern, secular equivalent of entering a monastery and sometimes the only way out. If we are to survive then our self-awareness will probably have involuntary, necessary gaps.[35]

Never does Freud present the object–libido problem with more complexity than when he suggests how easy it is to fall prey to either perversion or neurosis. Hysteria, anxiety and compulsive activity are never far off, if our desires to be in the world on our own terms are too much thwarted:

> We began with the aberrations of the sex drive in relation to its object and goal . . . insights into the circumstances of the sex drive in psychoneurotics, who are a numerous group not far distant from healthy people . . . [showed that] . . . with these people there are inclinations to all perversions as unconscious powers and that these disclose themselves as the creators of symptoms; we can say that neurosis is as it were a negative of perversion . . . [it is our view that] the disposition to perversion is the original general disposition of the human sexual drive, out of which normal sexual behavior develops with a series of organic changes and psychic inhibitions in the course of maturity. We hoped to show the original disposition in childhood: amongst the powers constraining the direction of the sex drive we emphasized shame, disgust, pity and the social constructions of

morality and authority. So we have to see in every fixated aberration from the normal sex life a bit of inhibited development and infantilism...since the original disposition must have been a complex one, it seemed to us that the sex drive itself is made up of many factors, which in the case of perversions as it were collapses into its component parts. The perversions showed themselves to be inhibitions on the one hand and on the other dissociations from normal development. Both conceptions came together in the assumption that the sexual drive of adults grows into a unity, a striving with a single goal, out of the combination of the many diverse impulses of the child's life.

In our beginnings we were "naturally" perverted – this is the force of the use by psychoanalysis of the Oedipal myth – and the possibility of regression to an earlier stage of development, under later pressure from society and personal circumstances, always lingers.[36]

A blockage in ego-libido means on the other hand that we never get beyond taking *ourselves* as the ultimate love-object. This state of being which Freud calls narcissism looks like a more grown-up approach to the world than sexual infantilism, because it is the next stage on, the necessary transition between infantile autoeroticism and mature object love. But it is also an incomplete stage which many people never leave, and which accounts for their choice of loved one, their sense of family and religion, and all they "stand for."[37]

The more we have a sense of self, and that capacity for self-observation which reaches its height in self-conscious philosophy, the more we are prey to narcissism, which diverts libido into a particularly worked-over form of self-preservation: it bolsters our sense of identity and our self-esteem. Freud answers earlier theorists who have used the term to label a perversion, and also observes that we all have *some* narcissism in us:

Narcissism in this sense would not be a perversion, but the libidinous complement, to the point of egoism, of the self-preservation drive, of which a portion can be ascribed to every living being.[38]

Later he simply calls narcissism the libidinous complement to egoism. Not all egoists, who want their own good, are narcissists; they may need passionately to love a distinct other. An egoist who is also a narcissist may however have very little desire for a full sexual love, and be content with *either* sex *or* a "love" that does without it.[39]

In narcissism we are literally full of ourselves. The state is comparable with when, for some subject, intense physical pain blots out the outside world. The sick notoriously live in a world limited by their affliction, as Tolstoy showed in *The Death of Ivan Ilyich*. Hypochondria follows this narcissistic pattern, in which the subject, like Proust's Aunt Léonie, is fixated on herself. As for narcissistic men and women, they either love themselves within their chosen other, or love the person they would like to be; or they do not love, but receive abundant love exactly because of their disdainful "feline" behavior. All the world apparently admires a narcissist, who loses none of her completeness when we advance towards her; as people say, she is never dislodged from her perch. Men love these infallibly self-contained women, Freud says, because they would like themselves to be emotionally so untouchable. In truth these perfect women are so problematic. Too often, unable to love outside themselves, they find a false love object in their children. Children do suffer so from the psychic imperfections of adults. Adults who have not fully matured are causes of disaster. The narcissism of both parents comes out in relation to the way they unload huge ambitions and emotional expectations on their offspring. "Loving" parental ambitions (and expenditure) are often gestures of self-duplication and self-aggrandizement on the part of the parent.

Freud's extreme examples of object-love and self-love are cultural legends: the man and woman who lose themselves in each other to the point of extinction and the man who draws the whole world into his ego-orbit. The first might be said to have a Tristan and Isolde complex, while the second is a megalomaniac. Megalomaniacs are the tycoons whose huge egos are every now and again exposed in our newspapers. For every one of these there must be a thousand private family tyrants and a thousand romantic tragedies.[40]

But for many people probably the greatest narcissism they face, without recognizing it, is in what they call their idealism or their conscience. With self-observation we set up an ideal of ourselves, which encourages us to make high demands; repression often follows in that we do not love ourselves as we are and cannot bear to contemplate what we are not. Idealism can be highly problematic and wasteful, says Freud. It includes the over-estimation of ourselves and others as sexual objects. Idealism has an interesting opposite in *sublimation*. Freud thinks sublimation can find genuine other objects to use up sexually unfocused energy, because the mechanism reaches back to the pre-genital age of the personality. But the idealist, who is a fully-grown but thwarted sexual being, is always unsatisfied, and demands ever more of himself. If only he were capable of more genuinely childlike passions and thus a sublimated outlet for his vitality the tight rein on his life might ease.

> Above all with neurotics one finds the greatest tension in differences between the education of the Ego-ideal and the measure of sublimation of their primitive libidinous drives. Generally it is much harder to persuade the idealist that this is a pointless waste of his libido than it is a simple person who has remained content with his aspirations.[41]

Freud claims he has no cure for narcissism. In the late works *Civilization and Its Discontents* (1930) and *Moses and Monotheism* (1939), he speaks of that "narcissism of small differences" which leads to so much conflict in the world as individuals assert that they belong to this or that class or group. He mentions the Bolshevik persecution of the bourgeoisie and the Germanic dream of world conquest primed by anti-Semitism. The unintelligible moment (which the Holocaust would surely have enlightened) is how in *Civilization*, amid such historical detail, Freud can speak of this rampant institutional narcissism masquerading as national culture as "a comfortable and relatively harmless satisfaction of aggression." Narcissism is not only a great hurdle to full erotic love but also to Christian humanist *caritas*. It is fundamental to war, I deduce from Freud, and one of the roots of human evil.[42]

No one should imagine there is no moral position evident in Freud's work. The therapist who posits a love free from fantasy and narcissism paints a picture of a better world. A partnership of unclouded and disinterested love is evidently Freud's version of the *Paradiso*, something to work towards, though by definition unattainable. But not only the therapist is at work in sustaining a qualified positive vision. Freud has an intellectual desire to purify love. It is again a neglected moral aspect of Freud's work, that we should try to clarify our motives for preferring one kind of "love" feeling over another.

One precedent for this search for correct and incorrect emotions he might have found in Aristotle:

> What avoidance and negation are in thinking, pursuit and avoidance are in desire; so that since moral virtue is a state of character concerned with choice, and choice is deliberate desire, therefore both the reasoning must be true and the desire right, if the choice is to be good, and the latter must pursue just what the former asserts...

But once again it turns out that Brentano was the modern spokesman for the ethics of desire:

> Now we have reached the point where the concepts of good and bad, as well as those of true and false, which we have been seeking, have their source. We say that something is true when its relation of affirmation is right. We call something good when its affirmation of love is right. That which is to be loved with a right love, that which is worthy of love, is good in the widest sense of the word.[43]

Under Freud's tutelage even in love we examine our feelings towards our parents, our unfulfilled ambitions and the basis of our self-esteem. Not systematically, and not too much perhaps. Woody Allen's worried New York Jewish male intellectual is the measure of modern post-Freudian excess. But perhaps we can enquire after ourselves in the Shakespearian spirit. Shakespeare seems to have reveled in the difficulty of "right" choices in love. Shakespeare's characters appear in disguise, or some playful spirit annoints their eyes with a misleading potion to remind us of what a difficult game getting the right partner is. According to Harold Bloom, Freud translated Shakespeare into prose. But whether we approach the love bond with sixteenth-century brio or twentieth-century pessimism, it seems wise to consider the origins and the objects of our most cherished feelings at the moment when they matter most to us.[44]

Freud has been reproached for being too normal; above all for not respecting solitude. It is a fair criticism of the positive, therapeutic project that Freud assumes that love is always love of *something*, which is a specific thing, and that its objects can be rated in quality. But I think Freud's view, again under the influence of Brentano, is rooted in emotional commonsense. I love my husband, I love an airplane, I love an elephant, I love old coins and lost cats, I love my brother. Are all these loves the same? Hardly. Warmth and tenderness may be appropriate towards elephants and brothers and cats, while coins and airplanes may make my day; but if these are the only outlets for my libido, without a main erotic focus (my husband or lover), then my sexual personality has either begun to split into its many component parts, more like when I was a child (in the latency stage), or it has become sublime. These disintegrations are fine causes. They probably often occur in exceptional personalities, and they remind us how lovely the diverse passions of childhood were, undisturbed by a concentrated and self-conscious sexuality. Normality should not spread too far and banish the recurrence of this strange bliss in adulthood. As for sublimity, it hardly needs any advocacy. These grand and poignant cases for eccentricity naturally question the need for Freudian, or any, therapy on a general basis. Over-convinced by the need for ubiquitous "treatment by successful relationship," we look as a culture as if we have become afraid of character and genius. Yet love would not be its urgent self if it did not, during the most nubile years, insist on a way through to its goal and cry for help if it can't get there. Freud answered that cry in so many people.[45]

Freud is anyway so complex that no adequate reading of him could end up with only the case for "normality." But here is a shocking turning-point in his thinking, like those two-way mirrors in a 1960s' sex scandal which made one realize illicit love was not only wicked in itself but further undermined the sanctity of the sexual by turning it into a show for covert spectators. I hate to say it. Where love is concerned, beyond the noble intentions of his positive project, much of Freud's work is taken up with substitutes. Substitutes, after our hymn to the real thing! Life can be so disappointing, and Freud is so honest.

Substitutes include as many kinds of perversity as Pieter Brueghel or Flaubert presented as temptations to St Anthony, or they displace normal sexual activity with excitement from its margins: fetishism, voyeurism. But all the more shocking are the small substitutes from imagination we are barely aware of. It is not that these are perverted, but that there is no guarantee of their reality outside the individual psyche. And this roughly becomes Freud's stance on normality.

Freud moves freely back and forth between his position as the healer and the curator of our neurosis. As our doctor he would like us to develop suitable responses to material reality, but otherwise he is fascinated by what we see from within. That it may be impossible to determine whether this psychic reality is fact or fiction makes Freud's thinking radically unstable. On the one hand he holds out reality to us as a firm goal in our fragility, on the other he offers reality as at best only a hypothetical and impermanent marker. After Freud the real thing is really in doubt: it has become "the real thing" or perhaps "this reality thing you talk about." We have to manage with that shadow hanging over "love."[46]

III Superabundant Substitutes

At his most radical Freud suggests all loves not directed at parents are substitutes. We are organically constituted for something less than bliss.[47] With the chaos of our emotional launch into the world, we begin a lifelong cruise through the realms of fantasy and illusion to try to match the receding coast of Ur-satisfaction with the discovery of an invented joy. Here, where only psychic reality matters, Freud's negative project is a damage-limitation exercise, daunting in what it says about truth, virtue and the future of humanity. He makes Flying Dutchmen out of all of us by seeming to say: if you can sustain the illusion, and the illusion can sustain you, then go with it, try it, it will be your personal reality, and the key to your survival. Just don't try to anchor in the material world, otherwise you will be astonished at what is not there. We might imagine a moment Freud turned his double-focus scrutiny on himself and saw the truth: that the respected doctor and professional man was also a paranoid fantasist, a condition which tended to lift all of his achievements as a good man into the air. His "true beliefs" float there untethered, like Socrates' balloon loaded with claims to knowledge which reason cannot substantiate.[48]

The problem of Freud's unresolved and differential vision was first stated then denied by Lionel Trilling fifty years ago:

> Love, morality, honor, esteem – these are the components of a created reality. If we are to call art an illusion then we must most of the activities and satisfactions of the ego illusions: Freud of course has no desire to call them that.[49]

Freud had no immediate *conscious* desire to undermine love, morality, honor and esteem. But Trilling was writing before it was evident that psychoanalysis would need to be turned on its creator; before the liberal Anglo-American establishment which bought Freud as science had been asked to look again and see that this "science" was really autobiography.[50]

It is of course an unprecedented *style* of autobiography, which is what made it difficult to recognize. As we have been talking about reality we should notice that at its heart is a particular relation of illusion to reality which Freud calls "*ein Zerrbild*" – a distortion, in which outside forces tug the known out of shape like a reflection in a fairground mirror. Freud sees normative reality as susceptible to constant distortion; paranoid fantasy makes sport with it, dreams turn it on its head, and sheer human craftiness undermines it. Perhaps this is what it felt like to have Freud's mind: to feel that nothing in language, or perception, or culture was stable, because of the tugs on their integrity exercised by the unconscious.[51]

The forces that threaten to pull love apart include competitiveness, the desire for power, and sheer need in craving an other. They work through charm and manipulation. Here I am thinking of those terms central to Freud's psychology of aesthetic reception, *Vorlust* and *Übertragung*, and which turn out also to be the main stations on the electric circuit of love. The desire for *mastery* through love seems to lie in Freud's unconscious as part of his infantile competitiveness with John and his experience of the (ab)use of power with Philipp. The temptation to charm and secure power is what Freud transfers to situations which, according to material reality, require love. What we get from Freud then is an apparently scientific analysis of love in society, deformed – and de-formed – by an underlying psychic drama which is his own.

The notion of *Vorlust* or forepleasure situates love midway between the Darwinian mating game and the illusions of art. Transference meanwhile is a psychic habit which emphasizes love's convertability, its almost parasitic nature, latching on to any apparently suitable object for its delivery, as itself, or as its opposite. Putting forepleasure and transference together we realize that love is simply a translation of energy, effected when certain expectations are fulfilled; those expectations include a screening of its own harsher reality; otherwise the desire for love happily falls for imitations.

The most brazen experiment built into Freud's teaching is that the bond between the analyst and the patient should be a kind of temporary substitute for "real" love. The gist of this relationship is transference, which plays upon "the credulity of love."[52] Transference consists in those deferred expectations which show themselves in the mixture of positive and negative feelings with which the patient responds to the analyst. Technically, the analyst will look out for positive and negative transference and for resistance to the promptings of transference, so as to understand what blocks any other new relationship the patient might form in reality. Ideally, as it seems was not at all difficult with Freud's teenage patient Dora, he will immerse himself with love in the patient's problems, in order to show patience and close the authority gap.[53]

To requote at greater length, with my emphasis, from *The Dynamics of Transference*:

Our experiments have shown that of the promptings which determine our love lives only a proportion achieve full psychic development; this proportion is turned towards reality, is at the disposal of the conscious personality and comprises a part of it. Another part of these libidinous promptings has got arrested in its development, it is turned away from the conscious personality as it is from reality, can only extend itself in fantasy or remains entirely in the unconscious, so that it is unknown to the person's consciousness. *Any person whose need for love is not incessantly satisfied in reality is bound to turn to each new person with libidinous expectations, and it is thoroughly probable that both portions of his libido, the one capable of reaching consciousness and the unconscious one, will form part of the approach.*[54]

What might be called the transference test is, at least in theory, a very neat, quasi-chemical experiment to observe what fundamental but invisible qualities of the individual psychic substance come into play to adulterate the reality of any encountered "other." Once the unconscious needs have been identified and recognized by the patient for what they are, they will stop clouding the picture. The patient's psychic substance will admit more reality in future. There is clearly something right Freud is getting at here.[55]

In the transference an occasion of two people falling in love is acted out and we are left in no doubt that this is a theatrical occasion. When Charcot carried out his experiments they too must have seemed like mime acts on a stage, during which the patient could be induced to lose her symptoms. But the problem with this healing drama which embraces Socratic questioning and Aristotelian catharsis is that the actual love bond is caught between life and artifice. The moment the patient really opens to the analyst (and the occasion does seem to be based on the heterosexual love act) is the signal for the analyst to cry off, to evade, to change his emotional clothes, leaving the patient to take her openness elsewhere. The patient should now realize what her real needs are and what feelings she has been repressing, and as part of her cure also realize that in the analyst she has chosen a wrong object. But how can psychoanalysis proceed honestly in practice? Only if the analyst is like Socrates, who remains motionless when the beautiful Alcibiades lies down beside him. Otherwise, especially in the light of Freud's unconscious, so full of the desire for mastery, transference looks very tricky. It leads one to suppose that psychoanalysis may be only a cover for a form of escapology; that escapology is Freud's real skill, which psychoanalysis only grants him the official license to practice. Psychoanalysis is the publicly sanctioned critical activity, while escapology is the risky secret pleasure.

Freud enjoyed and acknowledged playing through love dramas with his women patients; enjoyed them, one imagines, rather like chess games in which he was guaranteed to be the better player. He guessed he might have an unconscious desire to see "Irma" naked. He caught himself not forgoing the opportunity to fondle a young woman friend of the family who excited him. He minded that Dora cut short her treatment. But as long as the control and self-awareness were there he believed his procedure was correct. Emphasizing in his theoretical writings a high degree of self-knowledge in the analyst, Freud evidently thought he could have the pleasure without losing control. But his dangerous love hammock is strung between these two trees of pleasure and control, both of which bend in the emotional wind. The pleasure risks being illicit, the self-knowledge can fail. Today he stands accused of "using hermeneutics as a way of engaging in a form of sexual fantasy which involves his patient." Moreover, by flirting with a method based on alternating pleasure and control, Freud seems once again to replicate the act of love, this time from the viewpoint of the male.[56]

One problem with his defense is that Freud never properly developed a technical literature to accompany the theory of transference, though he set out the problem of temptation quite starkly.[57] A man playing love as a game to liberate an inhibited woman must keep his mind on his therapeutic goal, and, Freud says, unlike some prankster watching a dog race, resist throwing in a real sausage for the boys to devour midway:

> I don't want to claim that it will always be easy for the doctor to confine himself within the limits prescribed by ethics and technique. Particularly a young and not yet committed man may experience it as a hard task...On the other hand it is a painful role for a man, when a woman seeks love, to play the one who rejects and denies, and from a noble woman who can face up to her passion there emanates an incomparable magic, despite neurosis and resistance. It is not the crudely sensual demands of the patient which present the temptation. This is rather more offputting, and requires tolerance to be left to stand as a natural phenomenon. The finer and more inhibited stirrings of the woman with regard to what she wants are perhaps what bring the danger of forgetting technique and medical agenda for the sake of beautiful experience.[58]

If the analyst's – or at least Freud's – practical temptation here is palpable, one feels they were asking for it, weren't they, these Puckish fools like Freud and Jung who had affairs with patients, and Breuer, who could only register terror when a patient fell in love with him? The Freudian analyst as he comes off the drawing-board is an amorous *agent provocateur*. The most sympathetic view of his potential plight might be extracted from the closing moments of Schnitzler's *Paracelsus*, when we realize the healer himself *is* in love, but can now only leave the married woman he loves, having cured her of her interest in him. But mostly the analyst as a substitute lover who runs away from consummation at the last moment is in an odious practical position whatever the justification of the theory.

Otto Rank called this scientific sanctification of the male tease "technical emotional virginity" and it seems like a set of symptoms in itself, this way of forging relationships and avoiding loneliness without becoming involved. Henry James is said to have behaved this way with woman friends, and I believe Freud, who probably confined himself to marriage after an exaggeratedly long real virginity, and lacked chances to know other women, also played the *fort/da* game with patients. With the transference he pushed psychoanalysis to the edge of perversion.[59]

We know more about the behavior of Jung and Jones and later Lacan in respect of their flirtations with couch-reality because they did let go.[60] But here is a shaded area of Freud's psyche about which we shall never know much, mainly because, when his sexuality got the better of his professionalism, Freud's demonstrations went no further than moods and words. I would guess that he was impelled to try out his sexual charm, in which, having confided to Jung he lacked such attractiveness, he gained a little confidence in his late fifties. But his disparaging comments on his colleague Rank's chances of being a successful analyst because he wasn't good-looking suggest Freud never quite grasped what women want. Anaïs Nin found round-faced, goggle-eyed Rank so engrossing that the Bogartish Henry Miller had to sail the Atlantic to get her back. The real truth, which Plato understood, and Freud evidently did not, is that beauty doesn't need beauty. But women don't like escapologists and cowards.[61]

The imperfect involvement Freud dreamt up under the name of transference *could* be liberating for the patient. It might be like a freely chosen "wrong" affair to get one going again after a real disaster of the heart.

Or it might just be useful as the offer of a temporary relationship in which high emotion will be traded and secrets revealed and depths plummeted and heights scaled. You might take it, if it were culturally disguised, to fill your life. Or, if you were a philosophical pilgrim, mostly busily occupied elsewhere, you might want to use this spiritual love-which-can-be-bought as a passing stage on the way to truth. Many analysts who are not sexual predators would also say that the truth and potential curative value of the transference lies with the benefit of having a substitute loved one to talk to: a truth no less true for being obvious.

Indeed the process can be fine, and there does not need to be the sexual complication from, say, the heterosexual patient's point of view if a same-sex analyst is chosen. But the great problem, moral and technical, if the transference still works, is the end. *How* does the absence of a loving consummation wake the patient up to a new sense of selfhood and separateness? The only illustration I can find in Freud comes in his essay on the novella which so closely demonstrated his technique. The author Jensen, animating the self-searching delusions of the young academic Hanold, is like the analyst watching over the patient's erratic progress towards the real love object. Love heals Hanold even when it has become neurotically invested in an ancient picture:

> We readily entertain the idea that our medical case could end in a conventional "love story," but one shouldn't disdain love as a healing medium [*Heilpotenz*] against madness; and wasn't our hero's captivation by his picture of Gradiva a case of being completely in love, even if directed at the past and the lifeless?[62]

Art is all about endings. *Gradiva* uses what one might borrow from Brechtian theatre and call *Verfremdungseffekte* – alienation techniques – to release Hanold. Hanold transfers his fantasies from one object to another, creating the illusion of a logical pattern, until finally he experiences love, albeit for the wrong object, and wakes up to his madness. But it seems very difficult for Freudian analysis to extricate itself from a situation where it has created emotional dependency.[63]

Some aspects of the transference, for so long as he was untouched himself, struck Freud as funny. He gave in his lectures examples of a patient throwing her arms round his neck, or her family telling him "she talks all the time about you and about no one else." There is a touch of Victorian melodrama about a set-up in which patients leap out from behind the psychological arras and either knife you (for there is much negative transference of hate) or kiss you suddenly; so long as the stabbing is not real. But the fact is that there is nothing to stop the patient being "really" in love. What might it not do to her, to find her emotional home at last, only to be told the right address is one house farther on? Transference remains a perilous and uncertain dramatic enterprise like a re-enactment of a crime that risks going wrong.[64]

We see indeed, with regard to love, that the problem of how real feelings can be known, and real love objects found, can hardly be solved, nor even properly stated, given the propensity of the psyche to transfer its energy freely to unconscious substitutes. For the fact that something was once hidden does not make it materially real when it is uncovered; it is still only psychically real. And yet here Freud's two projects cross over, for he needs a definition of the real: what really happened in the patient's life to cause neurosis. There has to be something commodifiable that the patient can take away in exchange for her fee. So Freud's definition of the real becomes what the analyst and the patient agree on. The fantasist in him knows that this is just a story: the story of how Freud believed he charmed the patient *as if* into bed; but the patient must believe she has discovered her true self.[65]

Freud's whole system has been seen as a caricature of a philosophical system based upon the truth-seeking of the ego, because of the flimsiness of the reality test; because love may be just an imitation of love. Freud does talk, much more than Strachey's translation allows him to do in English, of the soul, but it is philosophically bewildering for his readers to be given, in practice, something less than ontologically guaranteed personal identity to work with. I, with my bundle of drives and inhibitions hitched to experience, am real to the extent that I feel the modifying effect of the social. Freud speaks of the Ego we present to the world as "a modified layer of the apparatus of the soul, the

Id." It is as if "I" am the skin which forms on the hot milk of a portion of human life, as it cools in the social breeze. And yet Freud wants us to have a strong sense of self.[66]

Let me take up that idea of caricature, emanating from the unconscious and predicated on the desire to secure some kind of delivery of one's needs. Neurosis, according to Freud, creates deceptive circumstances difficult for science to measure. Neurotic symptoms even imitate the symptoms of organic diseases to secure an outlet. Hysteria is a caricature of a work of art and an obsessional neurosis a caricature of religion; a paranoiac delusion is a caricature of a philosophical system.[67] Something in us says that if truth is so shaky, how much less reliable can be a concept of "love."

Serious critics have often been tempted to use an artistic metaphor for Freud's manipulative position in the transference. The analyst managing abreaction and catharsis (abreaction is the acting out of complexes) in the patient works like a painter whose palette is people's lives; or, less severely, the analytic patient resembles the artist's model.[68] These contentions are forcefully confirmed when we remember Freud's view of the artist as a master of charm through disguise. The writer seduces his reader into confronting otherwise unpalatable, raw, repellent wishes from his unconscious.

Consciously Freud sees in the artist a man *unlike* himself, and belabors the difference in their work. The artist can simplify to suit his presentational purposes; also he works with beauty and the Apollonian image while Freud has constantly to wade through the Dionysian psychic mud. Nor can a Dora turn round to the artist in mid-session and say: "You would say that, wouldn't you!" Still the idea of charming the patient, and thus dominating him, seems to have captivated Freud from within the inspiration he drew from hypnosis and art.

To recap, the artist when he produces not only frees his audience, but liberates repressed material from his own psyche. Both participants in the artistic contract obtain pleasure and delivery.[69] Now it seems barely a step on from here to see that in the psychoanalytic contract, when the analyst puts up interpretations, the moment of delivery will come when the patient assents to the truth of that story. Analysis will be successful and complete when the analyst has told a good story, which can be believed by his client. Freud, so often accused of bullying his clients, wanted confirmation that he was a good storyteller. It was not sexually that he couldn't hold back in the transference, but "artistically."

Freud mimics art, specifically the transaction between reader and writer/work, to practice psychic medicine. When he builds a *Verlockungsprämie* – the incentive of some reward or bonus – into his own technique it is the promise of a cure, if only the patient will trust the word-spinner and go where he leads. Evidently what is required of the patient is the willing suspension of disbelief. Where originally it was a question of the relationship between a work of art and its recipient, however, now we are dealing with a searching relationship between two people, one of whom is an exceedingly good talker.

Psyche is a Greek word which is translated in German as *Seele* (soul). Accordingly psychic treatment is called *soul-treatment*. One might suppose that what that means is treatment of the morbid manifestations of the life of the soul. But this isn't the meaning of the word. Psychic treatment means rather treatment starting from within the soul, treatment of disturbances of body or soul with means which primarily and directly work on what is of the human soul.

Such a means is above all the word, and words are the essential tools of the treatment of the soul. The layman may find it hard to believe that the morbid disturbances of the body and the soul can be overcome through the "mere" words of the doctor. He will say he is being asked to believe in magic. He is not so wrong; the words of our daily speech are nothing other than etiolated magic. But it will be necessary to go on a long detour in order to make people understand how science proposes to go about restoring to words at least a part of their original magic power.[70]

Reading this impassioned statement of intent, one begins to

understand why Freudian analysis tried so hard to counter its inherent wildness and soulfulness by insisting on "scientific" impersonality. Freud after all was strict as to the duration of the consultation; he insisted on the ritual of the analyst sitting behind the patient, who would lie on the couch; and the fee was always due at the end of each month and non-negotiable.

Freud admired art's capacity to open up a way through to the unconscious; he saw that art can break down normal human reserve. We can re-examine an earlier quoted passage in this light:

> When the writer displays his tricks or tells us something which we are inclined to believe are his personal daydreams, we experience a high pleasure which probably flows together from many sources. How the writer does that is his most intimate secret. The technique for overcoming that repulsion [which we feel at the personal source, LC] no doubt has something to do with the limits arising between every individual "I" and the other. In it lies the actual *ars poetica*.[71]

The truth was psychoanalysis could never replicate the impersonal yet passionate and intimate bond between a person and a work of art which it based itself upon. Still Freud hoped an *ars psychologica* could have the same disinhibiting effect as the *ars poetica*.

There is a theory here of the attractiveness of certain kinds of art and personality, which Schiller investigated under the heading of play. Freud adopted this aesthetic theory with his view that the artist is a liberating force who makes us feel free because we suspend our judgements. This translates in life into a feeling that successful relationships are all a question of adopting and furnishing the right disguises; of not coming straight out with it and frightening the other person away.

And perhaps the best beginnings for love are disguise; certainly for "love." For normally we prefer to encounter a social persona rather than immediately another naked psyche. Normally humor, jokes, role-playing, and even Freudian slips keep the ball in the air and keep us feeling free. At the same time jokes and slips have a cunning tendency to reveal more than is proper, and as such remind us that the dialectic of concealment and revelation is what Freud really has in mind as the healthy mechanism and the substance of culture. The detailed attention Freud gives to disguise at the heart of cultured behavior and verbal dexterity makes us think of why the Ancients invented rhetoric. To have spoken *directly* of the gods would have spelt disaster.[72]

The trick/untrick dialectic accounts for many patterns our emotions follow and from which we extract a sense of self. It is part of the accomplishment of the balanced human personality to be able to sustain forms of disguise and then in love to drop the disguise and find true release. It would be a Nietzschean view that there *are* no right objects, only right disguises, and Freud didn't quite get there. But he saw that the psychically sick can't disguise much; and that with sickness life loses its charm; whereas with art and culture it regains most of what it needs.[73]

Manufactured pyschoanalytic "love" replays this process in the laboratory. Analysis provides a temporary, artificial release from society, and consciousness, so we may know how things work within. We learn to examine our disguises for what they are, while the analyst helps us to understand those of which we are not yet conscious.

In fact love, or "love," or sexual energy can be disguised as almost anything. Our attitude to food, our pleasure in or dislike of driving and taking trains, our fondness for argument, our capacity to concentrate and the pleasure we take in intellectual work, our fascination with horror films, or scenes of cruelty, all relate to the fundamental drive in us for sexual pleasure, which in the course of our lives becomes stratified, diverted and sometimes sublimated. In his study of the compulsions of the indecisive Ratman, Freud observes that because this patient cannot take erotic action, his whole sexuality is transferred to the realm of thought. The pleasure a certain action would entail becomes the pleasure of having the thought.[74]

Much symbolic and semiological interpretation of modern and contemporary culture has built on Freud's pansexual revelation. Evidence for the diversion of sexual drives is unsubtly apparent in the compulsions and peacock displays of consumerism, the narcissism of the chic *quartiers* of our cities and the violence and prurience of the entertainment and news media. There is a massive diversion of sexual energy, with a large component of narcissism, into sophisticated post-twentieth-century food and foodways.

That the "charm" of this culture, in which love energy is displaced into myriad high and low forms, has to be weighed against its nature as illusion seems to me to be the unforced context into which the later Freud introduces Thanatos, the death drive, or the drive towards release. Thanatos is the counterweight to the intensity of Eros, which indefatigably churns out the illusions we need to keep us alive with a will.[75]

Freud's views on disguise, and almost all else I am concentrating on in this book, belong to the first decade of the twentieth century, some thirty years before he wrote *Civilization and Its Discontents*. Freud always had a feeling for a dialectic of instinct and illusion, force and façade. Parallels frequently drawn between Freud and Schopenhauer bring to mind the veil of Maya, which palliates the savage instincts beneath. In the beginning was the unconscious wish, striving blindly for fulfillment. Freud's Schopenhauerian view is of the whole world as one great appetite. Wishes collide. Civilization constrains them, and on the disguised, diverted wish, and on the suspension of real needs, rests the charm of polished society and of art.

The fate of love in the civilized but ideally non-neurotic world looks pretty: a triumph for Life. In *Amor*, both civilization (through disguise) and nature (through satisfaction) have their way. *Amor* organizes the perpetual glittering *ballo in maschera* where no one is stabbed. From Shakespeare to Cole Porter love trips a pretty ring dance. This love is magic, like the genuine, consoling, beautiful but not at all erotic love in Hugo von Hofmannsthal's *Die Frau ohne Schatten*. *Amor* happens in a fairyland where only occasionally the lights fuse. This love is a state into which disguise and magic help to lift us. It delivers the kiss of stage happiness. From the age of seventeen, when he defended the tinsel of a stage production of *La Dame aux camélias*, something of Freud's work was always to do with the search for *l'élisir d'amore*. He would have bottled it and sold it if he only could.[76]

The poetic strangeness of Freud's work consists in the charms of *Amor* pitted secretly against the howling and pounding of Eros; against the hot-blooded ordinariness of the need for a mate. This tension is built into a question which might be seen as arising particularly out of the crisis high bourgeois society faced at the beginning of the twentieth century. How can we suspend our most urgent wishes, without becoming neurotic? How much charming tension can we bear before we start baying for real satisfaction? To requote:

> It depends what quantity of unused libido a person can tolerate, and how much libido they can lead away from sexual matters towards the goals of sublimation. The final goal of the activity of the soul, which may be described as a striving to gain pleasure and avoid pain, presents itself from an economic point of view as the task of subduing the excitement-seeking quantities (whatever exists simply to be stimulated) which are at work in the apparatus of the soul, and avoiding the blockage which causes them pain.[77]

The question is: what can we civilized beings do about the tension in ourselves with which love, and its absence, and art and its (metaphysical) illusions, seem to tease us unmercifully? And the problematic answer from the past, and which we might improve upon in the future, is that we can take shelter in fantasy. The gods of Greece have departed, but let us anoint our own eyelids. Fantasy, as Freud says, is a halfway house on the way to neurosis, and if we can hover there, all may be well.[78]

6

REALITY RECONSIDERED

I have imagined Freud so far to have written a long narrative poem about nature, and two thick novels, *Vienna 1900* and *Love Story*. The imagined novels were written in the same style, centered on the compassionate observation of character, and were full of the joys and sorrows of social ambition in a status-conscious, hypocritical, middle-class society. The narrative of these works took no leaps beyond grammar and logic. But now, to pinpoint an alternative path in Freud's work which has nothing to do with chronology, but finds its reflection in the two radically different Freud traditions existing in Western culture, I want to invent a third novel, which I shall call *Look What I Can Do!* This journey into the far reaches of the imagination hardly seems by the same author, for in it Freud is passionately interested in that other outlet for our life energies, the unreal. He finds endlessly entertaining the prospect of what we could do and what we might have done. The possibilities of the unconscious suggest to him an alternative *way through* to satisfaction and psychic health. The resources of imagination and self-absorption are an option even set against the real need for love. I imagine Freud could have written *Look What I Can Do!* on the basis of what he speculated upon and secretly so enjoyed in *The Interpretation of Dreams*. But, remembering that Freud's work on dreams and much of his understanding of the unconscious stemmed from his self-analysis, I suggest love never was the goal of this third novel, but rather the solitary means to finding a place in the world. *Look What I Can Do!* is a voyage of discovery which involves transforming into beautiful or at least gripping or amusing pictures all that we find secretly problematic about ourselves. It is a journey towards the creativity that makes self-acceptance possible.[1] But it is also a discovery about language. If the first two imaginary novels based on Freud's real work in another domain were about success in the world, and love, the third is about the possibilities of language. Every night the narrator climbs down into the hold of his own mental ship to chart a new course in a world of infinite possibility, *behind* and *before* words. I imagine this interior journey called *Look What I Can Do!* so that the reader can move closer to Freud the secret artist, or the artist who might have been.[2]

To return to what Freud did actually write, he said that in dreams doors open to the unconscious which free the psyche from its conscious constraints and replace anxiety with entertainment.

> The unconscious is a particular realm of the soul with its own stirrings of desire, its own means of expression and its particular mechanisms of soul, which do not otherwise come into effect . . . Something, which originates in our conscious life and shares its character – we'll call them "residues of the day" – comes together with something from that realm of the unconscious to make dreams . . . The way the residues of the day are influenced by the unconscious coming to meet them contains, I would say, the condition for regression . . .[3]

and

> We call it regression, when in the dream the idea turns itself back into the sense picture which was its origin once upon a time.[4]

The unconscious dissolves our abstractions and concepts, our ideals and rules. Something happens so that another voice in us, besides our controlled and logical adult voice, can speak. The state of mind shared by the mental patient, the inspired artist and the dreamer is one of uncertainty, impressionability and withdrawal but also a starting-point for seeing the world differently.

Regression, though it temporarily reverses the story of human civilized progress, strengthens civilization. The artist needs to descend to the level of dreams to release his true inventiveness and genius. Ernst Gombrich convinces us that regression was the goal of the young Picasso when he found that the draughtsmanship inherited from his father made his work too perfect. Picasso wanted to tap something raw in himself, unshaped by skill and sentiment, so he went in his mind to where the world looked unshaped, fierce, daring, naughty, murderous, sensual and funny; to a place where we stand on our heads, entertain alien feelings and pass into other identities; where contradictions and opposites exist side by side; from where the world is pictured and language is only another picture. We see something of this world in the beliefs of primitive peoples, in fairy tales and in the eternal myths and legends.

He takes to carving where he can exploit his lack of skill . . . and now he pours into these regressive forms all the expression and savagery that was pent up in him. The great smashing begins. He invents the game of Cubism.

The force tapped from the unconscious gets transformed. Eventually it emerges in "these multiform crystals of miraculous complexity we call works of art," says Gombrich, understanding Picasso through reading Freud.[5]

Someone skeptical of the existence of an unconscious may say we are deluded; that there is no such place; that a folk memory can exist independently of an unconscious and that dreams only produce mental junk. Of these three points I am inclined to agree with the notion of an independent folk memory. I also observe that for Freud the unconscious was still only a hypothetical place, even if he thought science would one day show it to be a real one.[6] But what does seem to me defensible is Freud's notion of a dynamic unconscious, which was never well understood. The unconscious in this aspect is like a storehouse of shadows; like an archive of photographic negatives, Freud says somewhere. In its relation to reality the unconscious is a shadow, but of a special kind which we invent here, for unlike a shadow it is the primary *cause* of the conscious world, not its inferior bi-product. It is not an echo, or a blurred cast, but an infinite set of songlines. It is the imprint our psyche will give to all such future occasions that it has experienced as similar in the past.[7]

Freud's notion that the intensity of past impressions is stored indefinitely in the mind, and always threatening to make a new appearance in life, is intimately bound up with the dynamic unconscious. "Dead" impressions remain indefinitely effective alongside the living; only they live in Brentano's intentionally inexistent realm, as desires, the real existence of whose objects is not guaranteed by the assertion of the wish. So Hanold desires as his sweetheart Gradiva, the unreal girl on the bas relief from Pompeii, but whose unreal existence will one day make it possible for Hanold to love a real sweetheart. Freud much admired Jensen's *Gradiva* for taking as its theme the way the dead and the fictitious continue to dwell as effective forces among the living. The story seemed to illustrate most strikingly the dual mental citizenship Freud envisaged for humanity: not of minds in conflict within the self, but an existence conditioned by a foot in each camp, conscious and unconscious.[8]

Freud's unconscious is actually made of a theory of perception combined with a theory of causality and to grasp these philosophical origins is I think immediately to have a better idea of what Freud was trying to say. Essentially the unconscious contains the imprint of things before they are named. I have an imprint of love, which allows me to recognize renewed instances of that experience, so that when I say "I love P," what I really mean is that I recognize love as love and associate it with P. This way of linking up mind and world by suggesting that the mind has a corresponding inner notion for every notion it greets outwardly with a name in the world has been nicely described as knowing the world by watching a mental television in our heads. But it suits Freud, because it gives him a division between a realm of mental activity which is for itself, posited as the unconscious, and a realm where it is expressed, the conscious. Words used appropriately make the transition possible. This is Freud at his most technical, but also most fecund as far as his influence on French structuralism and post-structuralism is concerned. The interested reader should turn to the notes for remarks on the original German and in particular the relevance to the work of Jacques Lacan.[9]

All at once we believe we know what the difference is between an unconscious and a conscious representation. . . the conscious representation embraces the representation of the thing and the appropriate word-representation, the unconscious representation is the thing-representation alone. The system ucs [= The unconscious] contains the thing-as-energy-charge [*Sachbesetzung*], the first and real mental objects; the system pcs [= pre-consciousness] comes into being when the thing-as-energy-charge links up with its corresponding word-representation and becomes over-charged as a result. Such over-chargings are we imagine what bring about a higher psychic organization and make it possible for primary processes to be absorbed into the secondary process which prevails in preconsciousness. Now we can express more precisely what it is that repression refuses to a representation which is sent back in the case of transference neuroses: it refuses it translation into words which should remain linked with the object. The representation which is not rendered in words or the psychic activity which is not over-charged remain then repressed back in the ucs.[10]

The word plays a crucial role in separating out unconscious and conscious ideas or representations, and significantly Freud derives much empirical support for his theory from his early work on aphasia. What happens to brain-damaged patients suggests to Freud that links between the stored energy of an impression, its imprint as an idea and the word that corresponds to it go awry; and he surmises that this also happens in cases of psychoneurosis, when certain things can't be remembered. The ideal way is for ideas to pass freely from the unconscious through preconsciousness into consciousness. But physical damage to the brain, and also neurosis, can block the passage. Bundles of undercharged things-as-energy just accumulate, without the strength to find themselves an outlet in consciousness.

Surely because I used to work in a school I see these things-as-energy in search of a word or concept to bring them to consciousness as like the boys milling about downstairs in the cloakroom, ready to grab any blazer so long as that gets them out to play. On a wet day I get desperate because they can't go out. All their energy is used wrestling each other and playing with ways of representing themselves: hiding, reappearing, swapping caps and blazers, and jungle-painting their faces. Seen from upstairs, they seem to writhe and seethe in a world which on the one hand is driven by pleasure and where on the other it is difficult to pin down who is who and even more who did what. I know if I did apprehend a culprit for a misdeed the blazer he had grabbed for cover would instantly detach itself from the worm-like body inside and belong to someone else. When I watch the boys on a wet day I am like the spectator of repressed wishes seething and writhing in the unconscious, if such a view were only possible. Freud's system unconscious as a repository of energy and words and memories left over from consciousness is just such a vision of highly organized disorder: it is a *perpetuum mobile* of actions and impulses detached from agents; an everlasting storm of confetti made up of fragmented nametapes. This is the raw material of the thought factory.

On a dry day by contrast I see an illustration of psychic health, for most of the boys do go out to play. They find a blazer somewhere, like the repressed wish finds a word, and out they go, metaphorically past the headmaster, literally past the censorship which consciousness exercises. In the stampede to get outside only the weak boys or those without cunning are left behind without anything to wear. But this need not break our hearts, because we are really talking about repressed wishes, not human beings. It is only that Freud, as a consequence of transferring the principle of the constancy of matter to the psyche, attributes a kind of Darwinian impulse to survive to our repressed thoughts, and by bringing out that submerged metaphor of his I can perhaps underscore the relentless residual energy which characterizes the dynamic unconscious.[11]

But system is a misleading word, because it suggests something too tight and too perfect. In fact the Freudian mental machine is a deliberately loosely bolted construction, inspired by his insights into aphasia. This system embracing unconscious and conscious is like a badly assembled bit of flatpack furniture. Suddenly there just aren't two overlapping holes, they are inches apart. When aphasics have trouble correlating effective thinking with right speech the problem looks similar. Things don't line up properly. But supposing they did, still, in a loose system? Wouldn't this technical picture correspond to the ideal Freud established for the non-neurotic and probably artistic personality, which is loosely packed? Here is our way through to the curative value of regression as we feel it in art and dreams. Loose packing turns out to mean, to express the psychology in Freud's technical terms, keeping a channel open by which ideas can pass freely between the unconscious, pre-consciousness and consciousness. In the vernacular it means artists don't get fixated on things, but move on. Their mental insides don't get stuck in one relational position. So now we know: the ideal inner life disports an open pathway, *a way through*, which is reversible, from the unconscious to consciousness, and back again.

Freud writes on the last page of "The Unconscious" (1915):

The activity of our soul moves very generally in two opposite directions of flow, either originating with the drives and making its way through the unconscious system into the conscious business of thought or, at a prompt from without, moving through the systems of consciousness and preconsciousness to arrive at the unconscious energy charges of the "I" and of objects. This second way must remain *passable* despite the repression that has occurred and stands pretty wide open to the attempts of the neurosis to get its objects back.[12]

That word passable, *passierbar*, suggests a mountain pass. It also suggests the Greek philosophical term *aporia*, a–poria, meaning literally "*no* path through" and generally an insoluble logical quandary. As any tyro student of philsophy knows, Socrates pushes his rational arguments to the point where they can't be resolved, and don't pass through. They come up against the barriers of logic. Whereas each time there is a transition, or a crossing made from the unconscious to the preconscious, or in reverse, from conscious experience into repression, the Freudian analyst has a point of investigation. The crossing through into expression, even when the link is illogical, is made possible by the existence of the unconscious. Was Freud the Greek scholar and philosophy student aware of the contrast he was drawing here? Let's suppose so. The work of French structuralism, bringing into academic purview material which would not previously pass through in rational discourse, also seems to find a beginning here.[13]

The notion of the crossover is central to understanding the Freudian unconscious as dynamic and word-seeking. Freud himself tries to understand more about its extraordinary versatility by watching how the crossover works to form symptoms and dreams. It is one way in which a repressed wish finds itself a suitable disguise and hence a passport in the direction of consciousness. A man has repressed his desire to succeed in cricket. Instead he dreams of playing football. But both games use balls, so the unconscious can use the football to release the cricket (ball) thought. This very crudely is how dreams are formed and how we can interpret them by understanding the fording places which link the apparently disparate narratives in the dream. A woman featured in *The Interpretation of Dreams* dreams that she goes out shopping late and the *Fleischbank*, "the meat bank," is closed. Her night pictures deliver no meat for the family dinner then, but also, thanks to the Viennese slang expression, her repressed desire for a sexual advance from a man comes closer to the surface. Or, in another dream, a man dreams of the discomfort of putting on his thick winter coat. A coat in German can be something you put on or pull over: *ein Überzieher*. But so can a condom, and with that we are on quite a different track for the young man's thoughts. The unconscious through its dream-making tool the dreamwork is indeed adept at meaning-switching. I adopt the term from the point in *The Interpretation of Dreams* where Freud co-opts from his colleague Hanns Sachs the metaphor of railway-line points to describe the way the unconscious uses ambiguities in conscious speech to gets its message through.

> We know from *The Interpretation of Dreams* that the dreamwork knows various ways to portray a word or expression as a picture that can be directly apprehended by the senses. It can for example take advantage of the fact that the expression it wants to represent is ambiguous, and, using the double meaning as a set of points [*Weiche*], instead of the first meaning occurring in the dream thought, incorporate the second into the manifest dream content.[14]

Earlier Freud uses another image, of the interpretation of dreams offering a glimpse into the interior workings of the soul as if through a gap in the curtains, *wie durch eine Fensterlücke*. Only here the idea of "getting through" links up with his typical desire to *unveil* a prior reality.[15] It also reminds us of the fundamental voyeurism in his personality which greatly affects the nature of his "scientific" thoughts. But other examples lead back to the more philosophically inspired notion of message-switching. Freud speaks of "something in the middle in common" which facilitates the move from a recent minor event to a matter of deeper psychical importance.[16]

The Botanic Monograph Dream confirms that, with various ideas running on parallel tracks, the dream seems to wait for a crossing point so that it can make some kind of story out of their crossing-over and thus illustrate some deep meaning which is trying to escape from the unconscious. Freud sees the Botanic Monograph in a shop, and the dreamwork uses this glimpse into a shop-window as a switch to dredge up his memory of the fateful monograph on cocaine. The same "common middle" terminology recurs in renewed discussion of

Irma's Injection, and in a dream about Freud's Uncle Josef. The first crossing-point is verbal, the second visual.

The visual crossing-point comes when Freud's criminal Uncle Josef and his friend R merge into one person. Freud expressly thinks the dream works here like one of Galton's photomontages. In this "Uncle with the Yellow Beard" dream the crossover allows the dreaming Freud to cast his esteemed friend R in a negative light by merging him with Uncle Josef. Thus he can persuade himself that R hasn't got the job because he is not good enough, not because he is a Jew. This reconstruction in turn protects Freud's hopes for his own promotion, for it means he need only worry about being good enough, not about being a Jew.

The verbal crossing-point works similarly by superimposing word upon word, until slight changes build up. Freud dreams of Otto having given Irma an injection of Propyl or Propionic acid or Trimethyl. Why these words, which would be nonsensical substances to inject? Recently Otto gave the Freuds a bottle of liqueur which smelt like diesel fuel or *Amyl*. In the unconscious "Amyl" prompted the near homonym "Propyl" which in turn summoned up an association with the Propyläen in Munich. That led the dreamer to Fließ, whom he had visited in the same city when he was ill, and both mental goads lead on to Trimethyl, which Fließ had identified as a substance mysteriously given off in sexual transactions.

In sum, cargoes of psychic energy change lines in the unconscious, in order quicker to arrive at their destination called self-expression; and they do so by exploiting overlapping associations to jump from one channel of thought to another. In this case Amyl-Propyl-Propyläen-Trimethyl correspond and create a way through, so that we know what is really bothering Freud in his unconscious: his professional doubts and mistakes.

> Close to Amyl for association lies Propyl; out of the "Wilhelm" sphere Munich with its Propyläen comes to meet it. In Propyl-Propyläen the two areas of representation unite. This middle element gets into the content of the dream as if by a compromise. Some middle thing which both sides have in common

is created here, which allows for multiple determination. We seem to have hands-on proof that multiple determination makes penetration of the dream content easier.[17]

And so we dream, and dreaming creates a temporary way through. Freud the therapist imagines that the dreamwork, as an agency of the unconscious mind, constantly conjures up pictures and makes a kind of story out of them which is designed at once to keep us asleep and soothe away the tensions of the day and the more distant past. We indulge ourselves with a temporary new reality.

I have something like a picture puzzle – a rebus – in front of me: a house, on the roof of which a boat is visible, then a single letter of the alphabet, then a figure running, whose head has been left out. I could go now with the criticism that this combination and its parts are nonsensical. A boat doesn't belong on the roof of a house, and a person without a head can't run; also the person is bigger than the house, and if the whole is supposed to represent a landscape, well then the individual letters of the alphabet don't fit in, because they don't occur in nature, do they? The right way to view the puzzle only becomes apparent when I don't raise such claims against the whole and its details, but apply myself to replacing each picture with a syllable or a word, which can be represented by the picture because of some context [namely, in which it has occurred]. *The words which come together like this are no longer senseless but can result in the most beautiful and richly meaningful tale.* The dream is this kind of picture puzzle, and our predecessors in the field of the interpretation of dreams have committed the error of judging the rebus as a piece of draughtsmanship. As such it appeared to them to be nonsensical and worthless.[18]

The dreamwork compresses past and present experiences, elides them, and displaces the various elements, so that we don't immediately recognize what's going on in the manifest dream, which is the one we remember. The dreamwork frequently also substitutes one thing or person for another, the further to conceal the real latent content of the dream. But what we immediately realize with the dreamwork is that we have moved out of experimental science and into the worlds of language and poetry. Also we are back in our familiar realm of disguise and revelation. For the dreamwork is in effect a master of rhetoric, with every possible means of verbal disguise at its disposal when unconscious stirrings urge us to dream of what we cannot face.

> The actual work done by dreams is far removed from the model of waking thought... It's not as if it were more careless, more incorrect, more forgettable, less complete than waking thought; it is something qualitatively quite different and for that reason not immediately comparable. It doesn't think, calculate or judge at all, but limits itself to a work of *transformation* [my italics]. It can be described exhaustively, if one fixes on the conditions which what it manufactures must satisfy. This product, the dream, must above all be spared censorship, and to this aim the dream work avails itself of a shifting of psychic intensities to the point where all psychic values are transvalued; thoughts are to be exclusively or predominantly reproduced in the material of visual and acoustic memory residues, and out of this requirement arises the dreamwork's concern for representability, to which the dreamwork's shifting of the psychic accent corresponds... [19]

Freud's two hundred and fifty dream interpretations are funny, illogical, apparently inscrutable tableaux. The *manifest* dream is relatively short and has no emotional content. It "is like the peace of a corpse-strewn field; no traces remain of the rage of the battle."[20] But the *latent* dream reveals layers of rage and desire, and moving slowly towards it, picking up bloody scraps of cast-off psychological clothing, we piece together great conflicts. We do so because the conflicts and ambiguities inherent in the psyche present themselves in dreams as conflicts of signification, with teams of words (*Vorstellungsgruppen*) pulling this way and that. Whatever words come to us to tell our dream in, therefore, are highly charged, as are any alterations we feel driven to make. Every phoneme and morpheme is significant, every alliteration or half-rhyme can point to a train of associations. Freud especially loved to portray the unconscious, that unstable undersurface of our lives, as a never-ending chain of signs, and then to ask: what kind of thought is it that links Mr. Jocelyn with Mr. Joyeuse? What links a sense of *déjà vu* with the mother's genitals, and a journey Italy-wards with male genitals? That must be how the dreamwork functions: not logically to be sure, but by extraordinary leaps of association, which encapsulate a drama.[21]

Each dream encapsulates a drama, and each dream of Freud's own encapsulates a vital aspect of his life, as we have already seen in earlier chapters, where we have used them for evidence. Within the two hundred and fifty analyzed dreams the fifty interpretations of his own dreams in the dreambook are one of Freud's greatest actual artistic achievements. He invents a new vehicle for auto-biography. But let us continue for the moment as if Freud were only functioning as a critic and a classifier of something existing quite separate from himself, this dreamwork.

The dreamwork is poetically inspired, but it also shows that Freud as a schoolboy has been well taught, for essentially it puts classical rhetoric into practice. It represents things which cause other things, or the qualities of things, as simply sequences of events (*hendiadys*). It presents alternatives alongside each other. No two things are incompatible (*zeugma*). It reverses the order of events or the relations of things (*chiasmus*). Or it simply behaves like a writer and makes one character out of three, or turns things into their opposites.

Understanding how all these devices work, Freud patiently decodes from the manifest dream back to the latent wish. His procedure re-enacts in reverse, he claims, the way the dreamwork originally disguised the repressed wish. But in fact the dreamwork is hard to describe divorced from particular dreams, so let us return to them.

A woman dreams that:

she is sitting with her husband in the theatre; a whole side of the front stalls is empty. Her husband tells her that Elise L and her fiancé would also like to have come, but could only have got bad seats, three for one florint fifty crowns, and of course they couldn't take those. She says it wouldn't have been a tragedy [to take them].

Freud focuses on that "one florint fifty crowns." The woman's sister-in-law recently received a present from her husband of a hundred and fifty florints — a hundred times more. Then that "three": the young woman known to her in the dream is three months younger than the dreamer is; and the couple wanted three theatre tickets. But why three tickets for two people? It's absurd. (That is, the dream wants to say *something* is absurd.) Think then of the theatre that was half-empty when they came in. The woman had bought tickets in advance, but saw that it wasn't necessary. The latent dream unravels as this: it was crazy of me to marry so young, I didn't need to. The example of Elise L shows I could still have got a man, had I waited, and he would have been worth a hundred times what my present husband is worth. I could have had three husbands for the same money. On the other hand it's not a tragedy to be married to this one.[22]

In another dream, which Pabst used as the centerpiece of his wonderful silent film about psychoneurosis, *Geheimniße einer Seele*, the absurdity is visual:

[A woman I know] dreams she is at the opera. It's a performance of Wagner, which has lasted until quarter to eight in the morning. In the front and rear stall there are tables, where people are eating and drinking. Her cousin, who has just come back from his honeymoon, is sitting at one of the tables with his young wife; next to them is an aristocrat. People say that the young wife brought this man back with her from the honeymoon, quite openly, the way one brings a hat back from a honeymoon. In the middle of the stalls there is a tall tower, which has a platform on top, surrounded by an iron railing.

High up there is the conductor, with the features of Hans Richter; he keeps running about behind his railing, sweating terribly, and from this outpost conducts the orchestra, which is seated around the base of the tower. She herself is sitting with a friend (whom I also know) in a box. Her younger sister is trying to pass up to her from the stalls a large piece of coal, with the motivation that she didn't realize how long it would take and she must be freezing by now. (As if the boxes ought to have been heated during the long performance.)[23]

The dreamer's love is secret, unlike the bold young wife's. At the same time, because this love is unavailable, the dreamer is afraid that like her friend, but unlike her married younger sister, she has been left on the shelf. The sister didn't realize how long it would take to find the dreamer a husband. The coal is a token of fire to keep the heart warm, but, in Freud's interpretation via a folksong, also betokens secret love. In fact, the dreamer has her ideal man, who stands high over all other musicians. But he paces behind bars, as if in a cage, and the dream picture, in both a play on the man's name and a reference to his insanity, turns out to be a representation of the composer Hugo Wolf. The tower, says Freud, is a "mixed depiction through apposition." It says the man the woman loves is both great and mad.

Because Freud's own dreams and their interpretations are such fun, and so stimulating, I can't resist citing two more. The first is a self-portrait of the child in the man. In the interpretation which follows I have brought out some of the meanings Freud leaves hanging.

I'm going in a state of considerable undress out of one flat on the ground floor up the staircase on to a higher floor. When I do that I always leap up three steps, and am happy that I'm nimble at climbing stairs. Suddenly I see that a maid is coming down the stairs and therefore towards me. I'm embarrassed, want to hurry up, when a feeling of inhibition sets in, I'm stuck on the stairs and can't move.[24]

The situation is Freud's own as the owner of two flats, but takes place in the house of a patient where the staircase lacks a spittoon and is covered with gobs of saliva. Recently a maid there has complained about Dr. Freud not wiping his feet. Of the two directions in which the dream is interpreted the second is more interesting. Freud's leaping is a piece of exhibitionism. Exhibitionism belongs in childhood. So who is the maid who has complained about him being dirty? She turns out to be a nanny who looked after him up to the age of two and a half, and whom he probably loved, despite her sometimes harsh ways. Hence the shame and dependence he brings to the maid in the dream. There is also a super-interpretation (*Überdeutung*) Freud offers in a footnote: *spücken* (to spit) recalls *Spuken* (spooks). I would add that spooks, in his favorite quote from Goethe, are what he has devoted his life's work to driving out of people's heads. Further, the tie-in with spitting and saliva reminds us, like the Latrine Dream, that this is dirty work, which he needs the energy of youth to sustain. But to return to this dream, in which Freud seems very energetic and confident, he points out that spooks are also spirits (*Geister*), and spirits are also wits. Wits on the stairs leads roughly to the French *esprit d'escalier*, which means one hasn't been able to say what one wanted to at the right time, one's wits were not quick enough to be charming in society. In German this could be diagnosed as a lack of *Schlagfertigkeit*, and brings us back to Freud's old worries about his defective charm. But in its literal meaning *Schlagfertigkeit* also denotes "readiness to strike blows" and its absence in the dream may be saying that actually his nanny didn't lack this quality at all, and used it to reinforce her message that some habit or other of Freud's as a child was dirty. Hence the present acute sense of prohibition, which halts him in his tracks as a man and as a doctor. There is a striking contrast between the leaping at the beginning of the dream and the lack of motion at the end. It establishes a picture of internalized culture wreaking its repressive worst. The man has become inhibited in adulthood because of some dirtiness he was chastised for in childhood and because of a frustrated desire to please. He has become exaggeratedly self-disciplined.

The two glories of this dream, a mixture of wordplay for its own sake and devastating self-discovery, are repeated with redoubled energy in the Three Fates Dream.

I go into a kitchen, to get something to eat. Three women are standing there, one of whom is the proprietor. She is fashioning something in her hands, as if she were making dumplings (*Knödel*). She replies that I'll have to wait till she's ready (that this was spoken isn't clear). I get impatient and walk away offended. I put on an overcoat, but the first one I try is too long. I take it off, rather surprised to see it has fur trimmings. A second one I put on has a long piece of braiding with a Turkish design. A stranger with a long face and short goatee beard tries to stop me putting it on, saying it's his. Then I show him that it has Turkish embroidery all over it. He asks: what business of yours are these Turkish designs, this Turkish braiding...? But then we're quite friendly with each other.[25]

The Three Fates Dream shows Freud playing with language to an unprecedented degree to understand his inner life. At thirteen Freud had been impressed by a novel in which, when the hero finally went *mad*, he called out the names of *three women* who had brought him the most happiness and woe in his life. One was *Pélagie*. In the dream the three women seem to a classically educated mind like the Three Fates who spin men's lives. Only one, the proprietor of the inn, is the *mother*. (The grammar does not have to be specific even in normal speech for this mother to be Freud's, but he seems to welcome the faint evasion which is also a generalization.) Mothers give life and first *sustenance*. We understand why this figure might be dispensing food. But then thinking about how mothers feed children, a young man's *joke* comes to mind that since his wet nurse was so pretty he wishes he'd taken more advantage of his *infant situation*.

The women in the dream *rub their hands* together making the dough. His mother did that when he was six, to illustrate that we *all* return to dust in the end; she rubbed some flakes of skin off her hands. The young Freud was stricken with the inevitability of *death*. But now the dreamer thinks of something else. He learned what he knows about *human tissue* (histology) from a Professor *Knödl*, who brought a case against someone for *plagiarism*. At the university at that time, moreover, there had been an *overcoat* thief, the kind Freud is being treated as in the dream. *Pélagie – plagiarism* links the novel enjoyed in his youth with the Knödl case.

The chain leads on to *Plagiostomen*, the technical word for sharks (*Haifische*), over which Knödl was embarrassed during a lecture, and from those fish to fish bladder(s) (*Fischblase*). The latter can also be used as condoms, and condoms are pulled over, as some overcoats are.

The name of another teacher, *Brücke* (= "bridge'), comes to mind, and acts as a word-bridge to Freud's happy days at the Institute. There is a Goethe quote about drinking at the breasts of wisdom (*Brüsten*), and a contrast with the torment (*plagen*) of the dream. The name of a third teacher, Fleischl (= "Meaty') also comes to mind, and like Knödl sounds like something to eat. Finally memory alights on a sad scene in which the *flakes of skin* and *madness*, and a means from Roman cooking to take away hunger, *cocaine*, all play their part. Freud's guilt over Fleischl von Marxow's death, which has been running through the dream, surfaces most evidently here. The bearded man meanwhile recalls some shopping Freud's wife did in Dalmatia (Spalato) which reminded Freud of his own failure to close a bargain in Cattaro.

I have underlined key words to bring out the storm of associations here: between words and words, words and things, meanings and sounds, words and pictures, words and functions, and pictures and pictures. They lead Freud to pick up the trail of some of his recurrent anxieties: not only Fleischl von Marxow's death from cocaine, but desire for the breast and sexual frustration during his student years. Death and the missed bargain remind him to take his pleasures where he can. Freud tactfully doesn't explain the condom fixation, but it seems easy to read in another plausible interpretation of the dream, following Freud's technique.

I suggest the female provider in the kitchen is his fiancée. He wanted something. She said, no, wait. Cross and frustrated, he put something on to go out and satisfy his hunger elsewhere. Or, rather, he went out hungry, intending to put something on when he got there. Only a bearded man with a long face said no, it's foreign to you, so he didn't. He waited, and didn't quarrel with the man over this. The man, who evidently was a personification of morality and Freud's own father, also said: don't put that on, it's mine, meaning that sexual intercourse and contraception belong to marriage.

The ability of unconscious mind to produce pictures like these does seem to be a kind of miracle, which only descriptions of the use of poetic language can begin to keep track of. One understands one of the many impulses which seem to lie behind the composition of the seven-hundred-page volume *The Interpretation of Dreams*. There is a term in linguistics, the paradigmatic, which captures the relation between words which fulfill the same function across the vast spectrum of possible sentences, relating I to you and he and she and we and they. We've seen this dynamic relation at work in dreams, where the protagonist begins as M, is briefly Flieβ, but seems to end up as Freud. The story makes sense for all of them. There are also simple opposites in space and time and perception, like black/white and big/small, empty/full and day/night, and the fundamental difference of verb mood between active and passive which the unconscious feels free to move between to make its pictures. "Crossing over" is also a fertile means to generate twists of plot and generally bring new material into the story, and move the narrative on.

But where we feel Freud is disingenuous is in insisting that these patterns are the work of an unconscious agency. How much he is actually setting down his self-discoveries as a writer becomes clear when we see the way the "how" of the dreamwork is inseparable from "what" is dreamt and keeps leading him back to auto-biography.

Ideally a detailed, dedicated study of the dreambook would tease out where Freud seems to talk about one writer's imagination, namely his own, of which he is at least partly conscious, and where he speaks of mental operations genuinely attributable to a universal unconscious. As it stands, Freud seems to project his writerly imagination on to the unconscious. This is not just a question of one or two attributes of the dreamwork, like the "association compulsion," to bring together disparate ideas in a new narrative. It applies to the whole existence of the dreamwork and its language games.[26] It shows up splendidly and to seminal literary effect in Freud's absurd belief that the unconscious is polyglot. A German man whose English rival in love is called Richard suddenly goes on a manic diet although he is not at all overweight. This makes sense when we remember Dick, short for Richard, is also the German word for "fat." The poor man has to get rid of dick. There are many other amusing examples of the polyglot unconscious in *The Psychopathology*, the dreambook and the case studies. Vladimir Nabokov counted himself as one inspired by Freud's example.[27] Freud's unwitting association of his own imagination with the general nature of the unconscious also seems to be reflected in the projection of a censor into the unconscious, as if Freud readily endorses, and displays, the apparent truth of the claim that censorship encourages greater writing because of the demands it makes on a writer's capacity for disguise.

We are left with two unknowns: one is whether these processes are really "unconscious" and the other is whether they aren't chiefly the result of Freud's self-observation which, in so far as he is an artist, may coincide with other writers' and artists' experience but doesn't justify the belief in a universal human creative agency at work in the unconscious. Characteristically Freud leaves us on the muddled borders dividing philosophy and psychology, autobiography and fiction.

If Freud is a writer the muddle is not so important. The dreambook is a study of imagination. It is also where Freud discovers his own creativity and displays what he can do. But what remains confusing is the element of prescription contained, in line with the whole therapeutic conception of psychoanalysis. For there is, at least as a gesture to science, a question implicit in Freud's confession of his dreams and his publicly conducted enquiry into how to liberate himself. The question is, isn't it like that for you too? Isn't it like that for everyone?

One reason why Freud the writer enquires into and displays the fruits of imagination is the sheer joy of it. But the other reason appealing to the therapist in Freud is that when we dream there is a basic conversion of forces from the defensive to the creative, that is from repression to release. *The Interpretation*, as a therapeutic text, is thus an advertisement for what psychoanalysis can do for any patient, if this is what it has done for Freud.

The Interpretation of Dreams conveys the general message that culture, laden with hypocrisy, is an unsatisfactory way of containing our real natures. It suggests strongly that art and dreams, which accommodate the unconscious happily, are far superior outlets for our individuality and inventiveness. We might even see *The Interpretation of Dreams* in this sense as the handbook to a cultural revolution, in which people learn to use their imagination for the sake of a happier and richer life. Freud teaches dream interpretation, he teaches dreaming, and, bar the confusion over whether he is actually talking about unconscious or conscious processes, he also seems to teach "creative writing." "Creative writing" took shape as an Anglo-American tradition of psycho-therapeutic self-making. Though barely recognizable, it is distinctly related to the creative freedom Freud's French structural linguistic heirs sought to map by defining the limits of the sign. The first tradition is democratic, the second intellectually difficult, but they are relatives.[28]

As a would-be writer, why not, after all, break up words, play with them, to create a new and amusing perspective on life? Why not forge an unlikely association between ideas, then write a story explaining how it might come about? Why not create a new composite fictional character out of three you know well from life? And finally, why not use symbols to render the inner life of your characters, and gradually reveal the meaning of those symbols? All these are interesting formal possibilities to do with creative writing, though not with Freudian writing as such. There is an incitement to create in Freud's love of language games, which goes far beyond whatever initial stimulus came into literature from psychoanalysis. It is borne out by those who have paid attention to Freud's love of word play on behalf of the unconscious, like Joyce and Nabokov and Burgess.

But always what seems to happen is that Freud's concept of the unconscious draws attention to the inner life and the place of the imagination within a general framework of therapy and self-help. Freudian dream expression is a personal funfair always open. In his novel *Therapy*, David Lodge suggests somewhat tongue-in-cheek that the patient senses a constant source of entertainment playing in his head, like a private television station to which we can always tune in. There is a sense in which Freud teaches the possibility of escape from reality. But the dreamer may also reap the harvest of his night pictures in enhanced self-knowledge, and may even move on to daytime creativity.

In fact there is a division in Freud which runs throughout his work, between indulging the imagination as such and repatriating the errant psyche in the world of the real. His is "a philosophical system . . . [or] an ego philosophy whose psychology is always at war with the autology it proposes." This I would call once again Freud's Binary Touch and say that it affects all he considers. Thus we may see learning to dream as belonging to the quest for a permanent diversion from reality into self-sustaining fantasy, *or* we may see it as fitting in to a scheme of self-improvement.[29]

But whichever way we look at it, Freud does have something specific to teach through teaching how to dream, which makes the notion that the unconscious is "an intellectual hallucination created by language" seem particularly wide of the mark. For Freud's lesson in relation to creativity and the unconscious, which comes with reading many dreams and their interpretations, resembles teaching us to write poetry in a particular form. Freud has created a form into which we can fit many experiences and ideas, often with results that we could never have predicted, had we not gone through the imaginative exercise. Insight into the way the form works comes from learning to ask the Freudian first question about dreams: "What is it I wish?"[30]

I had a simple enough dream myself last night. I dreamt I saw my name in print twice in a literary paper I write for, and on each occasion I was cast in a negative light. The first sentence read, "Lesley Chamberlain has an odious view of art," while the second bracketed my name after an example of a literary critical trap which the unwary always fall into. Because I am full of strong feelings about these things, the dream was very clear, and I knew which paper was meant, because the same typeface had figured in the dream as I had been examining the previous day on a sheet of proofs. I was particularly aware of it because the proof layout and type had recently changed, and this was the first time I had seen the new version. So what was my wish in this dream? To see myself pilloried for insensitivity and incompetence in my professional work?

There were two minor events from the day, *Tagesreste*, "day residues." The first was receipt of the proofs, the second was reading a passage in which Lionel Trilling said Freud held art in contempt. Freud says dreams are made with such residues, which offer themselves as carrier words for the bundles of repressed energy waiting to escape our unconscious. I read this again and it made things clear. What the dreamwork had done was to replace Freud with me. I was under attack from Trilling, not Freud. Yet this is still not what I wish, surely? No, let the interpretation rotate the dream meaning just a little further round in the light. No, it's not that I wish myself failure, but quite the opposite: that I wish myself so much success that my name will appear twice in the same paper; indeed it will be equal to Freud's.

Another far more complex dream I had while writing this book probably belongs in the same psychic basket, which I am only scraping the surface of here. It featured the partly nonsensical, but evidently German sentence: *Sie war in Ambuß*. She was in Ambuß. Others were saying it about me. The first of many suspicions must be that my desire for glory is bound up with a love of the German language. *Amb–* heralds ambition. On the other hand it also prefixes ambivalence, while the whole word suggests the German *Amboß*, meaning anvil, and the English *am*bush. Might I not fear falling victim to outside forces which would thwart the plan? Is this not what the dream is about? Freud would probably readily take that syllable *boß*, only disguised as "German," and weigh up its possibilities as the English "boss," "The Boss." The word expresses my love of foreign languages, especially German, as a neurotic shield and disguise in life, giving me places to go and hide where no one familiar to me can follow. It also indulges my secret megalomania, which only my ambivalence about the power project ensures functions at half-capacity. Suffice to say the ambitious type of dream Freud found to be just as prevalent as the sexual dream; though the two are not necessarily separate.[31]

I put in this dream and its interpretation for readers to know that Freud's work, ostensibly on dreams, encourages the imagination generally to run and run. It is maieutic. It helps at the moment of the birth of self-discovery, and it does this by promoting "free association." This happens naturally in dreams, and is encouraged on the couch. It's true that Freud's unconscious dreamwork is a conjectural structure, but creative practice comes towards it to confirm the rightness of a kind of human experience which, if it does not happen spontaneously, can be brought into being by practice, and is certainly no mere hallucination.[32]

What a strange beast is *The Interpretation of Dreams*! A less disingenuous writer would have written the novel *Look What I Can Do!* instead just to show us how these processes and experiences were born in himself. The novel, narrated in the first person, would have told the story of a critic or a doctor who, in writing about imagination, discovers that he possesses it. Since he now wants to keep track of what his imagination is producing even while he carries on with the critical project, his book becomes multi-layered, multi-annotated and vast. The novel takes a twist when we realize that because imagination is released through self-interpretation, much of what we have already read as happening to someone else now turns out to be the autobiography of the narrator himself. But also the novel in progress has become a novel about writing because the author has discovered he *is* a writer. We classify and reclassify, but in the end *Look What I Can*

Do! seems to show a writer of great talent and some mental disturbance weighing up his accommodation with reality, and changing the parameters of art on the way.

7

FREUD AS A WRITER: STUDYING THE CASE

Loosely I have suggested that a substantial part of *The Interpretation of Dreams* as a voyage of artistic self-discovery could have been repackaged as the modernist novel *Look What I Can Do!* and in that guise would give Freud an artistic reputation closer to the one he deserves. There would have been material left over for a writers' and even a general self-healing-through-creativity manual besides. Yet still some things remain, for besides generating new content Freud is also pioneering a new form of writing. In *The Interpretation*, under a *Decameron*-like umbrella of scientific research which is already a novel invention, Freud tells a series of unusually shaped stories. They alternate passages of third-person narrative and passages of self-reflexivity, and they have dreams as their turning-points. The narrative is double, like a two-welled condiment reservoir, and the dream sits on the divide. Freud sets up a model for the narrative which is both symbolic and constantly self-interpreting, in a way which gradually distills meaning out of pictures suggested by the unconscious.

The double-well is an artistic form with a moral component, because it rests on the view that the richest meaning we can have of our lives includes what is stored as potential in our unconscious. What we would like to do, what we fantasize about, comprises much of our identity, and should be part of our self-knowledge, though many of the mental objects we toy with are unreal. The dream-plus-its-interpretation gives us a model for how to emancipate those irrealia for the purposes of storytelling *and* living: how to bring them into our lives from the margins of rationality in a way that society finds acceptable and even desirable. The double-well form features in *The Interpretation of Dreams*, but comes into its own in the case-studies, which might, by an avowed and unabashed writer, have been written up as ground-breaking novellas.

The case-studies are, at their most controversial, assisted autobiographies. Otherwise, as semi-fictions invented by the inventor of psychoanalysis, they are stories of the lives of people governed by a very strong unconscious imprint, such that it disrupts normal patterns of behavior. "Dora" for instance describes a disturbed adolescence. The eponymous heroine has catarrh and a nervous cough; sometimes she loses her voice completely, and has threatened to kill herself. She has reacted with exaggerated horror to a kiss stolen by her father's friend, Herr K, and Freud has detected a powerful problem in her not accepting that she loves or desires this man.[1]

Freud then tells us that Dora's father is wealthy, mid-forties, and "of not quite ordinary industriousness and talent." Freud has been treating this man for a syphilis-related condition, and the father, whose excesses flag a further trouble to the analyst, has himself introduced his problematic daughter to therapy.

"Dora" exemplifies a typical Freudian invitation to the reader, to pull the love thread and see where it leads. All Freud's case-history and dream-interpretation narratives have this shape of a "cat's cradle" of threads, which, with one final weave and tug, suddenly resolve into a simple, definite and clever pattern.

We keep the father in mind. Dora is both particularly affectionate and highly critical towards this lamed but otherwise loved figure. The father has a lover, Frau K. Dora's brother has suggested they should not mind this liaison, if father is happy. Father may have a good reason and Dora certainly doesn't like her mother. Dora though moves from being a close friend of Frau K, silently complicit in her father's affair, to a creature quite distant. Eventually she will go to Frau K and say yes, I know, without condemning her father's lover, but there is much repressed material between her and that small, not entirely successful action post-analysis.

Freud extracts from Dora's dreams love for all three adults in whose lives she has become enmeshed – Herr K, Frau K, and her father – as well as the desire to get revenge against them. To go along just one track a short way: she has taken refuge in a childhood love for her father to evade her love for Herr K and Freud feels he has been punished as a father substitute along the way. But at this point, bringing her attack on Freud to a head, Dora abandons the analysis.

Apart from the ultimate disappointment, the lack of an ending, the foreshortened perspective of "Dora" and the focus on parallel households give an almost soap-opera feel to this story of continuing relationships and tensions. Here is an everyday tale of upper-middle-class folk, helped to enjoy life by money and cultural education but plagued by syphilis and other illnesses and by sexual frustration. Freud lifts the lid on propriety to reveal the scheming and curiosity of children, and the unhappiness, shame and complicity of their parents. An undertow of dark, contradictory emotions is revealed by reading the cast of the unconscious shadow.

"The Wolfman" by contrast is the story of a memory of a disturbed childhood. It happens at a greater remove from the present than "Dora," and thus, through the greater reach of its memories-cum-fantasies, has a different feel. It is the history of an individual, set against changing times.[2]

The young man, who breaks down at seventeen and first enters analysis at twenty-three comes from a Russian aristocratic family. His father is a manic depressive and his mother suffers from a painful gynecological condition. His relationships with his mischievous older sister, his Russian nanny, and an English governess dominate his early life on an isolated country estate.

At first he was said to be a very gentle, obedient and rather quiet child, of whom people used to remark that he should have been the girl and his older sister the boy. But all of a sudden, when his parents came back from their summer travels, they found him transformed. He had become discontented, irritable, and flew into violent tempers, availed himself of every opportunity to take offense, raged and shrieked like a wild animal, so that his parents expressed the fear, with the condition lasting, that it wouldn't be possible to send him to school when the time came. It was the summer when the English governess was there, a woman who turned out to be a foolish and unbearable creature who, incidentally, tended to hit the bottle.[3]

Freud's "The Wolfman" recalls Turgenev's *First Love* or L.P. Hartley's *The Go-Between* in the way it highlights an unconventional sexual awakening leading to adult repression. But Freud begins much earlier in his character's life, in infancy, and invests each of the young child's relationships with an explicit and conflictual sexual content, laying down a model for a new literary genre. Before the Wolfman is five he is a compulsive neurotic suffering from hallucinations; new outbreaks of neurosis hit him when he is eight and ten. The child's entire inner life seems to be sexual, and sexually confused, and such is this magnified and unusual perspective of Freud's that we are unsurprised to learn that the boy grows up passive, evasive and afraid of an independent existence.

The story is one of glittering symbolism, beginning with the boy sharing a birthday with Jesus, moving back and forth through a fear of wolves in books and stories which his sister exploits, and passing through his alternating passions for tormenting, loving and fearing animals and insects. There is a dream of a transfigured Christmas tree laden with the wrong presents. As a five-year-old the too-pious little Wolfman switches between devotion and "dirty" thoughts about the possibility of Christ having a rear end. Three piles of horse shit remind him of the Trinity. It is his mother who has instructed her son in religious matters (though *this* association is never explored), but otherwise the mother holds herself distant from her children because of her illness. The boy's good relationship with his father, tender in infancy, steadily declines until it is replaced by fear.

There is a family history of mental illness, but Freud persists with the sexual etiology of this childhood neurosis, zigzagging between instances of passive and active participation in sexual acts.[4] Since the sexually precocious sister had "seduced" the boy – he was then just over three and she was five – he had become enraged by the sexual passivity inflicted on him, Freud surmised. The family wrongly blamed the governess. The child had attempted to recover the initiative by playing with himself in front of his nanny, but she threatened him with a wound instead of a penis. So he repressed his active wishes, and took to cruelty to animals. Freud's interpretation jars: both seduction and masturbation (the come-hither display) seem to be exaggerated ways of characterizing small children's behavior. Yet I think justifiably Freud wants to capture those moments when the child's sense of himself, as incorporated in his body's capacity to give and receive pleasure, is infringed. Either the child's autonomy is taken away from him or his wishes are refused, and these are decisive moments for the future of his soul.

In puberty, when the Wolfman's sister rejected him as a sexual partner, he satisfied himself with a servant girl. His consequent pursuit of women who were his social and intellectual inferiors seemed then like acts of revenge against his clever sister, Freud thought. For while the sister pleased their father, the Wolfman went ever further downhill: his mental development impeded by neurosis meant that he could make fewer and fewer investments in the real world.

The sister blossomed until her early twenties; but then anxieties about her appearance and her sexuality set in and she poisoned herself. Her death brought an exaggeratedly empty response from the Wolfman; he congratulated himself on becoming the sole inheritor of the estate. But later he wept copiously at the grave of Lermontov, to whose poetry their father had compared his sister's.

As more and more material comes into the story, Freud concedes that his narrative freely mixes the patient's memory with the analyst's surmises. This is particularly evident to the reader in the two central chapters which concentrate on the child's early sexual experience. What is reported by the patient "gives the impression," writes Freud,

> that seduction by his sister had forced a passive role upon him and given him a passive sexual goal. Under the continuing influence of this experience, he described the way from his sister via his nanny to his father, from a passive attitude towards a woman to the same towards a man. With that nevertheless he found the link with his earlier, spontaneous development [admiration for his father].[5]

We are asked to follow extraordinary unconscious sexual fantasies involving parents. With Dora we are funnelled back to her childhood love for her father, and to imaginings which include his infecting her, like mama, with syphilis; and wanting to be her father's lover. The Wolfman's story equally prepares us to move backwards, down the tunnel of personal history, into the revelation of a dramatic father-love. But the Wolfman's case seems so much worse, for Dora's is a case of teenage hysteria, while the other is one of lifelong compulsive neurosis.

Aged four, the Wolfman has that crucial dream of six or seven white wolves sitting in that tree outside his bedroom window which he later figures as a Christmas tree, hence his ability to date the occasion. Freud, at his writerly best as a semiotic Cupid linking estranged objects of desire, fires a signifying arrow from the whiteness of the wolves to the rumpled white linen the man "remembers" on his parents' bed one hot summer afternoon. This, Freud reads off from the symbolic evidence, is where a repressed homosexual desire for his father began. For during that *Urszene* – the primal scene – Freud supposes the one-and-a-half-year-old infant not only sees intercourse, but father enters mother from behind. The child, whose alleged ability to keep track of both penis and vagina in this act has been disputed as physically as well as psychically impossible, thereafter unconsciously conceives the desire for his father similarly to love him – but here under Freud's disjunctive narrative influence, I break off, just when the action approaches sodomy, to make some theoretical observations.

Both "Dora" and "The Wolfman" include in their subject matter fact and fantasy and memory and interpretation, plus reverberations from the relationship between the patient and his interpreter. They also interweave several time-frames, demanding that the reader move back and forward.

The toing and froing movement is vital. Vital for sexual intercourse, as some critics have pointed out, but also vital for Freud to convey what it is to have a mind. The shared action, literal in the first case, symbolic in the second, is a way of capturing the theme of creativity which links them by analogy. Freud's narratives cross-stitch their way between the embedded structure of a man's psyche and the content of his present actions. The narratives move by cross-stitch because our minds have a natural tendency to create, adopt or otherwise attach themselves to symbols past and present which form a network of references for self-understanding and decision-making. Only the sewing metaphor doesn't go far enough, for all the surfaces hooked together temporarily also change.

Our inner life is a mesh which leaves its print. The mesh moves, which means "printed" mental life on the surface is constantly threatened by a contradiction moving into play underneath, or by a parallel on a different plane, or by something diverting happening on the periphery. With all this Freud is not so much saying reality is uncertain as, by virtue of being disunited and dis-centered, it is constantly moving back and forth in more than one dimension. The German verb *wandeln* and the noun *Wandlung*, which come into play here, literally mean change, metamorphosis, transubstantiation, but also turn or trope and are hence closely related to metaphor.[6]

Though Walter Jensen was not impressed by Freud's praise, Freud found that *Gradiva* employed a depth-to-surface technique. For that novella not only tells a good story; it is a graphic demonstration of how human beings stumble into symbolic activity on the surface of their lives in order to express their thwarted deeper needs:

What are repressed with Norbert Hanold are his erotic feelings, and since his eroticism neither knows nor has known another object except Zoë Bertgang in his childhood, so the memories of her are forgotten. The ancient bas relief awakens in him his slumbering eroticism and activates his memories of childhood. Because of an existing resistance to eroticism these memories can only become active in his unconscious. What ensues in him is a battle between the power of eroticism and the forces that are repressing it; what communicates itself of this battle is a delusion [*Wahn*].[7]

Hanold's story may be compared with that of the Ratman, Freud's most likeable character. The Ratman leads a decent life, yet a life done a disservice by the painful and otiose compulsions which have stepped in with his upbringing and education. Freud's advice to his kind, especially in sexual matters, is to be a little less good. Someone should reinvent, retell and continue the Ratman's story, for it belongs among the compelling novels of the twentieth century.

The Ratman has grown up with a great love but a concomitant unconscious hatred for his father (fathers in Freud standing, besides for themselves, for the cultural heritage, tradition and power). Freud shows how the opposition between loyalty to the father and sexual happiness constantly sets itself up in the Ratman's mind, directing his libido into compulsive alternating actions which get him nowhere. The situation comes to a head when he is on army maneuvers in Austro-Hungarian Poland and loses his pince-nez. Away from Vienna he also becomes aware of how much he wants a woman, and also a wife to have children with. At the railway station, at the post office, wherever he goes women pay him generous attention, so his prospects don't look bleak. But the feeling that he should please his father keeps pulling the Ratman back from any woman; even though the father is already dead. The Ratman is a study in misplaced imperatives and wasted moral seriousness. The Ratman suffered, one feels, so that Freud might liberate the twentieth-century middle class.

The Ratman literally pendulates between women, and between places, while the narrative pendles to show us how inner uncertainty blocks his way forward towards a real love object; and how the Ratman is taken in by the disguises adopted by his unconscious. Freud's task is to alleviate this highly intelligent man's plight, which he will do by getting him to confront the complexity of his feelings towards his father and stop them harming his future life.

Pendling ensures that all Freud's depictions of our inner lives are ambivalent. It is the structural equivalent of the analyst's assumption that we often feel the opposite of how we think we feel. One reels a bit from this. Does love really always imply unconscious hate, piety blasphemy, and so on? Surely not. But then we don't know what is in our unconscious until it surfaces to wreck that love, and this fundamental ambivalence Freud attributes to our psychic life. In any case whatever we decide to believe about human nature, ambivalence must be grasped as the key to the structure of Freud's transformational stories. It is as if the psyche is figured as a dance between constantly changing partners; and when we remember Freud was exploring what Nietzsche called the Dionysian, the dance motif seems right. We follow the whirl of dancing pairs of ideas, as love sets to hate, and piety goes arm in arm with blasphemy.

Polar opposites usefully establish the parameters of the psychic story. This is what it is to be a Freudian animal: to be in two minds, one of which we are unaware of. Freud is the chronicler and reader of a distorted universe, where all strong feelings come from somewhere only indirectly related to where they are going. Signs of this unconscious structure will surface perhaps when we excessively praise someone we hate, or are the recipients of such praise. Our all-too-human ambivalence begins when quite naturally we prefer one parent to the other, and from that Ur-contrariness of our emotions Freud derives a model for the contrariness of all our concepts. Deep/shallow, love/hate, strong/weak, water/fire, patient/analyst, passive/active, collective/individual are some of the dyads he plays with. Reality is issued to us as a two-sided coinage.

Another structural feature of Freud's stories is the fan of time, such that the narrative seems to grow according to lines emanating from a series of points on a double graph. The vertical central axis, down the fold of an open double page, is the analyst's two-way glance. On the left he plots the patient's progress in material reality, which is inevitably a Sisyphean slide back to nought. On the right the lines rise as analyst and patient recreate, or invent, the progress of the patient's psychic reality. The inventive "Dora" and "Ratman" narratives, but supremely "The Wolfman," splay out in multiple discourses, the patient's version, the analyst's version, and the results of their interaction, in pursuit of realities r, $r^1 \ldots r^n$. Since Freud believes that in infancy we work through primitive fears and desires, to which we later regress when too much challenged by lack of erotic fulfillment, the end-point of the developmental story is not stable; the goal may be reached and lost again. Nought to a hundred in thirty-five years perhaps, then back to two. Each line of development may be redrawn as a spiral, which may rise and collapse.

The course of the analysis itself contributes a further set of temporal reference points and line of growth. Nor are the time coordinates of "Dora," "The Ratman" and "The Wolfman" just monolinear, but overlay one another, as they duplicate and reduplicate queer psychosomatic stories of how one becomes what one is. By all these means the cases are drawn in outline then closely cross-hatched.

The density of the sexually-saturated stories owes much to Freud's interpretation of every last, apparently insignificant detail and his insistence on making it relevant as fact or symbol to his sexual point. The theory is that nothing in the unconscious is accidental. The effect in the stories is an incredible series of links between what repeats itself in the phenomena of a pear, a wasp, a butterfly and a dress; a butterfly's wings and a girl's legs; a snake, a barley-sugar stick, a wolf's tail torn off in a story and a man's penis disappearing inside a woman. Out of these the Wolfman's psychic fate is constructed and constantly reannounced, for as a device in the text the psychoanalytical symbol works like a leitmotif in music. In the case of Dora, like clues in a bizarre quiz-show, we have to conjure with catarrh, a jewelry box and a fear of fire. Tales of convulsive secret passion spring forth. Just now I borrowed from Freud the idea of a mesh to convey the psychic density of this narrated reality, for in "Dora" he uses such an image. A wire trellis interwoven with flower garlands signifies the furious network of organic life through which unconscious ideas become threaded. I think we can see (and almost hear, Wagnerian fashion) each symbol we come across in the stories as a significant blossom raised against the background of the text or score which is the continuing life of the patient.[8]

Structure leads us back to content. The content of Freud's stories is one of common humanity, however bizarre that humanity seems. The patient is himself or herself, but also an example of the general sufferings of cultivated humanity in love. As Freud says in "The Ratman," we too often confuse *this*, being in love, with character. There is no new love story on earth, nor was there ever. The patient's entire life history is his, but can also be invoked as a model of the psychological development of mankind from primitive tribal being to cultivated member of society.[9]

Thus Freud's characters' lives all are potentially mythical. Dora loves her father, which imprisons her as a maiden, while the Ratman, tied to his father, cannot marry. Before they existed as examples of Freudian analysis such stories were fairy tales and legends, and now we read the stories of Freud's analysands as literature. Together these writings illuminate the human path. Here I borrow a picture from Rider Haggard's *She*, an adventure story Freud loved. A brilliant young man has to travel back to his remote and cannibalistic ancestors to learn the truth about himself, and find love. In one magnificent scene the way is lit by torches fuelled by the bodies of the dead. The value of the phylogenetic human story for Freud is just like that. It is a backdrop, spectacular when visible, equally effective when invisible, to the little histories Freud tells of Dora, Wolfman and Ratman, and to the little stories told to friends by anyone else who has ever had parents.

So to finish [Totem and Taboo] I would like to articulate the result of an enquiry undertaken in a greatly shortened form: that the beginnings of religion, morality, society and art meet in the Oedipus complex, in complete agreement with what psychoanalysis has discovered, [namely] that this complex forms the kernel of all neuroses so far as we understand them. It comes as a great surprise to me that even the problems of the spirits of peoples should allow a solution from a single concrete stand-point such as the relationship to the father is. Perhaps another psychological problem should be brought into the picture in this connection. We have so often had the opportunity to reveal the ambivalence of feeling in a real sense, that is the coincidence of love and hate towards the same object, at the root of important cultural manifestations. We know nothing of the origins of this ambivalence. One can assume that it is a fundamental phenomenon of our emotional life. But the other possibility also seems to me worth noticing, that it was originally alien to emotional life, but was acquired by humanity with the father complex, where today the psychoanalytical investigation of individuals reveals the strongest stamp left behind.[10]

That all children should lust for one parent, usually of the opposite sex, and long to kill the other, allows Freud to set up the fixed, constantly repeating pattern which makes his "anthro-pological romances," whether told as theory or story, relentless. There is bliss at the maternal breast, followed by the inevitable wrench away; self-pleasuring follows, then curiosity leading to a choice of pleasure objects beyond the self. During these experiments girls, who seem to have a wound instead of a penis, suffer penis envy, while boys fear castration. Freud says neurotic patients later tend to remember or imagine scenes of parental intercourse, seduction by an older person and this threat of castration. Freudian sexuality seems like the original imperfect gift, and memories surrounding its discovery saturate the unconscious and keep returning in fragments to consciousness. This is what it is like to be born on the human wheel. This is what made Schopenhauer despair of appetite.[11]

The constant regressive element in Freud's stories, to the infantile and the primitive, makes them necessarily studies in perversion. The erotic life rests on a fundament of perversion, seen from the standpoint of the cultivated adult life. The stories look through a window into a character's past and see moral chaos. The child for Freud lives in a sensual jungle, his mind an associative blur. This childhood is always potentially with us. We tap back into it in dreams and mental sickness. It is with us because of the inevitable always-active network of unconscious associations guiding our conscious choices. An opening in the body, for instance: the child's confusion about where babies come from; the boy's puzzle over the difference between anus and vagina. These affect the Wolfman's imagination lastingly, though not necessarily in a sexual way. "He chose the anus over the vagina in the same way and for similar reasons as he later took his father's part against God." And were the Wolfman a scientist, or a philosopher, his thinking might be similarly unconsciously led in those spheres too.[12] Then again we have Dora, sucking the nipple, then her thumb, then one day fantasizing about sucking a penis. Freud says of Dora that there is nothing perverted about her adult fantasy (which is unconscious anyway), just a necessary concatenation of ideas which we should understand in order to grasp the workings of the psyche. He might say the same about the content of his stories. Our early sensual preoccupations return in later life as a scheme to shape our unconscious thoughts, and what other form could such "memories" take, since in infancy we only react sensually. The corollary is that only via primary sexual shapes can we get at the content of diverse later troubles.

The need to write about the unconscious in the only way possible, as if it were conscious, means however that the stories *are* full of sexual fantasies which can excite the reader's imagination. The reader may wonder about Freud and pornography. Nabokov, Freud's fellow Modernist, ran into the same difficulty over *Lolita*. Was that extraordinary novel about love or perversion? Nabokov tells us he often wrote with an erection; Freud, who is a voyeur given to homosexual and masturbatory fantasies, can be similarly stirring, whether or not he aroused himself. But I have no doubt both wrote about love, and tried to give in the form of their work a kind of literary guarantee. Freud goes out of his way to include irony, disengagement and self-ridicule in his texts.[13]

In "Dora" for instance the girl is lying down on Freud's couch (explicitly noted) and is fingering her funnel-shaped purse.

> I watched her for a while, then I explained to her what a symptomatic action was. I call symptomatic actions those things a person carries out, as one says, automatically, unconsciously, without being aware of them, as if playing, and which he would be inclined to attribute no meaning to and which he explains as indifferent and coincidental if he is asked about them. More careful observation shows that such actions of which consciousness knows nothing, or wants to know nothing, express unconscious thoughts and impulses...
>
> "Why shouldn't I carry a little purse-bag like this? It's the latest fashion," [retorted Dora].
>
> Such a justification does not cancel out the possibility of an unconscious origin for the action in question...Dora's two-leaved little purse-bag is nothing other than a genital representation, and her playing with it, opening it and sticking her finger in it, is a downright unembarrassed but absolutely recognizable pantomime communication of what she would like to do...

Insinuating? Melodramatic? Voyeuristic? These are frequent characteristics, and condemnations, of Freud's writing. Yet this passage is followed by a masterly change of mood, for the analyst remembers as if by chance a much older patient interrupting an analytic session by getting out a little bone box. It's "difficult to open," she complains, and hands it to Freud to see if he can do it, whereupon he expresses surprise that he has never seen it before, since she has been coming to him for a year.

The woman began hastily: "I always carry this box with me, I take it everywhere I go!" She only calmed down after I made her laughingly aware how well her words suited another meaning. The box is . . . once again only a representative of the Mount of Venus, a woman's genitals.

Freud, hardly the misogynist here, realizes something about women's omnipresent potential for pleasure which has not yet struck all men on earth. As for the writing, the titillation the Dora scene affords is matched by the comedy of the second scene. Albeit at the expense of the implied no-longer-attractive older woman, the effect is to cool the sexual tension in the text. But the writing is also psychologically clever, for although the contrast in the two stories hardly exonerates Freud from our feeling that he has been harboring illicit thoughts, it invites us to laugh with him at himself.[14]

Furthermore he rounds off these episodes with a statement of theory so eloquent that, having assured ourselves of our urbanity and self-awareness, we still feel Freud's wilder claims have the ring of Attic truth:

There is much symbolism like this in life, which we normally walk past without noticing. When I took upon myself the task to bring to light what people hide, not through the compulsion of hypnosis but through what they say and show, I considered it a harder task than it really is. Whoever has eyes to see and ears to hear will be persuaded that mortals can hide no secret. He whose lips are silent speaks with his fingertips; betrayal threatens from every pore. That's why the task of making conscious the most hidden business of the soul can certainly be resolved.

Nothing human is alien to Freud. I write about him as a writer now. *Nihil humanum alienum a se putat.* And that insight delivers him from the burden of himself.

Wittgenstein was wrong to think Freud was saying "this is merely this" when he set up this double-welled scheme for the necessary workings of disguise in culture and the psyche. Freud's approach is expansive rather than reductive, for the forms coexist and intermingle to form a torrent of possible motivation. The extent of "doubled" territory this opens up for art and criticism, not to mention psychology, makes Freud's work a landmark in the history of human self-reflection.[15]

"Doubled" means that beside the conscious inner life there is a worked-over version of previous outer life which has settled in the unconscious and comprises a readiness to respond to new situations in an old way, based on the history of the subject's real collisions with the world. The collisions are available for excavation if the subject wants to try to change his life, or just understand himself better. But what is excavated may or may not coincide with what really happened, because the excavated thing is already a subjective product. So versions of the subject's life multiply, with more or less appeal. And what we quickly see is that while the Freudian cure begins and ends with the needs of the individual to survive in society, the poetry he discovers in his subject's unconscious threatens to distract the doctor from his purpose. For the poetry that comes to the fore in a Freudian cure, such as he wrote up in his case-histories, is self-sufficient: it is a product of fascination and amusement. This suggests the real route the cure will take. The hope, hardly conscious on Freud's part, but embedded in the power of the transference, is that the story will be good enough for the patient to say: yes, that will do for me, and not to worry about whether it is "real" or not. I refer the reader to the notes here, which try to make sense of the accusations of fabulation against Freud, and at the same time suggest the Platonic tradition he is coming from, and the twin traditions he inspires, of intertextuality and *différance* in writing, and distrust of his messianic personality, "manipulative rhetoric (*sic*)" and "totalizing worldview" in the therapeutic domain.[16]

In pursuit of the true story of the patient's distress, meanwhile, the spark which sets the tinder alight and makes the poetry blaze up in the psychonanalytical encounter, and which entitles the patient to hope, is Freud's belief that repression always leaves a visible trail behind it; that there *is* a truth to pursue. Nothing human is entirely invisible or silent, he says. Nothing in the psychic life is accidental. Just tell me what occurs to you and the unconscious will speak through you. The transformations which guarantee the process of repression can be traced, you see, because they are energy, and because the nature of the unconscious is as a hiding place and a refuge, but not a mortuary. That free radical energy buried in there is forever seeking words to lift it into consciousness as a feeling. For like a guilty felon or a reluctant suicide, the repressed wish *wants* to be found out. This incidentally is the deep sense in which Freud's case-studies demand comparison with a detective on the trail. Repression is a crime against oneself, worth tracing back.

> The Ego undertakes a repression of . . . instinctive stirrings. For the moment it manages to keep the danger at bay, but one cannot confuse the inner and the outer and go unpunished. One cannot run away from oneself.[17]

To underscore the key borrowing from physics which gives neurosis its detectable character: Freud applies the principle of the constancy of matter to the psychic life. Repressed material will out. If we defer the confrontation, the momentum of conflict will be stored only to emerge in some stranger than ever form.

And so the formal Freudian story possibilities rush forward: matters of danger, escape, hiding, detection, revelation and trial are conveyed to us as forming the netherworld of our personality, but presented as if they were the conscious forefront of our lives; and with the engine of sexual desire behind them. What we read *is* a story, because of its "as if" quality. The analyst's symbolic pictures of our hiding places can only provide a simulacrum and imperfect reconstruction of what happens beneath our consciousness. Yet what Freud can capture directly is the rhythm of the unconscious, one might say the whole business of deferral. He uses the bodies of his patients – Dora's taut and angry young figure (we are left in no doubt she is attractive) comes to mind – to inject this tension into his narratives, yearning towards release.[18]

Deferred energy insisting on resolution is embodied in the principle of *Nachträglichkeit*, and it means that Freud's stories are never simply chronological and never follow a single line of causality. Spiritual and physiological processes overlap, and the rhythms of memory and narration run close by. The infant Wolfman saw his parents make love and this has affected his whole psycho-sexual life. We don't learn until towards the end that this moment was accompanied by a great physical release. The child had a bowel motion. This retrospectively is what makes his chronic constipation so significant. It is a literal fixation on that early trauma, and it parallels his reluctance to give much in analysis. He is holding the main thing back, while dropping little hints and clues here and there. Finally he discloses that he has the lofty sense of the world being veiled to him, a common enough symptom of compulsive neurosis and paranoia, except when he opens up down below.

To excrete/express or not to excrete/express. In this rhythmic challenge faced daily by body and soul we find the form and the content of Freud's Wolfman story. As a way of writing it is a disturbing parody of "spiritual" values; and yet it only enlarges what we mean by the human, by "body and soul."

Need and Cunning characterize the unconscious. For Freud as for Plato they are the parents of Eros who set their malnourished child from early infancy on the criminal road.[19] We shouldn't be sentimental about this Freudian Eros. It is about getting what one needs, and if the repressed need is great enough no contrivance or disguise is too elaborate to express it. Our love lives but also our art and dreams and neuroses are driven by deep needs which engender their own versatility. I turn myself into a writer; Zeus changes into a swan.

How does Eros work as an unconscious drive? The primacy of the unconscious suggests a boomerang action. The original erotic frustration which carried us far from our goal catches us up when it boomerangs us back to some replacement situation in later life. Here again *Nachträglichkeit* is at work, which is to say the fury, the passion which grabs us, only seems to come from nowhere.[20]

Nachträglichkeit refutes Wittgenstein's spoilsport view of Freud, for the way in which disguised and revealed layers of our lives coexist is like a vision in which the dead remain effective alongside the living; only they "live" in a strange way; in virtual reality, we might say today. The importance of this view for understanding how we make and mar our relationships with others can hardly be underestimated psychologically, while artistically it makes possible potentially infinite doubling, as a character lays one encounter over the next, both outlining and blurring the nature of his personality for us. Freud knew well those overlays of photographic negatives designed by Galton to show how physical characteristics evolve, and here it seems is the model for his depiction of the way character evolves.[21]

But now I must say something negative about the case-studies as stories. Freud keeps reminding us that his narratives are only "as if conscious"; and he punctuates them with theory. These interruptions dilute the pornographic value of his adventures, but also the appeal of the stories as literature, since Freud is a lesser writer than Nabokov. The stories have a magical forward impetus for a few pages, then dismantle themselves; a symbol is isolated, a scene or a sentence or a word analyzed and reanalyzed; the result is that the dynamic stops while the motor is examined. We stop enjoying the easy story, while learning how the unconscious provides the fuel line. We follow the writer as he assembles and reassembles patterns of symbols which correspond to body parts and processes long ago discovered and enjoyed, but now stored up for use in a new reality still being written. With apologies to Courbet, with a Freudian case history we do not find ourselves quite in a work of art, but in a workshop, *dans l'atelier du psychopeintre*.

Symbolic ideas carry the stored energy of desire. They enshrine the longing which is the stuff of erotic life, and the whole Freudian case-study narrative would in theory capture the bizarre nature of the erotic animal's thoughts when he is in mental trouble. But the associative links are so strange we don't find it easy to keep reading.

Freud refers to the clusters of associations he plays with as "Thought Rows" – *Gedankenreihen* – which makes one think of the *Tonreihen* of Freud's Viennese contemporaries Schoenberg and Webern. Each note in the scale is of equal value. This new music is not travelling towards a classical aesthetic climax and resolution, but aims to explore associations of contiguity and repetition for their own sake. The music of the Second Viennese School comes in short bursts, is difficult, with easier interludes, and imitations and parodies of older styles, and that is exactly how Freud's stories feel. The most immediately seductive passages, at the openings and scattered through the narratives, are those which belong in an outstanding nineteenth-century novel: Flaubert or Dostoevsky perhaps.[22] The easy transitions, such as when Dora hurriedly puts away a letter when Freud comes into the room, are stock scenes from melodrama. But then come the theoretical passages, which, with the *Gedankenreihen*, seem to belong to a different century of reading. Imaginative input from the reader is required to read them and must not fail if the same reader is to grasp what kind of reality is being portrayed.

A well-known Freudian *Gedankenreihe* is this. The primitive mind of the infant Wolfman sees no difference between giving shit as a present and producing a baby. After all both are expelled from the body and are the most personal thing which can be given. Furthermore, the pleasure of passing a stool and the pleasure of gripping an erect penis fixes itself so firmly in the Wolfman's unconscious that his later neurosis, exacerbated by his resistance to analysis, is accompanied by that chronic constipation of which we have already heard. Freud then reads the Wolfman's relishing of his financial inheritance, as it were his hoarding of money, as a symbolic expression of his repressed homosexual wishes.

In the stories generally we get to the causal power expressed by a symbol by bringing in surrounding associations from cultural and personal life. Children are never at ease when stealing a glance at their parents' medical encyclopedias, supplies Freud, for example, to make sense of one of Dora's dreams. In the Wolfman's case the retentions of the miser provide the link with the pleasure that anal withholding gives this man. But only a resolution of the whole story of the Wolfman will tell us what real primary experience his anal obsessions reproduce, which is the associative *Endstation*, and this resolution Freud defers and defers, while bringing in ever more passing links. Deferring resolution, already illustrated with reference to the infant Wolfman's bowels, and suspiciously close to anal retention as a literary habit, does not always maintain our attention because there is not enough momentum built up behind it.[23]

The power of the psychic symbol to affect the organism also challenges credulity, and our attention to the text wanders, as Freud rightly feared it might. Is it really the memory of lust for the father's penis that causes the Wolfman to hold on so tight, and wouldn't a change of diet force him to open up? Was the memorable single occasion when he gave money away and experienced while walking along the street the most momentous relief of his life really linked in his unconscious with the desire to outdo his mother and give his father a baby? One is generally happy to give the benefit of the doubt to psychosomatic explanations of headaches, palpitations, constipation, nausea and so on in the context of that most closely examined life which is one's own. But the connections Freud supplies in his necessarily abbreviated writing, with its many flat surfaces, don't help the reader *read* on. The leitmotiv as cause makes for hard going and we have to suspend our disbelief.

Dora's catarrh and coughing present similar problems. In the beginning there is a real cough which is associated with a part of the body, the mouth and throat, which has retained a strong erogenous meaning for this thumb-sucking girl. She is *therefore* inclined to use it to express libido, says Freud. Because this inclination is unconscious we can't immediately gainsay it, but to believe it demands a suspension of disbelief which the *Gedankenreihe* doesn't necessarily reward. The habit is fixed when Dora *imitates* her father's syphilitic cough out of sympathy; it is also fixed when she reproaches herself over her catarrh, for, this being the upper-body equivalent of a lower body discharge, whether caused by masturbation or syphilitic infection, it is equally to be hidden. The cough and its psychic allies further express a reaction to the absence of the secretly loved Herr K, for they disappear when he comes back, Dora thus outdoing Frau K, who gets ill when her husband *is* around. Finally the catarrh represents sexual intercourse with the father through identification with Frau K. The story does move on, but we follow it as a thinly upholstered puzzle, not with the investment we would bring to more traditional literary fiction.

Some last impossible examples set the seal on what kind of content Freud's stories have. Dora's appendicitis is interpreted as hysterical because this pain which simulates childbirth occurs nine months after the lakeside scene when, instead of paving the way to marry him, Dora turned Herr K down. This causality is entirely by uncontrolled association. *a* makes one think of *b*, therefore *ab* is the psychic reality. Dora also has a "hysterical" limp. She last had a real one in childhood, when she sprained her ankle. I missed my footing, she told Freud; in German, I took a wrong step (*ein Fehltritt*). Freud is now sure that the somatic hieroglyphs of the unconscious doubly add up to an expression of regret that she did not yield to the sexual demands of Herr K.[24]

Somewhere between psychodiagnosis and fiction, however, the symbolic *Gedankenreihe* is liberated as a principle for making up an indefinite number of funny and wonderful narratives, which are more than scientific texts, but less than works of art. The fundamental idea is an endless process of imitation, *Nachahmung*, which begins in the way the psyche preys on the body to find ways to express its unconscious wishes, and continues into the highest forms of culture.

The patient has physical symptoms, like stuttering and twitching and having a pain; the doctor wonders why neurosis is miming stuttering or twitching or having a pain: what is the real content of these *mimicked* organic symptoms? Why is Dora's psyche hiding behind the mantle of appendicitis, and the Wolfman's behind constipation? There is a case for enquiry here, but also a sign of comedy, which is the artistic clue. The neurotic patient is used by the unconscious so that he resembles a puppet or a stooge; a parody of a human being. Exploring the minds of neurotic characters, Freud's stories expose either passing comic incidents or elaborately constructed neurotic alternatives to nature. We see how his patients assemble not quite fake lives, but way-off-beam pseudo-mimeses of material reality, like Borges' land of Tlön.

By these psycho-mimetic stories alone we may be seduced. Certainly together with Freud's analytic commentary they raise an extraordinary challenge to a normally proud and unambiguous world.

> Neuroses show on the one hand obvious and deep conformities with the great social productions of art, religion and philosophy, on the other hand they seem like caricatures of them. One might dare to say that a case of hysteria is a caricature of a work of art, a compulsive neurosis a caricature of a religion, and paranoiac madness a caricature of a philosophic system.[25]

Here we have a deep metatextual reason for following a Freud story with the same fascination as art, philosophy or religion; a key to its intellectual allure as the reconstruction of a necessary crime. The Freudian vision seems to expose an intellectual criminality at the heart of things. Neurosis leaves a trail of psychic fraud and theft through everything we believe in. Mimicry is the great crime against rational authenticity, and even against the authenticity of our organic illnesses; even the body is dishonest. Because this is the way the unconscious behaves in his view, Freud's teaching has a tendency to reduce our conscious life to fantasy or ridicule.

Yet why is Freud so terrible, except that he tells of the worm in the intellectual and cultural bud, which is the domination of the unconscious over consciousness? Is it not that he does so with such an exposé of *sexual* detail? I think it is his examples that have done for him, rather than his true message. For what Freud sees is what Hume saw, in a surreal vision whose darkness was thoroughly overlooked by the Logical Positivists around Wittgenstein who latched on to him in Freud's day: he saw that there are no rational causes, only rather haphazard associations of ideas. To call Freud's stories science fiction after the *déluge* of Hume, and surreal of their own making, would be no slight on their worth.

In the end, what we have in Freud's case-studies is endless associative play; playschemes which create illusions of progress back and forth, and of one thing causing another, and of repetitions having a meaning beyond themselves. Freud, against the Humian darkness, does give his human stories a meaning: a psychoanalytical one which gives the afflicted subject a temporary purchase on life; but finally one feels that fantasy exists in Freud, both in himself and his patient, for its own sake: to get things out, to make patterns.

In *The Psychopathology* the theory which underlies Freudian stories is clearly stated:

A constant stream of self-reference goes through my thoughts, of which I normally have no cognizance, but which betrays its presence when I forget someone's name. It is as if I were obliged to compare everything I hear about others with myself, as if my personal complexes would come alive every time I took in another person. It is impossible that this should be a peculiarity of my being alone; rather it must contain an indication of the way generally that we understand "the other." I have reason to assume that others undergo a very similar process to the one I do.[26]

In our subjective reworking of the outside world, determined by libido, lurks a danger of complete misunderstanding and self-alienation, and even madness, but also the great fun of being alive.

8

MUSIC, PAINTING AND COMEDY OF THE NIGHT

It is as if Freud were trying to create a new music. He creates meaning by supplementing grammar and logic with the wisdom of the dream. The dream unites opposites and beautifies the absurd. It twists original experience into new shapes and forges new links, according to its boundless capacity to generate and animate metaphor. In the case-studies it is the symptoms which do the transformational work, and the analyst who reduces their ways to tropes of the unconscious. The meaning of a person's life emerges somewhere between his lived imaginings and "what really happened." It is the "how" of this process, through the animation of metaphor, which makes for brilliantly idiosyncratic, *concentrated*, if imperfect stories.[1]

The stories are written as if written by a literary critic applying his ideas to life. They work by a multiplication of psycho-rhetorical twists and turns whereby one idea, mental or physical, associates with the next: by copying it, by reversing it, by adding it to something else, by inverting it. These *Gedankenreihen* cross over each other at points where they have something in common: the unconscious switches track to achieve its expressive aims. To dynamize Freud's garden-mesh image in "Dora," we might say that character and action are made up from the clusters of flowers – rhetorical ornaments – which form on the surface of this moving tangle of signs.

Unconscious meanings are often the opposite of their conscious counterparts. Dora tells Freud that Frau K loves her father only because he is *ein vermögender Mann*, a man of means, and Freud immediately inverts this to "a man without means" and puts it to Dora that she knows otherwise. Yes, she replies, he's impotent, but it's still a normal relationship. Impotence is normal? Dora replies she knows there is more than one way to make love. Using the mouth and the throat? presses Freud. Dora says these do not form part of her thoughts. But Freud notices that her cough has stopped while they have been talking: the cough which represents her fantasy of oral intercourse between her father and Frau K, whom she would like to replace.

Alongside the trope of inversion sit less radical, more elusive shifts of meaning sideways, *Verschiebungen*, but also wholesale replacements, *Ersetzungen* or *Ersatzbildungen*. If a thought is too unpalatable it is replaced by one more acceptable to consciousness, and a physical experience in one part of the body is shifted to another:

> I think that she felt in the passionate embrace [of Herr K.] not only the kiss on her lips but the pressure of the erect member against her body. This repellant perception was pushed out of her memory, repressed and replaced by the harmless sensation of pressure on her thorax, which acquires a disproportionate intensity out of its repressed source. Here we have another displacement from the lower body to the upper body.[2]

Freud writes of the "hysterical conversions" he unveils in Dora's case. Ideas "leap out of the realm of the soul and into somatic innervation . . . we can never empathize through our understanding." His stories are an attempt to persuade us of the reality of these conversions, though he is often in doubt that he can.[3]

Hysteria for instance is barely intelligible, and, if it resembles a work of art, then the genre in question is surreal or absurd. Compulsive neurosis generates more meanings, but the wrong ones. The compulsive Ratman is *aware* of being gripped by fantasies but can't get free of them. A sadistic Czech army captain told him the tale of an "Oriental" torture in which rats burrow into a man's anus (the anus as object of sexual penetration being one of *Freud's* obsessions). The Ratman, who takes his nickname from this anecdote which sticks in his mind, "fears" such a punishment being inflicted on his father, and on his girlfriend. But he recoils in horror from his own imaginings. He forces himself to do a self-imposed penance or "sanction" for his thought-crime. But when he is told by the same captain that he must return some money to a colleague, the imperative gets split: he must return the money to redeem his besmirched girlfriend and his father, but also he mustn't, because the sadistic officer must be resisted. Such oppositions set up a real polarity in the text, between actions enlisted in the aid of the dangerous wish and those in aid of its prevention. Moreover their psychology, because it *is* psychology with a certain logic to it and not the anthropomorphized rhetoric of Dora's cough or the Wolfman's tailless wolf or chopped-up snake, make it easier for us to read the story as such.

Because the thinking is always daring, though the *Gedankenreihen* meander, Freudian cameos work well. In one case Freud starts from a man's desire, like the Ratman's, to rescue the loved one, and finds its origins in a fundamental unconscious response to a parent. Told that we owe our lives to our mother and father, it seems to be part of growing up that we fantasize about giving life back to them. This is a dream of gratitude but also one of independence. The man wants to square his existential debt by saving or defending a life, as his parents succored his. For Freud this crusading passion is then easily transferred "to a Kaiser, a king or some other great master and after this distortion becomes viable to enter consciousness and can be used by poets." Indeed. By a credible inversion of a simple idea about life, Freud would retell brilliantly the classic journey a man makes from birth to fighting for his country. The cameo is a novel in embryo.[4]

As a description of the unconscious life what I am calling "anthropomorphized rhetoric" *is* more difficult to accept, however, than the perverse tergiversations of a psyche in conflict, because we don't recognize it, and we don't recognize it because the process is thoroughly impersonal. In the unconscious our passions are headless, with detachable identities, like live parts kept in stock in a joke shop, which we can draw on at any time we need to assemble an identity. This is what I mean about Freud's stories being like workshops full of the parts that would make up a story if properly fitted together.

As it is, our unconscious minds, unconstrained by the need to produce a grammatical or logical structure, behave like circus acts, throwing all definite reality into the air. Senator Schreber's manuscript juggles with the subjects and objects of actions. What goes up as "I hate him" comes down as "He hates me." "I don't love him/I love her/She loves me" is a pedestrian sequence, but there are some acrobatic leaps in "I don't love this woman/I love this man/I don't love this man/She loves this man/She is to blame." Paradigmatic shifts underscore at once the impersonality and the enormous poetic scope of Freud's unconscious. They surely revitalize every writer's capacity to invent a plot.[5]

The Wolfman dreams of six or seven white wolves staring at him motionless from a tree outside his bedroom window. Later he adds that the window opened of itself. Freud extends the psychic arena, makes those paradigmatic shifts, with a few deft flicks of the pen: not the window opens, but the child's eyes. Not the wolves stare, but the child. And it is not a motionless moment, but one of intensive movement. To this new picture Freud then adds an inversion: in the dream the wolves are in the tree, whereas in a story the boy knows, they are on the ground, and can only get up the tree by climbing on each other's backs. The wolves are "reared up" in one picture, on all fours in another, all of which helps tell the Wolfman's story. The transformations of the unconscious are transient assemblages of those spare parts lying around in the psychic unconscious. They are the symbols literature and psycho-analysis depend upon.[6]

In "Schreber" and in "The Wolfman" we get inversions of mode combined with paradigmatic changes: They are looking at me/I am looking at them. The embedded rhetorical figure here is a diagonal crossover or chiasmus. A chiasmus is inscribed in the Oedipal family situation where, against the norm, son loves mother and daughter loves father. This is the prime instance of animated rhetoric lying at the heart of Freud's view of the world.[7]

The unconscious also doubles and splits existing material to create that arena for action which we call our personality. This is graphically expressed in the case of the man so keen to repay his existential debt to his mother that he wishes her a child just like himself. Unconsciously he yearns to become his own father and thus to impregnate his mother and make this true.[8] The intermittently "rational" Senator Schreber perceives that he has a persecution complex and asks himself why. He decides that it is because he *is* a great man, and by this recreates himself as Schreber One. It is an unconscious ploy to disguise his illness, and it leaves the original Schreber to get sicker and sicker, believing that he is someone else. In his text Schreber splits to inhabit a whole series of identities, each of which springs mythically to independent life.[9] The result is a doubling or tripling of the same basic relationship, with the roles apportioned to different sets of people, and it seems to be a characteristic of paranoia. We also get interesting examples of doubling in "Dora." Her father, discovered with Frau K in the woods, invents a suicide attempt, claiming that this woman, his neighbor, had merely rushed to this hidden spot to save him. Dora then unconsciously incorporates a suicide attempt into her own story. A few pages later Dora accuses her father of using his illnesses as means and excuses to get what he wants, which is exactly what she is doing herself. Further, when she comes to Freud with a new symptom, stomach pains, he artfully asks: "Whom are you copying?" (which we might reword as "Whom are you doubling?'). This instantly drives home, for when her younger cousin has just got married, the jealous older one collapses with stomach pains. Dora unconsciously learned that stomach pains can express sexual jealousy.[10]

Wholes become parts in the unconscious so that the same person can feel love and hostility, attraction and the desire to gain revenge. Splitting and doubling seem to be approximate psychic mobilizations of the synecdoche, another trope by which the name of part of an object stands in for the whole (or the whole stands for the part) but then acquires a new verbal life of its own in the poetic text. If I introduce examples that have recently struck me in life here, it is to show that Freud, for all his final explanatory resort to thwarted sexual desire for a parent, at least aims his intermediate gaze at those tricks of the psyche which are still, and always will be, the stuff of our daily lives. My mother-in-law has an unfortunate habit of switching on all the lights in the middle of the night. She can't help it, but it makes me very cross. A week later my husband makes an irritating remark in bed. Furious, I leap out and switch on all the lights. A man lavishes praise on another for being so at ease with the world. The speaker himself is manifestly *not* at ease. The unconscious splits what is perceived as good so that the anxious subject can share in it. By this means, without being aware of it, he finds a psychological hiding place and avoids confronting his real self, which he does not admire. In argument those who want us to believe them, but don't entirely believe themselves, consciously isolate that group of thinkers to whom they expressly don't want to belong, and the unconscious uses this means to cover the fact that they do.

"Identification" is another curious process which to the psychoanalytical eye belongs among the inevitable mimetic habits that generate our behavior. Its rhetorical parallel lies in the internal rhymes linking otherwise quite different lines of a poem. A man may see in his wife both his mother and his sister. In audible terms, he hears the rhyme of one in the other. Freud explains the quasi-musical procedure of associations, which can also produce *mistakes* in behavior, in *The Psychopathology*

Besides the motives for forgetting names, the mechanism by which it happens is worthy of our interest. In many cases a name is forgotten, not because of the motives it invokes itself, but because through harmony [*Gleichklang*] and homophony [*Lautähnlichkeit*] it touches upon another, towards which these motives direct themselves.[11]

Freud amplifies the unconscious; he creates a fantastic arena for what, in a desperate attempt at meaning, we call our personality; like Nietzsche he shows the sustaining power of metaphor, but also that we live in the depths of delusion. Nietzsche and Freud tell us that the human mind primarily has a gift for the ornamentation of life, *not* the analytical confrontation of which Western culture was for so long proud. Exploring those realms of delusion in terms of impersonal forces that dance a jig of rhetorical devices is sometimes like being asked to study the choreography of a Totentanz. A chill comes over one at the spectacle of so much unconscious mimicry ruling once proud human autonomy.[12]

Freud pulls back from killing the soul, but he does so only in a way we can appreciate as literature, by stretching words to their limits. When he mixes literal, metaphorical and etymological meanings, and also homophones, as he does in tracing the *Gedankenreihe* of the Wolfman's breath, he is writing perhaps the most bizarre poems to life ever to have entered the Western canon, for they are close to nonsense.[13]

But also close to art. The initial darkness of the symbols of the unconscious makes Freudian narratives seem like a Cubist painting, the reading of which Gombrich pitches at the highest degree of complexity:

> In [Picasso's Cubist paintings] primitive representational cues turn up, but only to tease and misdirect us – we try to integrate the guitar [in the *Still Life Painting*] as we integrated [Raphael's] Galatea or [Titian's] Europa, but find that we are everywhere brought up against a contradiction, till our mind is set in motion like a squirrel in the cage. But look at the premium of regression that is offered us if we let ourselves be whirled by the merry-go-round. In the dizzy chase after Humpty Dumpty the primary process comes into full play – anything is possible in this crazy world...

Gombrich underscores the ultimate unfathomability of the new symbol which *art* creates:

Instead of a fairly simple parallelogram of psychological forces we are here confronted with the highest type of organization of countless pulls and counterpulls on a hierarchy of levels that would baffle analysis even if we had greater insight into the kind of elements used.[14]

Freud's work is not on the same aesthetic level as Picasso's. Some less mysterious but still significant Cubist work like Fernand Léger's *Soldier with a Pipe* (1916) makes a better comparison with the case histories. That patch of red roughly identifies the soldier's hat, and from there head and face; it signals a way to go round the picture. Like the soldier, whom in a way civilization has turned into a machine, "The Wolfman" becomes clear once I grasp the way the primal scene disperses its effects through the story, because what Freud sees is also a kind of psychic machine at work in man. Freud shares the Cubist love of disguise, through fragmentation and a disturbed surface, because that is how his personality combined with his clinical study of dreams and symptoms has moved him to figure the workings of the unconscious. His case histories bring to mind another sometime Cubist painter Georges Braque, who as in *Woman with a Guitar* (1913) was fond of displaying flat surfaces where character might have been, and offering word fragments as clues. Freud, as with Léger and Braque, functions artistically under Gombrich's genius level. On the other hand it is surely the newness of Freud's art which makes one want to describe it in terms of an art adjacent to his own. The same is the case with Nietzsche. Nietzsche is a musician. Freud is a painter.[15]

Freud is an artist fascinated by his own wit and inventiveness. He is a painter with a new vision of the personality and what can be seen of its many layers. But he is also a writer with that familiar pathological streak, popularly referred to as a huge ego, which drives him readily to assume the mantle of important characters. Freud once suggested Napoleon modeled himself on the biblical Joseph, but didn't Freud too?[16] His literary-psychoanalytic essays concentrated on historical and mythical figures like Moses and

Joseph, and Prometheus and Oedipus, into whose portraits he could read or build aspects of himself. Hamlet, Oedipus, Rider Haggard's "She Who Must Be Obeyed" resemble ready-made rhetorical decorations which he can use to embellish his own life saga. Notoriously Freud twisted plots and made far-fetched interpretations of Sophocles' and Shakespeare's plays to suit his own ends. Harold Bloom notes that Freud's Shakespeare criticism reveals an instinctive and profound rivalry with the Bard.[17] He took what he needed to write his own "analytical novel," says Sarah Kofman in a similar vein, when she investigates Freud's borrowing from Empedocles. If Freud had called himself a writer from the beginning, it surely wouldn't seem so strange that, short of plagiarism, he took what he needed from other writers. He borrowed their examples, and in his theory put to his own new ends the artist's perceived mastery of the grammar of charm and deep knowledge of human character and behavior.

In a late essay Freud asks a telling question:

> Myth creation tries its hand, as it were jestingly, by using disguises, at giving some bodily expression to generally known, though still highly interesting, processes of the soul: but the question arises whether one can see in this anything other than representation for the sheer pleasure of it [*bloße Darstellungslust*].[18]

"Representation for the sheer pleasure of it." *Bloße Darstellungslust!* I read the question as a confession: concealed, oblique, set in the margins of his work, but still a confession. Freud has written up himself as myth for the unadulterated joy of it.

Actually this would be enough, that we should go on reading him as a writer to know about his life and imagination. Only a touch of greatness means that unconsciously he renders the meaning of the age. Thinly textured, slow-moving, anti-realist fiction, brilliant but bizarre poetry, near-nonsense, a written style of Cubist art with forays into Surrealism and Expressionism and Escherian absurdity, silent-film slapstick and brutal comedy: how without Freud's contribution, and this must at last be seen as an active contribution, can we understand the nature of modern art, and especially the Modernist art of his day?

Artists of the word and the brush instantly loved Freud's dream world, for the way it celebrated the beauty of the illogical and the way it suggested the existence of an unconscious or automatic creative process; also the new expressive possibilities it opened up for language. From Dali to Magritte, the Surrealists made persistent attempts to represent a manifest dream content, while the whole phenomenon of the dislocated, disjunctive modern art object echoed Freud's fascination with psychic reality's oblique and obscure relation to material reality. Freud's interests were also, and more relevantly, obvious companion volumes to the attempts of the Russian Futurists to create a new poetic language "beyond reason" and of the flightier Italians to catch "the word-in-liberty." Freud's multiple perspectives on personality sat companionably alongside Cézanne's revolution in painting. Atonal music presented strange, harsh, seemingly disconnected sounds much the way Freud's unconscious revealed strange, harsh patterns of association at the core of the personality. The broadened territory psychoanalysis offered to art also had a curious though quite misleading reflection in the "stream of consciousness" novel.[19]

Freud was quite rude about modern painting in his day, but in his theory and practice he noted and did what much modern and contemporary art was and is still doing. Gombrich parodied the connection between psychoanalysis and the pursuit of the new in painting when he suggested that looking at any conventional canvas through beveled glass would make it instantly more interesting, closer to Picasso, because of the broken surface. A deliberately "Modernist" painter might deliberately aim at this effect and presumably fail for lack of real inspiration. At the same time what Picasso achieved in *Les Demoiselles d'Avignon* was a breakthrough for painting.[20] Coming from the other side, there are many intriguing details in Freud's description of the dreamwork, which equally seem to foreshadow where painting will move in future. For instance, the dreamwork likes to use "inappropriate" materials to express its ideas. What Freud includes in writing up his "scientific" notes also casts shadows ahead of itself in literature. "Dora," after all, has multiple endings. The character called Dora also suddenly challenges the narrator and walks out of the frame. As Trilling *rightly* put it on this occasion, the art of his day and after rose up to confirm Freud's insights into the unconscious.

> ... of all mental systems, the Freudian psychology is the one which makes poetry indigenous to the very constitution of the mind ... the mind is in the greater part of its tendency exactly a poetry-making organ ... Freud discovered in the very organization of the mind those mechanisms by which art makes its effects.[21]

Of his "night book" of displaced syllables and mixed languages *Finnegans Wake*, James Joyce said it would be written "to suit the esthetic of the dream, where the forms prolong and multiply themselves, where the visions pass from the trivial to the apocalyptic, where the brain uses the roots of vocables to make others from them which will be capable of naming its phantasms, its allegories, its allusions."[22] Critics aware of the difficulty of reading a text which meanders like a river and takes in the whole of Christendom, from St Augustine's City of God to Stephen Dedalus's City of Dublin, sound like Freud pleading for the character of the dreamwork to be understood when they insist that *Finnegans Wake* needs to be listened to, as much as pictured, and least of all subjected to rational analysis. Freud and Joyce seem to believe that the whole sweep of historical anthropology is embraced in the individual life, and that this is truly the realm of the mythical. They suggest that the way to convey how the past lives in the present, and the collective in the individual, is through language suggesting another realm of perception, beneath logical consciousness.[23]

Proust's *In Search of Lost Time*, which takes its literary unity from the unity of a single reverie, opens with a magnificent testament to the imaginative power of the dream, followed by a whole volume on Charles Swann's neurotic love for Odette de Crécy. But what is truly remarkable about Proust and Freud is the coincidence of a theory of mind which all but locks the individual in his subjectivity. This ontological limit to our being throws a shadow over the impossible ideals of friendship and love. The greater part of life therefore comprises thought, including the thought of desire. Proust's theory of mind cedes no complexity in making thought a reflex of the body yet in an echo of Freud's unconscious equally insists on "the displacement of invisible beliefs which affect how we feel things, and what we feel." For Proust the mind is "selfish, active, practical, mechanical, indolent, centrifugal" and "readily turns aside from the effort which is required if it is to analyze an impression in itself." In Proust's world self-knowledge is just as defective as it is in Freud's, a state of being perversely complemented by the craving of both individual and society for a suitable disguise.[24]

Franz Kafka in his fiction acts out the suffering rather than the aggressive aspect of the Freudian *Problematik* of the father. He explores the guilt the archetypal son feels and the punishment he inflicts on himself without ever knowing what he has done. But above all Kafka brings out as no other writer the mixture of comedy and terror implicit in the dominance of an unconscious that doesn't care for us, only wants to show its malign and illogical power by undermining the most humdrum everyday interactions between individuals. This was never Kafka's intention, but *The Castle* is such a powerful metaphor for the unconscious as the *malin génie* which governs over us that we are bound to think back to the Austro-Hungary where Freud was also a Jew in the social margin confronted by a hostile bureaucracy. We feel what it is to be ruled from "elsewhere." Kafka presupposes a state of affairs of which the effect undermines identity and memory, and the ability to see anything clearly. One way Kafka does this is to keep "doubling" characters, so that experience is only a chain of impressions hopelessly removed from the real thing. Reason's dominant place in this world otherwise like our own has been usurped. K's confident assertion early in the novel that, "Life at the

Castle wouldn't suit me. I like to be my own master," is made to seem immediately ridiculous.[25] Freud writes on the very last page of the dreambook:'It remains in every case something we can learn from, to get to know the very churned-up soil on which our virtues stand proud."

The study of defective self-knowledge, of the human being's ready resort to disguise, coupled with a natural desire for self-assertion lead Freud to understand the inner failure to connect with reality and the consequences of actions which can in turn explain criminality. When Robert Musil, another chronicler of Austro-Hungarian decline, calls his murderer protagonist "The Man without Qualities" one thinks ineluctably of a passage, again in the closing pages of *The Interpretation of Dreams*, which portrays the failure to connect in telling technical terms.

> For actually thought processes are in themselves without qualities until the excitations of pleasure and pain which accompany them and which must be kept within bounds as a possible disturbance of thought. To give them a quality, [thought processes] are associated by the human being with the memories of words. This is designed to attract the attention of consciousness and from there to give thought a new mobility and charge.[26]

In the previous sentence Freud describes the capacity to regulate the interventions of pain and pleasure on our thinking as to what distinguishes human beings from animals, and what gives thoughts quality as well as quantity. So that it seems to denote a fundamentally defective mental and moral state to describe a man as being without qualities, because he lives in a state of mental and moral numbness.

Nabokov meanwhile inherits Freud's exploration of the insufficient conditions for our self-knowledge as textual deviousness. He adopts as a strategy of the language of the narrator the elusive playfulness of Freud's unconscious, its sexual loadedness and its techniques of punning and splitting. Humbert Humbert, with his mixture of Rousseauan idealism and criminal perversion might as well have been a deviant analyst who fell in love with his child patient. As it is he is a literary critic. How can this sexually precocious child called Lolita, daughter of Dolores Haze, be viewed other than against the background of Freud's devastating sexualization of the child, a loss of innocence over which suburban America in the 1940s is still in a fog? Only Nabokov's skill and humanity show that she is nevertheless still a child. Overall though it is surely the loaded word surface which Nabokov could be seen as having learned from Freud's unconscious. The Idealist tradition which Freud brings with him also gets passed on, which is why some critics detect in Nabokov a metaphysical otherworld implied by the playful surface of his poetic words.

Generally in creative fiction we are immediately struck by this or that text being essentially pre- or post-Freudian, according to the nature and status of the symbolism and the use of language, and the degree of skepticism brought to questions of motivation and identity. Freud lent to Western literature a picture of consciousness as inherently sexy, clever and subverted, which it has since not wanted to give up.

9

POETRY, TRUTH AND FREEDOM

Freud found success in the world despite defective self-knowledge. He became successful by suggesting the scientific reasons why we can never know what we project on to others, and thus can never know the social world as it is. His autobiography reshaped the view of human nature held by millions of people.

One of its many effects was to undermine the public façade that shored up a society which cared more for appearances than the private well-being of the individuals it tormented. Freud's dream treatments and case histories rewrote the intimate history of bourgeois life by applying to it a sexualized *Naturphilosophie*.

The unconscious is Freud's ultimate weapon against social authority. Funny, naughty, subversive and shocking, it is a force in which mockery and revenge fight on the front line. It is a tool of rebellion against state, society and family; against the discreet charm of the bourgeoisie. It undermines public performances, gives away secrets, dares people to think the unthinkable. Further, it was in the nature of the primary unconscious that once invented it would undermine not only patriarchal authority and sexual restraint, but also any circumstances which might lead to the repression of the spontaneous impulse, including the ordering powers of reason and logic.

Historically, Freud's prototype psychoanalysis had no conscious political program. Trilling and Mann, not wanting to believe what was happening before their eyes, claimed Freud didn't really mean to foment revolution, or anarchy. His famous elder statesman's pronouncement that where Id was Ego shall be, and his borrowing of Plato's image of the mind as a chariot of horses whose wildness is under control because they are led by reason: both of these stands reinforce a picture of the later Freud increasingly aware of his role as a social diagnostician and wise man, who cautioned parents against bringing up their children as revolutionaries.

But as we have seen, as well as a "freedom from" one's own demons Freud's work demonstrates a "freedom to" explore one's own powers of fantasy to sustain an otherwise unsatisfying life, and this ambivalence makes it the case that Freud is simultaneously a conservative and a revolutionary. Only his revolutionary nature is not Marxist, but highly individual and anarchic and selfish, bound up with that repressed writer inside him. And this ultimately is where free association leads in Freud's case: to luxuriating in his own imagination, to substituting it for a dubiously available "reality."

Some of the ironies built into Freud's work can be explored by following the very notion of "freedom." Free association in its fearlessness and rejection of segregation for the individual ego offers an analogy for an ideal society perhaps, happily supplemented in English, if not in German, by wordplay. For *freedom of* association is one of the essential tenets of democracy, along with freedom of speech and freedom of belief, and these were the political freedoms which the men of Börne's and Heine's generation campaigned for in 1830 and 1848, together with a release of literature from the classical fold and the Idealist mould.

In the philosophical rather than the political domain, however, "free" association in consciousness is only the counterpart of what Freud calls the "association compulsion" in the unconscious and turns out to be nothing of the kind. When it opens a doorway into our unconscious, "free" association actually reveals the most determined aspect of our personality. The limits which an active storehouse of memories imposes on our future is such an irony that only a metaphor will do. I wash my trainers, symbols of my freedom, in the washing machine. As they spin, I sit listening to them thumping against the sides of the tub.

In the end Freud seems divided between the political radicalism which is latent in his disruptive unconscious and his private thoughts and the political quiescence which comes with occupying a professional position in society and seeing the unconscious as at best a private mental playground, an occasion for individual creativity, but not a force for undoing and remaking the world. What straddles the divide between these two political extremes, however, is an ideal for the personality that is at least free of its own worst demons, and therefore can function rationally and morally in the world, and by that means bring about indirect improvement.

This was Schiller's ideal in *The Aesthetic Education of Man*, a hundred years before Freud. The Freud scholar should be aware of Schiller, not only because his name, like Goethe's, crops up in many of Freud's essays and dreams, but also because his ideal for personality was based on a schematic analysis of its competing drives, or *Triebe*, that word for which Freud imagined other languages must be envious of German. The *Stofftrieb*, the drive to content, accounts for our hunger for the infinite variety of experience, whereas the *Formtrieb* is the desire to shape that experience and abstract from it. These are drives which Schiller identifies as fundamental in the artist, alternating in their effect, and which he sees generally at work in how any of us deal with the world in terms of a dialectic of freedom and constraint, sensual joy and intellectual principle, self-abandon and self-ordering. But what he wishes to avoid in his prescription for personality is a head-on clash between the two. The person should not be at war with herself. Rather, a third drive, the *Spieltrieb*, the drive to play, should supervene. Its effect, rather like Freud's undoing of neurosis, would be to loosen the adult personality, to return to it the child's capacity to receive diverse impressions without immediate fear or judgement. But it also sets up a general model for the whole, balanced, personality, developed in all its aspects, and neither uncivilized by never having emerged from raw nature nor unnatural for having moved too far away from it under the influence of rules and principles. Reinserted in the political context, the ideal of play allowed Schiller to assert wholeness of personality in individuals as the necessary prerequisite of general political change.[1]

After Schiller, first Marx then Freud picked up this notion of the wholeness of personality, conceived on a dynamic model. They were interested in how the personality was formed by active emotional forces or *Triebe*, which in turn structured needs other than the simplest for food and shelter and procreation. In Freud the more differentiated needs emanated from personal history; in Marx they emanated from a society which blocked fulfillment of those needs. Thus in Marx's view society should be changed to liberate the personality, whereas for Freud, as for Schiller, romantic conservatives both in this respect, the changes had to come from within.[2] But a common language with a common ideal remains to link Schiller and Marx and Freud. It rests on the belief that the personality can be more liberated under the right circumstances, which amounts to who is master of what. The individual should take more power over himself, the young Marx and Freud agree. Moreover, psychic health depends on finding a home for one's inner life in the outer world.

Erich Fromm, in an essay on psychoanalysis, puts this view emphatically on behalf of, and quoting, the young Marx. The brutish interpretation of Freud is a caricature, though it puts forward a view of Freud which will echo down the twentieth century, portraying him as a man of the Enlightenment who sets up rational ideals which plunder and distort nature.

"Passion is man's faculties striving to attain their objects." In this statement [of Marx's] passion is considered as a concept of relation, or relatedness. It is not, as in Freud's concept of drive, an inner, chemically produced striving which needs an object as a means for its satisfaction, but man's faculties themselves, his *Wesenskraft*, are endowed with the dynamic quality of having to strive for an object they can relate to and unite themselves with. *The dynamism of human nature is primarily rooted in this need of man to express his faculties towards the world, rather than in his need to use the world as a means for the satisfaction of his physiological necessities.*[3]

This may be right about the young Marx, but it is such a distortion of Freud that it misses the main point of his moral value *as a therapist* that he insists that seeking out the real, distinguishing it from fantasy objects, is an unequivocally virtuous impulse catering to the deepest human need to be at home in the world. Both Freud (b.1856) and Marx (b.1818) saw the need to reconfigure the relationship of the perceived "inner" to the "outer" life so that those terms no longer constituted a conflict. What Freud showed, like Marx, was that the authority of society to suppress the personality rested largely on hypocrisy and falsehood. In particular, received morality caused unnecessary misery by dividing the world into black and white, good and bad, sane and mad. If we see Freud as at one with Nietzsche here, then it becomes all the easier to throw out the accusation against Freud that he is just another tyrant executive of instrumental reason and welcome the view, expressed by Nietzsche, that the world is well rid of a spiritual-moral tradition whose effect is mainly to cause pain and estrangement:

> The general imprecise way of observing sees everywhere in nature opposites (as, e.g., "warm and cold') where there are, not opposites, but differences of degree. This bad habit has led us into wanting to comprehend and analyze the inner world, too, the spiritual-moral world, in terms of such opposites. An unspeakable amount of painfulness, arrogance, harshness, estrangement, frigidity, has entered into human feelings because we think we see opposites instead of transitions.[4]

Marxist dialectic, of course, aimed to overcome conflict and contradiction and promote the real scope of human nature by changing *material* reality. Freud would have treated as a symptom that confusion of ideas and life.

Both Freud and Marx founded "sciences" to try to realize an essentially metaphysical dream of human self-transcendence. Despite a great deal of havoc and exploitation of their writing by lesser minds and rabble-rousers, both Freud and Marx made intermediate gains for a more humane society. Freud did this through the very coming into being of dynamic psychology. Marx achieved it through the birth of sociology.[5]

The effect of Freud was to begin to emancipate the margins of intellectual and cultural society. The sick and the ill-fitting could begin to come home, as they did in literature.

As Freud interprets a dream called the Hollthurn Dream, for instance, we glimpse a world very familiar to us in literature from Dostoevsky through Musil to Camus. We get inside the mind of the criminal to understand not only the limits but also the limitations of the normal in a world too much conditioned by social injustice. Here once again is his account of the dream.

I'm travelling in the night of the 18th/19th July on the southern route of the railway and hear called out in my sleep: "Hollthurn, ten minutes." I think straight away of Holothurien, a natural-history museum, that here is a place where brave men fought in vain against the dominance of the ruler of their lands. – Yes, the counter-reformation in Austria! As if it were a place in Steiermark or the Tyrol. Now I can see indistinctly a little museum, in which the remains of these men or their conquests have been preserved. I want to get out, but I hesitate. Women are standing with fruit on the platform, they're crouching on the ground and holding out their baskets so invitingly. – I was hesitating because I doubted we had enough time and now we still haven't moved. – I am suddenly in another compartment, where the leather and the seat are so narrow that one knocks directly against the [wooden] back. I am puzzled, but I can of course have changed compartments while asleep. Several people, among them an English brother and sister; a row of books, clearly in a bookcase on the wall. I see *The Wealth of Nations*, *Matter and Motion* (by Clark-Maxwell) thickly bound in brown cloth. The man asks his sister about a book by Schiller, whether she has forgotten it. The books seem now to be mine, now to belong to those two. I want to intervene in the conversation to say something or agree with something – I wake up bathed in sweat all over my body, because the windows are closed. The train stops in Marburg.[6]

I should like to read this dream first as an allegory for the very coming into being of psychoanalysis and what it is for. Its origins lie in eighteenth-century individualism and liberalism and nineteenth-century materialism, in a theory of matter-*in*-motion and some book by Schiller with a forgotten title. It respects the struggle of the individual for the dignity of self-rule, while being fully aware of the psychic shadow cast by the individual and collective human past and the challenge to build on our natural inheritance. Psychoanalysis sees that life offers the overwhelming diversion of sexual fulfillment, enough to make a man miss trains and appointments, and perhaps not even bother with the political struggle. The fruits of life are there, if only the individual is psychologically free to pick them. But so often he behaves as if immobilized, and his personality gets stifled.

But other aspects of the second half of this as always over-determined dream induce Freud himself to leave a dark and less personal interpretation behind. A couple he had recently travelled with had behaved in a very unpleasant way to make him feel inferior. "In the dream I exact a fearful revenge upon my unlikeable travelling companions; it's not possible to imagine what curses and humiliations lurk behind the broken-off bits and pieces of the first half of the dream." Though the dream has reversed the sequence, the change of compartment would also seem to indicate his rejection of this woeful pair. But Freud has a more important idea, that to make this change his unconscious has borrowed the idea of sleepwalking from a patient; and not just any patient, but one intent on murder. Following the death of his parents this otherwise normal patient has developed such wishes and is afraid to go outside lest he carries them out. His murderous feelings mean that no sooner has he passed someone in the street than he wants satisfaction, and feels he could have chased them off the pavement. So he stays in reading newspapers, but the newspapers are full of murders which he feels he must have committed. In fact he hasn't been out for weeks, but gets the idea that he might have walked in his sleep. He gives the key to his landlady with strict instructions to keep the front door locked at all times and not to let him out.

Freud's patient suffered from enmity towards his father. He was now cured, but Freud identified with that anti-paternal feeling. The complex might be called the Underground Man Complex, for it almost exactly reproduces the state of mind of one of Dostoevsky's most persecuted and infantile characters. Moreover, Freud would later attribute to Dostoevsky himself a love/hate sadomasochistic father complex.

What we see then is that on the one hand Freud is a voluptuary, and a revolutionary like Danton in the name of pleasure, and on the other, because of his own psychology, he is a specialist in the deep psychology of deviant criminal behavior. He studies what it takes psychologically to commit acts of violence against oneself, against others, against society; and to be a revolutionary.

The social outsider dreams of making his mark through violence. The revolutionary wants both to kill his father and destroy the existing social order. In Freud's otherwise un-satisfactory Dostoevsky essay, there is a paragraph about "Dostoevsky the criminal" which emphasizes the enormous destructive powers emanating from Dostoevsky's unconscious, which tend to clothe themselves in characters driven by hate and rage, and the element of criminal sexual perversion which also seems to have been part of his makeup. Freud, while recognizing his genius as a psychological writer, didn't particularly welcome Dostoevsky's company on the grounds that he had already exhausted his capacity to accommodate neurosis with his patients. But it seems clear that in Dostoevsky he met elements of himself.[7]

For the place where envy and vengeance and perverted lust naturally live and toy with "freedom" is very much Dostoevsky's world, where it is only challenged by religious faith that the abominations of man will one day be overcome. Freud, very much the Westerner by contrast, believed in the very decent repression of such feelings by rational consciousness. Only, *against* his rational self, Freud's invention of the unconscious by its very existence legitimized such feelings as envy and vengeance and lust and perversion, which then became part of public and political discourse regardless of any distinction in quality between "conscious" and "unconscious" mind. After Freud, the most aggressive and perverted things were no longer wrong, only on the periphery of the norm.

His successful crusade here derived from the needs of therapy. To try to understand the psychic disorders, slight or advanced, which could ruin a life, it was useful to see their kinship with full-blown mental diseases. Freud is taken to task as a scientist for measuring the normal by the abnormal. But in matters of compassion and assessing moral duty we regularly gauge our good fortune by noticing the degree to which others are less fortunate. Here again is a strong ethical tinge to his "science" which is often forgotten. He takes the-less-than-perfect, the deformed, as the humane standard.

It is not our intention to deny the noble strivings of human nature, and we have never done anything to downgrade them in value. On the contrary: I show you not only the wicked dream wishes which have been censored, but also the censor, which suppresses them and makes them unrecognizable. We only linger with more emphasis on what is evil in human beings because others deny it, whereby the spiritual life of the human being doesn't get better, but becomes unintelligible. If we give up the one-sided ethical evaluation of man we will surely be able to find a more correct formula for the relation of good to evil in human nature.[8]

If examples of social rebellion and crime fit naturally into the pages of Freud's great unwritten novel about the state of Viennese society *circa* 1900, however, what seem to be missing are individuals who exemplify a sense of social responsibility. Freud's thinking privileges subjectivity as the great inner adventure, and here he radically departs from even the young Marx and turns into the doctor to the old, pampered, artistically inclined middle class. His work encourages everyman's journey into the interior. The novelists Thomas Mann and Italo Svevo understood Freud exactly in this, and where his shortcomings lay. They ended *their* novels of 1900-1914, Mann in German Switzerland, Svevo in Trieste, by contrasting the high intellectual entertainment value of psycho-analysis with the cold sharp shock of war. They identified a real problem, for what are we to do with an Eros which even as it sends us out into the world obscures our view of anything that might exist independently of ourselves?[9]

This is the essence of Freud's pessimism. In a super-sexualized, highly-determined, louche, unnatural-*naturphilosophisch* Freudian universe it is the nature of our minds to distort the world, and this tendency is mimicked in culture. If there is a reality it is either empty (metapsychological) or not to be faced (primitive). The determinism is dark, as it always has been in the Judaeo-Christian world:

> There is far less freedom and wilfulness in the life of the soul than we are inclined to assume; perhaps none at all. What we call coincidence in the world it is well known can be explained by laws; also what we call wilfulness in the sphere of the soul rests on laws, however darkly we begin to perceive them now. So let's look at what we have![10]

Our lives are spent in moving from one substitute for reality to another. If this can be represented as a reality of disproximate signs, it may sound like a version of "through a glass darkly." Except Freud does move on from Judaeo-Christian tradition, and no high, clear, unambiguous and stable realm exists in his mental or linguistic beyond. The play of meanings, like the play of disguises, is what we have. And this really is the limit of any comparison between Freud and Plato based on the harnessed rationality of the chariot, and the limit of any description of Freud as a rationalist and an Enlightenment thinker. It marks the assertion of Nietzschean fantasy – the power of metaphor to be our reality –

over metaphysical idealism in Freud's stories, and it seems to resonate with the shock of moving out of the nineteenth-century world of realism in literature and positivism in science, into Modernism and relativity.[11]

Let me recall what the metapsychological view is. Freudian stories are moments of endopsychic myth when we project our inner muddle on to the world and come to believe in it as real, whereas what we see is only imagined.

> Can you form an idea of what "endopsychic myths" are? The latest product of my thinking. An unclear inner perception of one's own psychic apparatus inspires mental illusions, which are naturally projected outwards and in characteristic manner towards the future and the beyond. Immortality, vengeance, the entire beyond are representations of our inner psyche... psycho-mythology.[12]

A Freudian narrative is a description of the psychic maze we get caught in, because we are all subject to mental illusions, not knowing what is inside us and what out there. This is expressly what religious belief, whether in a soi-disant religious or secular cause, looks like through metapsychological eyes. Because metapsychology also erodes the power of all external moralities, Freud stands wide open to charges of amorality and possibly moral irresponsibility.

The Ratman's story is a terrifying parody of morality because it undoes the value we would normally attach to the intelligent individual's desire and will to follow precepts. Not that the Ratman is not good, but his choice of good is shown to be full of illusions, as are the things he believes in to give his life "meaning." He has the intelligence to dismiss a fear of Fridays and the number 13, but cannot get beyond his doubter's need to believe in prophetic dreams and telepathy. He clings passionately to meaningful coincidences, and amongst these holds especially to those which solve his indecision by ordaining sexual denial. In other words the abstinence which might seem to be his "good" choice rests on unresolved unconscious conflicts which show up as haunted confusion. When he returns hopefully to a spa hotel where the proximity of his previous room to staff quarters had led to a sexual liaison with an employee, and finds the room already occupied, he seems quite intent on his goal. He curses the elderly professor who stands between him and his main chance and dreams of the man's death. But when a few days later the professor does die, and his body is carried out of the room, guilt moves into the Ratman. Guilt now confirms the rightness of the Ratman's "self-denial" all along.[13]

On another occasion in the Ratman's thwarted erotic life, a still young woman but "getting on in years" and "in need of love" asks him to bed and he refuses. Later he hears that she has jumped out of a window. Again he feels terrible guilt. Freud diagnoses that the Ratman overestimates the power of his thoughts to affect the outside world. The deaths of the old man and the young woman are not caused by him. But that he thinks they are matches his unawareness of how truly damaging are the inimical feelings he harbors within himself. At the end he is shown to have neither self-knowledge nor true morality.[14]

To try once more to get at the philosophical character of Freud's *Dichtung*: as their author says, compulsive neurosis such as the Ratman suffers is a parody of religion, Dora's hysteria caricatures a work of art, while the paranoia of Senator Schreber is a parody of a philosophical system. What we can see from these three examples is that Freud's stories first collapse the *bona fide* spiritual and traditional moral value of the so-called inner life which rests on art, religion and philosophy, then, as is the job of psychoanalysis, they try to recreate meaning by giving that inner life a new pattern.

The pattern comes from words. In Freud's view words – apparently without any necessary referents in the world – have ultimate power to determine happiness:

In the beginning words were magic, and the word still retains much of its magic power today. With words one person can make another blissful or drive them to despair, with words a teacher conveys his knowledge to pupils, with words the speaker carries with him the assembly of listeners and determines their judgements and decisions. Words evoke emotional states [*Affekte*] and are the general means by which people influence each other. Therefore we won't underestimate the use of words in psychotherapy and will be happy to listen in to the words exchanged by the patient and the analyst.

Happiness through words creates meaning:

> Words are the essential tools of psychic treatment. The layman will probably find it hard to grasp that morbid disturbances of the body and the soul can be overcome by "mere" words from the doctor. He will think he is being asked to believe in magic. And he's not so wrong in that: the words of our daily speech are none other than etiolated magic. But it will be a long haul to make people understand how science proposes to restore to the word at least a part of its previous magic power.[15]

With this relationship to words Freud rescues neurotics. He translates their woes into the language of another realm, with the result that their symptomatic actions and dream matter fall into place as versions of something they couldn't otherwise get at, something like the meaning of life.

But here Freud's interpretations of the soul become tinged with metaphysical mystery and begin to replace religion. The metaphysical tint contradicts the idea I advanced above that Freud persuades us to delight in metaphorical fantasy Nietzschean-style and have no further wants. But even Nietzsche did not really escape metaphysics, with his notion of self-overcoming. Freud's metaphysical strain is visible in his insistence that the unconscious does not have a language but that the interpreter invents a possible language with the help of "made-up medical words" or, literally, "medical art-words." Art and medicine together show the way forward.[16] Now we see through a glass darkly but one day there will be light. The Idealist and religious preoccupations left over from his classical education and Jewish background determine Freud's healing metaphysics. He has absorbed the Lutheran tradition of pastoral care, and inherited the Cabbalist tradition of symbolic exegesis and teaching the flock responsibility for self by moral tale. These inheritances lead him to betray himself as a metapsychologist. No sooner has he pared back the old religions to a state of the psyche close to disease than he promptly founds a new religion of psychoanalytical hermeneutics. In this respect Freud fulfills the worst fears of his best scientific critic, Wittgenstein, because he must mythologize.

Like mad Senator Schreber with his vision of the super-erotic universe, Freud tries in his middle period to apply very harsh metapsychological criticism to the system he seems to be building up.

If we think abstractly we are in danger of neglecting the relations of words to unconscious thing-representations, and it can't be denied that our philosophizing in that case takes an undesired similarity in expression and content to the way schizophrenics work. The other way round, one can venture of schizophrenics' way of thinking the characteristic that they treat concrete things as if they were abstract.[17]

Freud sees that his own system is in danger of becoming more like an expression of mental disease, for as he says, to conjure up a vast fantasy and call it a description of the world would be demented; so too would be to treat concrete lives as if they were mere examples of abstract problems. Thus his own system is just a description of the way metapsychology works: the way human intensity tends to produce certain imaginings about the world. He invites from his patients "benevolent skepticism" and open-mindedness from the public.[18] But Wittgenstein noted that metapsychology was impossible to sustain. A myth such as Freud created would always build up the impression of there being something there, not just a word but a fact about the world, and that would be a totally misleading description of what was real.

It's interesting to reflect where this mythologizing comes from.

I would say that the classical German tradition from Goethe to Thomas Mann is so utterly suffused by a concern with personal happiness, and so sure that the truth about the world is the truth about the individual drawn to art, that it cannot resist demonstrating its worship of imagination.[19]

In any case, the result is that morality is flung out. Art is what makes people happy and gives them self-insight in a certain special way. And the uncertainties of art as a relationship between work and reader, mingling with the even greater uncertainties which freight the relationship between a teacher and a pupil or a doctor and a patient, present the particular problem of Freud.

Freud bases the invention of psychoanalysis on the belief that he can mobilize that particular aspect of art which enshrines its relationship with its audience. His starting point is the belief that writers exercise a quasi-erotic hold on their readers through the power of words which somehow promise deeper pleasures of the soul. Perhaps, despite my earlier criticisms, we can read this as saying that sex is important in adult life because it gets things going. It helps us love art and pursue truth. Plato certainly had no objections to mobilizing it for truth's sake. But unlike in our appreciation of art and our reading and thinking, in psychoanalysis and in teaching we can never finally bypass the presence of sexual and emotional dependence because real people are involved. The Plato of *The Symposium* knew as well as the Freud who invented the method of transference that the *enacted* pursuit of truth via mutual attraction is a tainted enterprise. Freud, of course, is much more critical of the artist in this respect than he is of the psychoanalyst. He writes of the artist that *he* cannot avoid getting some personal pleasure out of hooking his fish with the right bait. When the artist produces the captivating goods he not only frees his audience, but liberates repressed material from his own psyche. *Both* participants in the artistic contract obtain pleasure and delivery. The art of words acts as a kind of unwritten erotic social contract by which we help each other to survive and flourish. But surely all this may be true of Freud the analyst, and other analysts too.

Freud is decidedly anti-metaphysical where happiness is

concerned: he thinks of the body. But he inclines towards metaphysics in the search for the meaning on which that happiness would still seem to depend. Art plays its part in both realms, by generating excitement and hope and new mental and emotional associations.

But the moral difficulty for psychoanalysis is that all this transacting is so uncertain in its promise of happiness, and Freud has meanwhile removed all the other supports in terms of traditional values on which the individual might depend. Freud is in the position of a man who has really made the Nietzschean decision to survive on fantasy alone, and this is what makes him culpable in many eyes.

Where Freud begins to make up moral ground is as self-help guru. He provides a description of imagination and accompanies it with a doctor's prescription: understand and exercise *this* and it will make you better. *The Interpretation of Dreams* has Hegel's *Phenomenology of Spirit* and Kant's *Critique of Aesthetic Judgement* as its precursors, and between them Schiller's *Aesthetic Letters*.

The crucial Kantian notion is that there is an activity of conscious mind not concerned with knowledge and truth, but rather directed at perceiving some purposiveness and wholeness in experience. That purposiveness in things does not exist, like I exist, nor is it an inherent quality of things; but the mind delights in perceiving the facts as so arranged or interpreted. Hegel, a generation after Kant, was thrilled by Kant's aesthetic vision. But then Hegel decided purposiveness and wholeness were indeed part of reality: of the reality of the human mind and of world history combined. Thus *The Phenomenology of Mind* describes how the purposeful evolution of individual conscious mind *does* entail the purposeful evolution of *reality*. It throws overboard all Kant's qualifications that "things only seem so" and invites us to believe that the inner world of men and women is gradually transforming itself into the nature of society.

Between Kant and Hegel resonates a tension which, as we have seen repeatedly, exists in Freud "like two souls in one breast." The limited therapeutic endeavor, governed by Enlightenment reason, leads to, but then struggles to accept a restorative Romantic position which delights in imagination for its own sake. Probably no tension has ever been so important in the history of German thought as that between Kant and Hegel. Marx and Freud tried to transcend it by changing the definition of reality, or mind. A fine problem, with brilliant but imperfect solutions thrown at it, has remained.

Schiller, Kant's poetic interpreter, is the prime example of how, in the century before Freud, German thought passionately pursued a happiness of the spirit which would be resilient in a real world of moral exigency, power and scientific knowledge. The glory of that problem, and the kinds of answers it prompted, are still part of how we live and think today.

On behalf of the individual, but with a tendency to create a Hegelian-style apparatus to explain the process, Freud continues the classic German pursuit of happiness. His aim is to suspend the tensions caused by inflexible principle, and in his day in effect to see German civilization partly undone, to allow men and women more happiness. But it seems as if, along with the way he undermines the authority of religion and the autonomy of conscious mind, Freud has to deal hefty blows at the intrinsic value of high art in order to carry out his project.

As the century over which Freud and Marx have predominated becomes a discrete entity behind us, we see how, as the art of self-making has risen to a position of extraordinary prominence in Western society, so the importance of high art has lost its broad social relevance. Freud neither intended this change of emphasis in society, nor crusaded for it; nor can it be said that an interest in discovering one's own creative potential necessarily militates against the study of the more difficult art of Virgil and Lucretius, Milton and Dante, Shakespeare and Racine, Corneille and Goethe, Rilke, Mann and Proust. But this is where we are, in an age of advanced self-making coupled with artistic mediocrity.[20]

Freud cannot be the sole cause of this great shift, which is above all the consequence of a hierarchical society giving way to a mass society. But since we seem able to pack the upstart twentieth-century jack back into the box of Freud's personality and teaching, his autobiography and his art seem to hold clues to the passions and preoccupations individuals must hold in order for such a sweeping change to take place.

One clue comes with what Freud himself identified as that disaster area in human psychology which he announced to the world on the occasion, of all places, of his receipt of the respected and revered Goethe Prize for Literature.

Our attitude to our fathers and teachers is after all an ambivalent one, for our respect for them regularly covers up an element of hostile rejection. That is a disastrous element in our psychology which can't be changed without a powerful suppression of the truth and which will inevitably feed into our relationship with the great men whose life stories we want to research.[21]

If Freud's conscious hostility to tradition is the main reason why he cannot straightforwardly compete to be recognized as an artist in an established school, then his envious demoting of the artist is the symptomatic expression of the desire to be an artist which he has repressed. That desire, as we have seen, is encapsulated in a mere two words in German as *bloße Darstellungslust*. It is, or would be, the simple joy of representing things.

Freud epitomized a natural tendency in a society growing ever less bound to the authority of State and Church, when he spoke of envy as the force which drives the new generation to take power. Pen envy, in which he was a specialist, was part of the democratic armory. Pen envious, he wishes destruction on high art in a way he can almost become conscious of as a *lover* of high art. This is because he knows that the stories told to him by neurotics are not art, but a form of aesthetic drudgery, mobilized for the first time in Western history as an ideal. Indeed the stories told to Freud are shit. Neurotics "confess their fantasies to the doctor," says Freud, a man who as the pioneer of psychoanalysis must also be the first connoisseur of the drudgery of self-making. Never mind what his hidden artistic talent is, his job now is to keep a record of his client's Nietzschean self-overcoming. He is a professional observer of *artistes manqués*; doctor to a world of epigones, because he has taught that what it takes to be creative holds the secret of the ideal personality. Since pen envy is my term for a complex I detect as present in Freud and symbolic of the *Zeitgeist*, I suggest it perfectly expresses the belief of a generation or more that power is to be acquired by becoming a writer; while all the while "writing" declines.[22]

One of the strangest things in Freud is the impersonality in which he clothes the storifying creativity which he has banished from his personal makeup. The Hegelian universality and impersonality of the figuring process is striking as Freud construes it in *Dreams*. As if he were claiming to have found the gene responsible for generating stories, he isolates a self-sufficient force at work in the unconscious Mind, the dreamwork, which creates networks of symbols. The ubiquitous Unconscious Spirit strives to express itself with the help of a bottomless dressing-up box and your soul or mine. Freud's thoughts about the Storifier were never collected in a volume called *The Phenomenology of the Untergeist* but this is what their force comprises in the history of German thought. Just as Hegel justified a belief in the increasingly rational development of human society, so Freud's unwritten *Phenomenology* both justifies and predicts why more and more individuals should become conscious of themselves as writers and *a fortiori* more fulfilled people. Becoming aware of the universal Storifier's presence in ourselves and how it holds the clue to our happiness is part of the scientific progress of humanity.

Freud's capacity as a Modernist writer, and his vision of the Writer giving way to the Storifier in a mass society, are equally virtually unknown components of his legacy, because they remain in the intentionally inexistent realm of books he might have written, projects he might have announced more loudly, had they not formed part of an elaborate mechanism of self-deception. That, in a sentence, is the reason behind this book about Freud's response to art. As we have seen, only Freud's subjective insights as a writer make it *possible* for him to imagine how such an impersonal storifying force might work. But such is the evasiveness and lack of awareness that shrouds his most creative project, and within it his moment of self-discovery, in a new science of the unconscious. It is a moot point whether by this route he acquired the "honor, power and the love of women" an artistic career would have brought, or whether pen envy maintained its hold on a secretly unsatisfied writer who used his talents under difficult constraints while ever dreaming that he might be free to write a novel in later life.[23]

On Freud's evasiveness *vis-à-vis* art, it is quite striking that apart from his explicit writings on the psychology of art and the artist, Freud either pushed art into the unconscious or to the periphery of his attention. He allows himself to function as *analyst to the writer/artist*, and even more tangentially and never disinterestedly as a critic; but never, despite "the pretty colorful order that obtains in my reproductions" which he recognized in "Dora" and the public praise he received for that and his other case–studies as stories, does he allow himself to believe that he is a writer.[24]

The split in Freud has been apparent for over half a century, and yet it has not somehow reached the prominence in the public mind which it should have, if we want to appreciate his great merits alongside his defects. As a scholar wrote fifty years ago:

The young Freud, in his student days, had subdued an almost incestuous eagerness to "unveil nature" by the compensatory concentration on laboratory work. He had thus postponed a conflict by realizing only one part of his identity. But when, in his words, he "touched on one of the secrets of nature," he was forced to realize that other, that more creative identity. For any refuge to the established disciplines of scientific enquiry was, as the project proved, closed.[25]

Freud splits himself, like Schreber does. The theory of a splitting like this is that it is a "rationalization" and a salient component of narcissism, to do with the ways in which the ego protects itself. So Freud is not Freud, but Freud One, because that persona makes it easier to survive the pressures of his surrounding culture. He is not a writer, but at his closest to creativity a critic after Aristotle, classifying the rhetorical ways of the Storifier. But when in "Dora" he huffishly dismisses the possibility that others will think he is writing a *roman-à-clef* rather than a medical case-study, and on other occasions of denial, he surely had a dim sense that his real business was poised between speculative philosophy and fiction.[26]

His self-camouflage and his disdaining the writerly label defend him unconsciously against something, though who can say what. Symptoms are like dreams, with an umbilical cord attaching them to somewhere unknown and unknowable. We can only come up with an interpretation. Apart from his destructive attitude to tradition, probably working in this area of his life unconsciously, Freud was probably also consciously deterred by the real uncertainty of the artistic enterprise. Further, he was unconsciously reluctant to base his professional life on his least governable qualities. Artists, after all, "have no occasion to submit their inner life to the strict control of reason." But this evasion of himself involved such strong repressions as to lead to pen envy and an original body of writing nevertheless.

Specifically on the feasibility of pen envy, we should remember that on his own admission Freud has a vengeful personality, envious and fixated. He is competitive, he wants to lead, and is thoroughly ambivalent about the great and the good. He is suspicious of charm, suspicious of what others might be concealing and what they are really like. A fear of "the artist," which surely was a fear of the artist within, but projected outside, made havoc of Freud's self-esteem when he was young. The panic with which he faced up to the "artists" who seemed to be rivals for Martha's hand was intense, even if there was never any real cause for it. In the work, meanwhile, the pen envy complex comes into play every time Freud positively insists that what he is doing is science. He projects his self-revisions out on to the world as scientific law. He conceives of science as hard and factual and dependent on evidence. Science is his neurotic hiding-place, camouflaging his fear of the uncertain nature of what he is doing. Even openly he confesses how much he relies on magic – as we have seen expressly, the magic of words. But when his analyst's or his public speaker's verbal charm didn't work he would always protect himself by stressing he was a humble scientist who did not work with magic. Freud defined his scientific position as an abstemious refusal to tell stories, despite the richness of the material that came his way. He wrote that "Science is quite the most perfect renunciation of the pleasure principle that is possible for our psychic work." Why he didn't cast a metapsychological eye over his assumptions at this point we cannot know. The "only science is reliable" strategy recalls Nietzsche's longing for philosophy to be *rough*, to counteract his vulnerability and compassion.

When Freud claims to be astonished to hear that "the case histories I write should sound like short stories and that, as one might say, they lack the serious stamp of science," his most serious scientific critic of recent years, Richard Webster makes a half-correct observation, for he calls Freud's words "almost like an oblique confession" of one "who has abandoned the role of the scientist for that of a novelist." But Webster misses Freud's neurosis: the fact that Freud's desire to give pleasure – including to himself – through words inches forwards, escaping deviously wherever it can.[27]

The signs of excess surrounding this complex include Freud's condemnation of artists as potential swindlers. This dislike of artists as confidence tricksters is powerful enough to rival that of Tolstoy and Plato. The little frustrations of a scientist who wants to write more freely meanwhile come out in an expression of regret that Freud is not free to charm the reader by better shaping his material. Where in the Botanic Monograph Dream he refers to "what my amateur passions cost me,"[28] he goes on to identify a lifetime's desire to compensate for physically destroying a book when he was young, the result being that reading passion he has long since condemned in himself.

Thus I would finally associate Freud's notorious interventions in his patients' lives less with moral turpitude and more with an aesthetic temptation gone wrong. Freud could not resist in analysis casting himself as both the controller of the story and a love object within it. His sessions were a kind of live story-making, and only later did he write them down as if he were a mere scribe for the storifying fabrications of the patient's unconscious. Hence my term for the case studies, "assisted autobiographies." In *The Psychopathology* Freud meanwhile made plain that he wanted love in return for his storytelling-within-analysis, and this strikes me as a supremely writerly ambition.[29]

And so we come back to love, and to Freud's body, and his intense sexuality. For an adult, abnormally unstable emotions possess him, such as his fury at being rejected by Dora. His sexuality is part of his energy and imagination, and irrepressibly projected outwards on to everyone and everything. The Ratman wants to sodomize him and Dora yearns for a taste of his smoky breath. He cannot stay out of the story.

There is a paradox in that Freud's physical vigour brings us closest to a notion of freedom in his thought, while his view of the sexual-familial origins of everything casts him as a determinist. The counterpoint of his instinctual, hungry body and his cultivated, pessimistic mind make him an excellent theorist of tension. His writing about sex, about emotional pain, and about humor, is true because it is full of the pressure of the load and the need to relieve it. In the context of humor, he talks of the pleasure of evading cultural restraint: the *Aufhebungslust* which makes a man feel free, and one knows what he means: it is whatever lightness a man who has just laughed and a dog that has just shat have in common.

Freud seems to me to survive the attacks on him as an immoralist and a fraud and to remain a well-motivated liberator who began to redraw boundaries in medicine and the humanities in a way which is still continuing. Only the scientific claims Freud made for his view of the psyche turn out to be so deeply rooted in his autobiography that we naturally feel unsure. We turn away and look for his merits elsewhere as a writer. Suddenly, looking for those other merits, we find them in such a way as threatens to overwhelm us. We find such a different set of qualities, such a different moral order, and such different uses for "freedom" in the exemplary exercise of his fantasy that our original rescue operation seems to drown the capsized genius nevertheless. We hold up the neurotic and the artist and the sinner in Freud for inspection by the ethical man, and find his presence in all those identities. Freud as neurotic, artist, sinner and moralist – to take the four faces he attributed to Dostoevsky – remains a puzzling multiple personality. In particular, the essential tension between a commitment to social reality and a love of fantasy, between freedom from inner and outer repression and freedom to live in a world of his own construction, choc-full of sex and violence, is never resolved.

Freud responded to the complexity of art, and perhaps storylines best capture who Freud was and what he did.

FREUDIPUS: Freud's natural parents were Art, and his adoptive parents Science. He took the name of his adoptive parents but unconsciously like Oedipus made his way back to his original parents. At a crossroads, but in ignorance, he killed his father. Later he married his mother. Should I explain this application of Oedipus to Freud? By unconsciously marrying itself to art, the science nominally founded by Freud does beget a new discipline, though it will be one Freud will gouge his eyes out rather than look at as something to do with him. Moreover, Art as tradition lies slain by the wayside.

CLEVER JOSEPH: There was once a learned family in which the youngest child was both very clever and very weak. He was so clever he had a new vision of reality, but he was afraid to express it, because he thought it would anger the strong. So he allied himself with the most popular brother in the family at that time, whose name was Science. His new vision emerged, half-hidden, under his brother's unwitting protection.

THE ELVES AND THE SHOEMAKER: A clever man strives for new insight and is very tired. He is glad when supernatural creatures come at night and finish his work for him. He just has to copy it up in the morning and he will be hailed a scientist of genius. But his wife, much as she wants him to succeed, is suspicious and stays up to try to catch the elves at work. She discovers that the husband she idealized as a great thinker can only make progress by magic, so she divorces and exposes him as a fraud, forgetting all the hard work he did by day. As Freud says, there is man and woman in all of us.

FREUD–PARACELSUS: A doctor who has found a new way of healing the soul does not understand the origin of his powers, still less his place in society. He arrives and leaves his home town as a mystery figure.

Freud's body, still stuffed with vital contradictions, was embalmed in twentieth-century Western social liberation. Lenin's body lay preserved in Red Square for the liberation of another culture. Great mummies, mixed gifts.

What Freud teaches is a hurdle to classical virtue: for every seeming white-crested outpouring of our hearts there is a black undertow. It flows from Freud, as it does for different reasons from Marx, that there can be no disinterest. For Marx because society determines consciousness; for Freud because the determinism comes from the unconscious. In either case the result is the same: there can be no such thing as goodness or beauty for its own sake. The reign of Kant comes to an end with these thinkers who epitomize the twentieth century. The kingdom of ends-in-themselves is partitioned or abolished. Freud-ism is a blight on love for the way it seems to disallow any *wholly* good feelings about our moral and loving selves. Freud further seems wrong to evaluate things according to their origins: a beautiful pot is no less beautiful for being made of mud. Because of Freud's strong streak of paranoia, the morally and the aesthetically ideal were easily contaminated in his mind, and man as such becomes suspect, because of the vastness of possible new motives for his actions, and because of the tendency of those residing in the unconscious to be murky.

The vision of body and spirit Freud bequeaths us might be called *Servitude et grandeur sexuels*, after Alfred de Vigny's strange tribute, after another revolution, to a lost way of life based on selflessness and discipline. The loss of disinterest and the loss of voluntary restraint with which Freud presented the twentieth century in art and society and morality seem like the fruits of the

Jacobin Revolution in France. Not everyone wants them, and for everyone there is a price to pay for the freedom Freud brings. We have read Freud and seen how to liberate and glorify our appetites, but perhaps as he himself said of the Latrine Dream, about washing away the piles of psychic shit, it is "as if something remained."[30]

What remains? Art for its own sake, certainly, and also the conscious desire not to go so far, and to respect the adult self. Freud was an extraordinary writer and psychologist, but he never quite understood the human need to cover up, not out of hypocrisy, but for beauty's sake, and modesty.

10

NOTES, ARGUMENTS AND EXPLANATIONS

These notes, though they do contain references, are mostly designed to be read as a continuation and recapitulation of the foregoing book.

I have based my study of Freud on the excellent *Studienausgabe* (Frankfurt am Main, 1969–79), ten volumes plus a supplementary *Ergänzungsband*, which also contains invaluable notes and cross-references. References to this edition are given first in the notes as SA followed by the volume number and page. A parallel reference is given for the *Standard Edition of The Complete Psychological Works of Sigmund Freud*, translated under the general editorship of James Strachey in twenty-four volumes (London, 1960), as SE followed by the volume number and page. Works not included in the *Studienausgabe* are cited as German texts in Sigmund Freud, *Gesammelte Werke*, eighteen volumes (London, 1940–68). These references are to GW followed by the volume and page number. Translations, including of the titles of Freud's papers, are mine unless otherwise indicated.

I have consulted Freud's letters in the following editions: *Briefe 1873–1939*, ausegewählt und herausgegeben von Ernst und Lucie Freud (Frankfurt am Main, 1968); *Sigmund Freud Arnold Zweig Briefwechsel*, herausgegeben von Ernst und Lucie Freud (Frankfurt, 1968); Freud, *Briefe an Wilhelm Fließ 1887–1904*, Ungekürzte Ausgabe, ed. Jeffrey Masson (Frankfurt, 1986) – this edition supersedes the selection of letters to Fließ published in

1950 (I have indicated where a letter has been used which was either not included or substantially cut in the 1950 edition which has come under exaggerated criticism); *The Freud–Jung Letters*, ed. William McGuire, tr. Ralph Mannheim and R.F.C. Hall (London, 1974).

Freud's case-studies are referred to by the names of their protagonists: "Fragments of an Analysis of Hysteria" = "Dora"; "Observations on a Case of Compulsive Neurosis" = "The Ratman"; "Psychoanalytical Observations on an Autobiographically Described Case of Paranoia" = "Schreber"; "From the Story of an Infantile Neurosis" = "The Wolfman."

NOTES TO THE **Introduction**

1 The vague claim is often made these days that *of course* Freud was a writer. But this is not a simple matter of showing he has an impressive literary style, which is in any case an exaggerated claim. Patrick Mahony in *Freud as a Writer* (1982) makes clear in reviewing earlier German and French commentaries by Muschg, Schönau and Roustang that defining Freud's claims on the word artistry is not merely a question of opposing the constraints of his chosen scientific form with aesthetic talents which might have been diverted into other channels. Freud's writing not only describes but produces knowledge. He contends for the title of *Dichter* in German, which is nominally a poet. However, Goethe's autobiography *Dichtung und Wahrheit*, referring to the Mythos and Logos of Plato's *Timeus*, opens up the scope of the word to mean something like a man who expresses his deep human insights through pictures. Freud creates a new mythology in Plato's sense. Alongside reason or *logos* this *mythos* can help pave the way to true knowledge.

Within psychoanalysis Adam Phillips has opened up new territory with his imaginative readings.

2 We may call a writer who a century ago laid claim to science an artist because we somehow value his writing, even if it

contains faulty science. Francis Wheen uses the same strategy in *Karl Marx* (London, 1999).

3 Freud nevertheless always felt writers were his close neighbors, which is why he relished the parallels between his theory and the *Gradiva* story told by Jensen (SAX 51, SE9 53).

4 Essentially Freud created a homeland for the new science of psychoanalysis by annexing territory which once belonged to art. But the result was then a rivalry between the worlds of art and therapy. Pen envy, or the idea that everyone can be, or can benefit from trying to become, a writer, is a marked feature of many latter-day ego therapies.

5 Of course the long failure of the Anglo-American world to read Freud as an artist also lies with the need to read him in translation. The Standard Edition of James Strachey is mostly very serviceable, but it deliberately scientized Freud on Ernest Jones's instructions. This strategy included replacing the homely terminology of Das Ich and Das Es with the pseudo-medical Latin of the Ego and the Id, writing "cathexis" where "charge" or "interest" might have been, and insisting on mind where soul was in Freud's German. Bruno Bettelheim in *Freud and the Soul of Man* was one of the first to draw attention to the false impression Strachey's Freud created in English.

A good example of where Strachey's pseudo-scientized Freud continues to mislead is Webster, whose admirably patient exposure of Freud's errors and false paths as a scientist is marred by a mistaken grasp of the nature of Freud's system overall. Webster writes in *Why Freud Was Wrong*, p.497: "We need an epistemology which does not repudiate or deny significance to any aspect of reality because it is emotionally laden, erotically charged or considered to be degraded by its ordinariness or its association with common humanity." This seems to adopt and carry forth Freud's own project, having argued it away from under his dead body. When in the pursuit of " a truly biological epistemology" we are asked to cast aside psychoanalysis with its "rationalism" and "mentalism" the extent of the error becomes apparent.

Other specific failures of the Strachey translation include "instinct" for *Trieb*, which would be less misleadingly rendered as drive, and failure to capture Freud's concept of deferred effectiveness or *Nachträglichkeit*. Strachey also tidied up Freud's style and rendered his dreams in the past instead of the present tense. Mahony in *Freud as a Writer* and also in *Cries of "The Wolfman"* (1984) has been influential in drawing attention to the predicament faced by readers of the Standard Edition, such that a revised translation is now in preparation. Ritchie Robertson summarizes the problems as they refer to one particular text in his Introduction to Joyce Crick's revised translation of *The Interpretation of Dreams* (Oxford, 1999).

Apart from translation, the gulf between Anglo-American and Continental responses to Freud is notorious: between those who deplore his science and those who revel in his imagination. Our study shows how amply Freud's work supports both kinds of reading, because of his effort to present himself as a scientist. It probes for the single "secret artist" making these diverse readings possible.

6 Few doubt that Freud's vision is valuable. Webster begins his book by identifying psychoanalysis (p.8) as, "with the increasingly fragile exception of literary criticism, the only branch of the human sciences which even begins to recognize the existence of the human imagination in all its emotional complexity," although by p.496 he is dismissing Freud himself as unnecessary reading.

With the object of keeping Freud in the canon of the humanities, the far subtler French scholar Sarah Kofman makes the point that Freud's intricacies need defending, and might have been defended had he himself chosen to present himself as a writer. "Reasons of strategy could have made [Freud] claim the title of novelist: the notion of the 'analytic novel' could be an inevitable weapon against the dogmatism of those new believers whose adherence to psychoanalysis becomes a new catechism" (*Freud and Fiction*, 1991, p.5).

Kofman's observation of what Freud was up against is exactly right. Webster worships evolutionary biology, while Frederick Crews has transferred his religious worship of psychoanalysis to worship of Science *sive* the Great Goddess of Rigour. This moves him to denounce any branch of learning which retains Freudian concepts as either a backwater or benighted by fashion. "Freudian concepts retain some currency in popular lore, the arts, and the academic humanities, three arenas in which flawed but once modish ideas, secure from the menace of rigorous testing, can be kept indefinitely in play" (*The Memory Wars*, 1997, p.34). Freud saw through those who clung to science like a religion (SAI 72, SE15 50).

Harold Bloom on the other hand in *The Western Canon* (1994) includes Freud's *Introductory Lectures on Psychoanalysis* and should have added *The Interpretation of Dreams* and *The Psychopathology of Everyday Life*, the latter which has long been sidelined as not part of the scientific body of the work, to his humanizing list.

The more interesting feature of Webster's position is that he picks up the fashionable critique of the Enlightenment as "instrumental reason" and accuses Freud of being part of this general forcing of life down unnatural paths. Compare his reference to the movement of ideas "from the Enlightenment to Stalin" (pp.443–5) and his insistence (p.475 and p.491) that Freud's system is a rationalization of the non-rational. D.H. Lawrence in *Psychoanalysis and the Unconscious* (1921) was amongst the first to vent rage (p.247) on what he saw as psychoanalysis forcing itself upon nature.

Kofman paints the wider and more intelligent picture when she writes, "Freud's gesture is related to the gesture of mastery which is symptomatic of philosophy, and a gesture Aristotle inaugurated by making myth the infancy of philosophy.'

Both of these views however should be measured against a notion of earlier and later Freuds. The Freud of the 1920s and

1930s was a spokesman for reason as the best guide we have to civilized human behavior. But he was always mindful of civilization's victims, including himself, and the great interest of his work as it has flourished particularly in France in the last fifty years stems from his codification of the non-rational as the devices and designs of the unconscious, mostly in their effect on language. These ideas were formulated by the earlier Freud of 1895–1917. They were never repudiated and Freud in old age continues to see the irrational as undermining the rational personality. But the experiences of the First World War and the rise of Hitler and anti-Semitism in Germany make it obvious why civilization at this moment of crisis needs to be supported by a conscious appreciation of its rationalizing ways.

NOTES TO *Chapter 1* **Beginnings**

1 *Briefe* (16.6.1873), p.5. Webster (p.205) picks up the strong desire for wealth and fame which both Clarke and Peter Gay, *Freud: A Life for Our Time*, observe in their subject.

2 "The Dynamics of The Transference": SA *Ergb.* 167, SE12 108; "Dora": SAVI 183, SE7 119; SA *Ergb.* 167, SE12 108; SA *Ergb.* 209, SE12 149; SAX 56, SE9 59. Freud sees psychoanalytic meaning as unfolding like a play.

3 Crews, *The Memory Wars* (1997), p.35, finds "a rapidly growing number of independent scholars...showing us a different Freud, darker...highly cultivated, sophisticated...but quite lacking in the empirical and ethical scruples that we would hope to find in any responsible scientist...Now we are beginning to discern a notably wilful and opportunistic Freud [who used] devious rhetorical maneuvers that disarmed criticism..." The former professor of English who thinks rhetoric can be accused of being devious may also have taken a step towards darkness by abandoning the dictionary.

    With his agenda Crews finds it most useful to lay at Freud's door the perceived shortcomings of psychoanalysis as a movement and a profession, and especially the Recovered Memory industry, which for a decade in the United States allowed adult children to accuse their parents of sex crimes on the flimsiest grounds of assisted memory. The movement's successes in conjunction with a defective legal system led to false imprisonments and destroyed lives which Crews's book quite rightly deplores. But the blame does not lie with Freud, who endowed humanity with the sharpest critical tools to deal with the recurring phenomenon of witch-hunting.

Webster's work is far superior to Crews," but there is a similar temptation to conflate Freud and the fate of psychoanalysis for evaluation purposes (p.3, pp.9–10) and to find Freud at fault (p.362) because psychoanalysis looks like a messianic cult, which would also make it an image of his perceivedly messianic personality. Webster bemoans Freud's moral shiftiness (p.132) as a scientist without taking into consideration his thorough awareness of the *problem* of self-deceit and what he has to say about it in *The Interpretation* and *The Psychopathology*. Then again he speaks (p.275) of Freud's analysis on occasions being "fraught with a quite extraordinary moral severity" and objects (p.318) to his use of the notion of evil. As a tolerant, liberal, laid-back, cool, populist and anti-confrontational figure, Freud evidently falls short.

4 SAII 466, SE5 484

5 Freud suggested that the moral principles and religious precepts imposed by society on the individual often caused harm, even spoilt lives, by stopping people from identifying their real needs. He saw that this was particularly the case with the sexual hypocrisy which characterized life in late-nineteenth-century Vienna. And so his social commitment to unmask the disguises of cultures, including "deep" and "shallow," took shape. Against Webster (p.212) and Masson, whom he cites, Freud's compassion underlying this project seems to me evident throughout his writing – see for instance

the concluding two pages of his essay "The Future Prospects of Psychoanalytic Therapy" (1910).

Judaeo-Christianity made "depth" a virtue because it required cultivation and discipline but for Freud the effects of that discipline called culture were most of the problem he encountered in his work as a soul doctor. The primacy of intensity as a quantitative force allowed him to dismiss the classical distinction between "deep" and "shallow" feeling as redundant. But Nietzsche saw the revolution coming a generation before and was also more radical in proposing to do away with the inner/outer distinction which Freud retained:

> As Democritus transferred the concepts Above and Below to infinite space, where they make no sense, so philosophers in general transfer the concept "inner and outer" to the essence and phenomena of the world; they believe that profound feelings take one deep into the interior, close to the heart of nature. But such feelings are profound only in so far as when they occur certain complex groups of thoughts which we call profound are, scarcely perceptibly, regularly aroused with them; a feeling is profound because we regard the thoughts that accompany it as profound. But a profound thought can none the less be very distant from the truth, as, for example, every metaphysical thought is; if one deducts from the profound feeling the element of thought mixed in with it, what remains is the *strong* feeling, and this has nothing to do with knowledge as such, just as strong belief demonstrates only its strength, not the truth of that which is believed. [*Human All Too Human*, "Of First and Last Things," Section 15, p.19]

Nietzsche used his insight immediately to dynamite the institutions of religion and philosophy which claimed depth, and therefore moral authority, over humanity. Freud continued the task of befriending the world "close to hand."

The effect of Freud's "anti-depth" crusade may be called postmodern because it effectively demotes the thinking world in favor of the body.

6 SAII 204, SE4 192; GWXIV 36, SE20 11

7 GWXIV 84, SE20 57; *Briefe an Fließ* (2.4.1896) p.190. "As a young man I had no other longing apart from that for philosophical understanding, and now I am about to fulfill it in moving over from medicine to psychology. I became a therapist against my will; I am convinced I can heal hysterical and compulsive neuroses, given certain conditions of the individual and the case." Similar sentiments are expressed on p.165 (1.1.1896).

8 Freud denied he was a philosopher in the same way as he denied he was an artist. He practiced both activities behind the front of psychoanalysis. The extent to which Freud's whole system is an investigation of the ways of deception, and the way, with the invention of the unconscious, he installs deception as the automatic process at the heart of man, suggests that self-deception was Freud's chief problem in facing the world.

9 Richard Wollheim, *Freud* (1991), provides (pp.20–4) a classic account of the influence of one "great man" on another. Webster (pp.312–13) counters that Charcot propagated "a basic medical misconception" with the concept of the "pathogenic unconscious" which Freud swallowed unskeptically. What we owe therapeutically to Freud's encounter with Charcot, however, is a far broader sense of illness, including psychosomatically caused "illness," which is essentially compassionate, even though it may have a decadent effect on society to extend the boundaries of "illness" so widely.

   As for Freud's reservations about hypnosis, Crews continues his negative picture of a disingenuous scientist (p.273) by stressing Freud's lack of personal skill as a hypnotist, and accusing him of bullying patients rather than coaxing them into playing an active role. As many have pointed out, Socrates, with a theory of knowledge founded on awakening lost memories, was also a "bully" and certainly not a liberal pedagogue.

10 John Huston's *Freud* (1961) was later subtitled "The Secret

Passion," to refer to Freud's discovery of infant sexuality. Jean-Paul Sartre wrote two scripts, but eventually asked for his name to be dropped from the credits. With sensual lips, bright eyes, fine hands and absolute integrity, Montgomery Clift plays a Christlike figure who overcomes a problematic relationship with his father and his Jewish heritage and finally makes the lame to walk.

Sartre and Huston were stimulated by the first publication of the Freud/Fließ letters in 1950, which in turn accentuated the intensity of Freud's years of self-analysis leading up to *The Interpretation of Dreams* and on to the case-studies and the works on love and on the unconscious. The film demands intense emotional and almost physical involvement from the audience and attention to the interpretation of every spoken word. It opens and closes by drawing attention to the ancient and quasi-biological problem of the way human vanity diverts us from the truth about ourselves. A score by Jerry Goldsmith emphasizes mystery, though the music "as if from another planet" isn't bold enough to be atonal.

11 GWXIV 52, SE20 27

12 Brentano taught Hume's mechanical view of perception and then added his own development of the argument. For Hume perception was a matter of accumulated impressions and ideas. Impressions are immediate experiences, and have great vivacity; the vivacity however fades as these experiences are stored as ideas, and is only reawakened by memory or, as those who read on in Hume's *Treatise of Human Nature* know, by art. Brentano's experiment with far and near lights, and the impression they leave on the mind of their brightness, or *vivacity*, or *intensity*, suggests that this theory interested him very much, and also that he came, as he thought empirically, to disagree with Hume, and to suggest that intensity doesn't fade; it remains influential; it is there in store, ready to go to work. Although Brentano's actual experiment, which showed that older, stronger associations prevailed over newer ones over the

course of time (McAlister, ed., *The Philosophy of Brentano*, p.37), doesn't seem to prove anything except a point about optics, how it might have inspired Freud is evident.

With the invention of *unconscious* memory, Freud would give the fullest account of how the intensity attached to our past perceptions gets stored as part of our mental equipment for the future. It is stored in the form of intentional energy as *Sachbesetzungen* (*The Unconscious*: SAIII 160, SE14 201). The coinage comes from *Sache* = thing and *Besetzung* = interest, occupying force, energy charge. Strachey translates it as cathexis. The unconscious is thus primary, in that it conditions the way we apprehend the present. For Derrida this entails Freud in overturning the entire prevailing metaphysics of *presentness* in Western thought.

> That the present in general is not primal, but, rather, reconstituted, that it is not the absolute, wholly living form which constitutes experience, that there is no purity of the living present — such is the theme, formidable for metaphysics, which Freud, in a conceptual scheme unequal to the thing itself, would have us pursue. This pursuit is doubtless the only one which is exhausted neither within metaphysics nor within science. [Derrida, "Freud and the Scene of Writing," in *Writing and Difference* (1978), p.212. Also quoted in Horden, ed., *Freud and the Humanities*, p.9]

13 Brentano's thesis of "not knowing what we know" strains what can be tested. Inner perception of what we know cannot be observed. Memory can be observed but is too unreliable to produce anything more than speculation about the truth of what is known (McAlister, ed., p.85). Brentano's problem in calling all his work empirical and founded in the methods of the natural sciences is inherited by Freud. Freud's therapy of anamnesis, or what can be recovered from the unconscious to enhance self-knowledge, rests on an immediately questionable truth footing. The affinity with Plato's theory of knowledge as

recovered memory has a certain bookish appeal, the more so as Freud seems to complete the ancient picture by adding in the notion of unconscious resistance to explain away persistent ignorance, but this affinity is no proof of anything but the continuation of a powerful myth. The "Memory Wars" would never have happened had the world been philosophically more literate. On the other hand, the temptation to give memory some status alongside confirmed fact would not lead well-intentioned therapeutic practitioners so far astray if Brentano's understanding could become generally accepted, that *there can be mental objects which exist in the mind but not in the world.*

14 This is the basis for Freud's theory of repression. Repressed ideas become known to us in disguised form as dreams or symptoms. We don't know them as themselves until analysis has shown us that they are there mixed up in our behavior and feelings. Intensity can often come out, disguised or displaced, in the semblance of passivity which actually masks a high degree of neurotic activity (SAI 79, SE15 59).

15 McAlister, ed., p.118. Another contributor to this excellent volume sets out the theory like this (pp.71ff.):

> Studying the mental phenomenon or the mental act means, first of all, emphasizing its essential characteristic, that is, according to Brentano, its relation to an object ...It was always his fundamental thesis in psychology: to think means to think of something ...The *Psychology [from an Empirical Standpoint]* of 1874 was a conscious attempt to revive a doctrine which dates back to the Scholastics, and even further back, to Aristotle. Like Scholastic philosophy it deals with intentional existence or a mental existence of the object in the mind. In his later years, Brentano dropped the expression "intentional existence" because he refused to attribute an existence to a thought-of object. But he always believed that an act of thinking is characterized by the relation to an object ...something in the terms of this relation must always

be something real, a thing which does not mean however that it must always be something that exists.

Intentional (in)existence gives Freud's thinking a Hegelian feel, for the state in which things are real to the mind but do not exist in the world resembles the negative moment in the life of a concept, when its effect is suspended or *aufgehoben*.

16 Proust, *In Search of Lost Time* (1992), Vol. II, p.61 (*Within a Budding Grove*, Part 1): "Let us then declare whether, in the communal life that is led by our ideas in the enclosure of our minds there is a single one of those that makes us most happy which has not first sought, like a real parasite, and won from an alien but neighboring idea the greater part of the strength that it originally lacked."

17 Freud fathered many cultural children. The self-help manual is one of them. *Power, Success and Greatness* and *How to Win Friends and Influence People* come to mind, but still more so Stephen Potter's *One-Upmanship*. The *One-Upmanship* books are manuals of well-guarded appearances, especially in the Freudian target areas of sex, money and honor, which one can turn to one's own advantage with a little psychological agility. Bluff and disguised aggression are two good means to coming out on top. The spirit of self-help is epitomized in these books – suspended, as Nietzsche might have said, in a *moraleinfrei* solution of determination and ambition. More opportunism than conscientiousness is the motive force, more journalism than art is the level. Something of this spirit went to make up the evasive Freud, economical with the truth, who wanted power, and the power a well-shored-up reputation brings.

18 GWXIV 36, SE20 12

19 Freud remembered it as two years, which Gay (p.43) shows to be a slip. Freud waited only one year, but evidently felt the burden so greatly.

20 GWXIV 40, SE20 16

21 Webster (pp.46–7 and p.50), otherwise judiciously playing off what others have seen as Freud's "mendacity" against his preference for detecting "some process of rationalization" on Freud's part, does not mention the cocaine regrets which recur over and over in Freud's dreams. Webster's partial exoneration (p.151) that Freud succumbed to self-deception on a vast scale but that he wasn't conscious of it is still not right. Crews (p.39) is all the more wrong to say that it would have been out of character for Freud to worry about destroying lives and that he didn't care, except from a public-relations angle, whether his patients improved as a result of his treatment. Freud, who believed in the professional value of being economical with the truth, only didn't confess his anxieties directly. This deep regret over a patient who died, therefore, is expressed in a footnote to *The Psychopathology* (GWIV 162, SE6 146).

During the days when I was first writing these pages the following almost incredible case of forgetting happened to me. On January 1st I examined my notes so that I could send out my bills. In the month of June I came across the name M—l, and could not recall the person to who it belonged. My surprise increased when I observed from my books that I treated the case in a sanatorium, and that for weeks I had called on the patient daily. A patient treated under such conditions is rarely forgotten by a physician in six months. I asked myself if it could have been a man – a paretic – a case without interest? Finally a note above the fee received brought to my memory all the knowledge which strove to elude it. M—l was a fourteen-year-old girl, the most remarkable case of my latter years, a case which taught me a lesson I am not likely ever to forget, a case whose upshot gave me many painful hours. The child became afflicted with an unmistakable hysteria, which quickly and thoroughly improved under my care. After this improvement the child was taken away from me by the parents. She still complained of abdominal pains which had played the part in the hysterical symptoms. Two months later she died of sarcoma of the abdominal glands. The hysteria, to which she was greatly predisposed, took the tumor formation as a provocative agent, and I, fascinated by the tumultuous but harmless manifestations of hysteria, overlooked the first sign of the insidious and incurable disease.

"Perhaps it is a consequence of my work with psychoanalysis that I can hardly lie any more" (*Psychopathology*: GWIV 247, SE6 221) still seems bold! Strachey's translation is marginally softer than the original, which I have rendered directly.

22 SAII 126ff., SE4 106ff.

23 SAII 131, SE4 111

24 Gay, p.84

25 SAII 328, SE4 332

26 Gay, p.156. Fließ's periodicity theory also formed part of the controversy with Weininger and Swoboda. *Briefe an Wilhelm Fließ* (1986), p.504.

27 Gay as above and also pp.95–6

28 GWIV 159–60, SE6 144

29 SAII 426, SE5 441

30 Crews, *The Memory Wars*, pp.40–1, writes: "Rice [*Dostoevsky and the Healing Art*; *Freud's Russia: National Identity in the Evolution of Psychoanalysis*] understands, however, that nihilism and spiritual extremism in general had another strong correlate in Freud's imagination: Russia. Freud's family roots lay in Lithuania, where he retained many kin, and where his imagination turned when he thought, as he continually did, about the persecution of the Jews and about their efforts to strike back. Up to the early years of Stalin's rule, Rice shows, Freud thrilled to revolutionism and looked to Russia for a political equivalent to his own assault on the tyranny of the despotic superego." Rice's comments and corrections (p.136) rightly stress Freud as generally skeptical and

ironic towards all political and religious authority but deny he was a disillusioned revolutionary.

31 SAII 218ff., SE4 208ff.

32 SAII 420, SE5 434

33 Note 3: SAII 226, SE4 218

34 in the speech in receipt of the Goethe Prize in 1930

NOTES TO *Chapter 2* **The Artist**

1 See for example the early article on "psychic treatment" (*Psychische Behandlung* (1890): *Ergb* 17, SE7 283). In fact, Freud was interested in words as such, in their etymology, in the use of language, and in the interaction of several languages. But this is a different point, to do with words acting as repositories for a whole history of meaning, and thus opening the door to the collective and the individual unconscious. This is Freud at his wildest and most exciting, generating a poetic critical literature which plays with split meanings and trick languages. See Chapter 8. It is where, *unconsciously*, he comes closest to being an artist himself, strutting about on the most unlikely territory.

But Freud's official position is that the artist is a man *unlike* himself.

2 Freud uses the word *Dichter* in the essay "Der Dichter und Das Phantasieren." This has been variously translated as "The Writer and Creative Imagination," "The Artist and Daydreaming" and "Creative Writers and Daydreaming." Both terms are difficult, because *Dichter* applies equally to poet, playwright and novelist, while *Das Phantasieren* can apply both to fantasy and to imagination in English, and thus cover a range of such activity which is wider than art itself. Daydreaming can be random or willed but there is more purposiveness and structure and an element of heightened consciousness in fantasy as play. Again Freud's use encompasses both. He also

adds in his view that most adults are ashamed of daydreaming/fantasizing. Fantasies can be the beginning of neuroses or psychoses, according to "Der Dichter und Das Phantasieren" (SAX 175, SE9 148), and one remembers the fashionable nineteenth-century worry that novels were bad for the health of young women. The energy in us which does not find a simple sexual discharge fuels introversion. On the other hand, all of us have wishes that are not fulfilled. Only when fantasy takes over the whole job of providing satisfaction, and the individual can no longer distinguish between fantasy and reality, do problems begin. (Cf. SAI 364, SE16 373.)

The point about *Dichter* is discussed by Gay (pp.307ff.). In the *Introductory Lectures* quoted below, Freud uses *Der Künstler*, which is also a general word for "artist," including writers and painters. The important qualities of the *Dichter/Künstler* from Freud's point of view seem to be those deriving from Plato's distinction between creators of *mythos* as opposed to *logos*. Freud as a scientist would see himself working in the tradition of *logos*, though there are times, as in "*Dora*" (SAVI 133, SE7 60) when he explicitly wishes he could cross the line, and "simplify and abstract" to make a better picture.

3   SAI 366, SE16 376. Strachey's literal version of the second paragraph ends by speaking of "a certain degree of laxity in the repressions which are decisive for conflict," but the sense of the German is hardly clear. This is one reason why although we have heard a great deal about neurosis and its cure we have never come to idealize the loosely packed soul as we should, though perhaps this is what was originally meant by having no hangups. Our free-moving "insides" don't get caught on anything for long.

In the third paragraph Freud writes *jeder Entbehrende*. I have kept the active voice. Strachey's passive "everyone suffering from some deprivation" makes for smoother English but loses Freud's point that neurotics are actively, though unconsciously, contributing to their own lack of satisfaction in life.

The word in the fifth paragraph is *Lustgewinn*, which Strachey translates as "a yield of pleasure." The idea is of a gain or profit or something extra and the word belongs to the vocabulary of early nineteenth-century utilitarianism and hedonism, with their concern to maximize general pleasure and minimize pain. When repressions are overcome and their effect suspended Freud uses the Hegelian term *aufgehoben*. See Chapter 1, note 15.

4 SAX 179, SE9 153

5 This makes a nice contrast with Stendhal's definition of beauty in *De l'Amour* as the promise of happiness.

6 Both Freud and Schiller before him believed primitive peoples had more freedom to *play* compared with modern self-conscious man, and Freud thought children were born with the original phylogenetic capacity. Freud pursues one of his anthropological fantasies here, and flirts with presenting a Rousseauistic ideal as a real event in the past (cf. Gay, p.326). Yet the idea that human beings benefit from a temporary release from the imperious demands of moral judgement and the factual nature of reality remains important. Schiller's ideal is of the personality maintained as far as possible by the *Spieltrieb* or the drive to play. When the drive to play is active, the force of moral and scientific imperatives is suspended or *aufgehoben*. In his essay *On Jokes and Their Relation to the Unconscious* Freud speaks of the *Aufhebungslust* of telling jokes, by which he means the pleasure of getting rid of a secret tension inside which has built up because of personal feelings in conflict with social taboos. He translates Schiller's Kantian aesthetics into the quantities of a mechanical view of the psyche and marries it to a vision of hedonism as man's natural way. What remains of the *Spieltrieb* is the possibility of regression from adulthood to a world in which a child's freedoms and pleasures are once again permitted, or can at least be covertly enjoyed. Regression happens in dreams, in delusion, and evidently also resembles the

freedom from the constraints of a familiar reality and the potential creative stimulus which drugs like opium can bring.

7   Here and below Freud marries the language of utilitarian hedonism to the language of Darwinism. *Prämie* is the Latinate equivalent of *Gewinn* and both point to the idea of a reward, bonus or premium. They are of course expressions of a capitalist economy within the body.

8   SAX 179, SE9 153. The temptation built into dreams to go on dreaming and fear that the dream might end is expressed in the *Gradiva* essay and modified in *Hemmung, Symptome und Angst* (1926), "Inhibitions, Symptoms and Anxiety."

9   Sebastiano Timpanaro, a Marxist who makes a linguistic analysis of *The Freudian Slip* (1976), pinpoints one of the central tensions in Freud: "An initially materialist and hedonist inspiration was so to speak 'smothered' by a social and cultural conditioning which then produced an idealist regression" (p.192). But regression into idealism is not necessarily bad from a non-Marxist point of view.

The influence of Darwin has been dismissed by Helena Cronin as amounting to "no more than a ragbag of pickings" in her review of Lucille B. Ritvo *Darwin's Influence on Freud*, *Daily Telegraph* 12.1.91. But Darwin is surely the essential background to Freud's whole enterprise in exploring why, given the biological need, we are so often unsuccessful in expressing our sexuality. For Freud culture inhibits the biological drive and as a result neuroses form. On the one hand neuroses are a form of adaptation. They stop further damage. They generate substitute satisfactions for our thwarted needs. But they also cause harm.

When Freud looks at how the artist delivers himself from potential neurosis the influence of Darwin is even more apparent. The artist through his work offers a *Verlockungsprämie*, which is bait with the promise of a reward of pleasure to come. Towards reader or spectator, through his creativity, he behaves like a peacock male luring a mate. Freud does not draw this last analogy at the end of the 23rd Introductory Lecture, but moves straight from the idea that the artist deals in "forepleasure" to the apparent observation that the successful artist does not want for lovers, nor wealth, nor respect. The artist, who is essentially a charmer and a master of self-disguise, is the most successful, best adapted man in present cultural circumstances.

Freud's fascination with disguises, and his understanding of neurosis as unconscious disguise, and art as conscious disguise, should surely be seen alongside Darwin's views on animal need and display.

10 This sounds like the myth and perhaps reality of a Victorian husband overcoming his wife's sexual fears on their wedding night. Freud was keen to end sexual ignorance as a source of ill-health, and for art to keep the secret passions company where no human company could reach. At the same time, disguise has an obvious connection with Freud's later theory of sublimation as essential to civilization.

11 SAX 292, SE21 208

12 SAX 173, SE9 146

13 SAX 171, SE9 143. In one way this desire "reduces" to the desire to be charming, as charming as art can be in securing its audience with something like an erotic promise of pleasure. But the effect is to open up our sense of Freud's complex personal input into his theories of artistic power, psychic health and success. Personally, Freud was always afraid that his writing lacked charm, yet experience taught him that his writing, but especially his public speaking, could be spellbinding. Evidently he could also charm some patients. In theory the desire and readiness to charm others is a sublimation of our egoism, and the desire to be charmed a casting off of narcissism. A character stuffed with Freudian charm seems to be Thomas Mann's Felix Krull (*Confessions of Felix Krull, Confidence Man*, 1954).

14 Lionel Trilling, *Freud and the Crisis in Our Culture* (p.15). When the loss of high culture in general becomes apparent to nostalgic critics of the present generation like Hilton Kramer the new world seems to be "devoid of inhibition, formality and other impediments to the unfettered expression of the self." Quoted by Kenneth Minogue, reviewing Kramer's *The Twilight of the Intellectuals* (1998), *Times Literary Supplement*, 30 April 1999, p.7. The link with Freud is not made, but all these social phenomena, and their equivalents in art, can be seen as a mixture of desired and unintended consequences of Freud's therapeutic vision.

15 SAX 176, SE9 150. Clarke (p.35) underscores Freud's affection for lightweight literature. His early fascination with *La Dame aux camélias* and with the way even lightweight art can point gratifyingly to a different morality from the one society officially upholds is evident in a letter to Eduard Silberstein, *Briefe* (22.8.1874), p.10. If poetry does its work, moral judgement is suspended.

16 *Human All Too Human*, "From the Souls of Artists and Writers," sections 222, 223, pp.105–6

17 Lieberman, *Acts of Will* (1985), p.282

18 In an essay, "The Prehistory of Psychoanalytic Technique," 1920 (SA *Ergb.*, SE18), Freud cites a letter from Schiller to Körner, in the form of advice on how to suspend judgement in order to let the creative ideas flow. As both a poet and philosopher, Schiller was exceptionally aware of the mental shifts that had to be made from one to the other realm, and he advocated free association. His advice was think whatever; just let the thoughts flow. Rank brought this passage to Freud's attention, and he used it in several of his works and letters. But the other important source for psychoanalysis in creative writing was the technique of free association or *freier Einfall*. When Freud was fourteen he received as a present Ludwig Börne's *How to be a Writer in Three Days*. This was a four-page essay advocating free association to liberate the mind, and any

trip to the library today would produce the same standard advice, enshrined in one of those diagrams where you write your topic in the middle and everything that occurs to you round about, and afterwards link them with arrows. Freud was there at the beginning of mass self-help-for-would-be-writers, acting first as a bridge between Schiller and Börne, and then between Börne and the present day. He took a classic-become-popular technique for liberating the pen, and applied it to the whole personality. Since then creative writing has clawed back material from psychotherapy in general, much of which was implicit in Freud's position, and echoed his own interest in the creative personality. Most recently a book which says of itself that it "helps demystify the creative process by making it part of your daily life" (Julia Cameron, *The Artist's Way*, 1992) has sold more than one and a quarter million copies.

NOTES TO *Chapter 3* **Self-Revelation**

1   GWIV 194–5, SE6 175–6

2   Freud, as has often been observed, was a kind of crime-fiction writer, who also looked at his psychoanalytic cases in those terms. See also his letter to Jung (*The Freud–Jung Letters*, 147F). The marriage that makes his writing creative is a combination of detective-on-the-trail suspense combined with a mechanical theory of psychic energy based on the principle of the constancy of matter. Dorothy L. Sayers' remark (Introduction to *Detection, Mystery and Horror*, 1928, p.27) that "The true detective has a passion for machinery" obviously applies to Freud. We might add that with a passion for puzzles (SA *Ergb.* 82, SE2 289; and *passim The Joke and Its Relations to the Unconscious*) he knows how to create a good trail for other would-be sleuths to follow. In this respect it should also be remembered that dreams resemble those guess what? objects photographed at odd angles, close up and so on. With a bit of twisting and turning one can recognize what the object really is.

3   GWIV 58–60, SE6 49–51

4   Freud develops character-types from childhood attitudes to and experiences of bedwetting and defecation. In "Character and Anal Eroticism" (1908), while the orderly, parsimonious character-type and his or her sexuality is an obvious candidate for analytical scrutiny, the connection with the pleasure of delaying defecation in infancy seems to be an arbitrary association on Freud's part, sparked by the linguistic overlap in which money and defecation commonly share the epithet "dirty." Thus (SAVII 27, SE9 172), "The inner necessity of this connection is of course not transparent to me either..." At the same time Freud links *his* childhood misdemeanor, that wrongful emission of urine, with a character dominated by ambition. The arbitrariness of Freud turning bedwetting, from which he also suffered around the age of two, into a sign of the opposite of his father's prediction is apparent, even while the whole theory reinforces the notion of Freud as an extremely ambitious man, greedy for success. The episode is commented on by Gay (p.23).

5   The Unconscious is above all a release from authority. Jokes and witticisms of all kinds are among its manifestations. GWIV 99, SE6 90.

6   Sexual pleasure *per os* is another euphemism used by Freud. But what an indictment of Crews' inverted prissiness and popularist banality (p.46) that he should replace intercourse *a tergo* with "copulating doggystyle." There must be better things for a professor of English to get up to. Crews (p.296) goes on to expose the "vulgar thematic affinities... residing in Freud's own prurient mind." One wonders would he similarly indict James Joyce and Anthony Burgess? And Shakespeare?

7   SAII 452, SE5 469

8   SAII 423, SE5 438

9   In "Justice, Envy and Psychoanalysis," *Dispatches from the Freud Wars* (1997), John Forrester observes that the uncovered

underlying motive of envy behind an instance of the pursuit of justice illustrates how Freud's theory of the unconscious reduces all motivation to the personal. But the further question to be asked is whether we should read Freud on primary envy as a defeat for the human, or only a standing warning against misplaced self-idealization.

10 According to Webster (p.224), Freud could have been the patient who went to Fließ with migraine because of excessive masturbation, while Otto Rank (Lieberman, *Acts of Will*, pp.112–13) proposed a masturbatory character-type whose characteristics closely fitted Freud. For *Aktualneurosen*, see SAI 374–8 SE16 385–90.

> The symptoms of the immediate neurosis... express themselves not only predominantly in the body... but are also themselves bodily processes, in the origins of which all the complicated mechanisms of the soul which we have come to know [in studying psychoneuroses] play no part.

> A person only falls neurotically ill when his ego has lost the capacity to accommodate his libido somehow.

Crews (p.64) is one who doesn't seem to distinguish between these two categories of neurosis. The distinction is often overlooked, perhaps because the wrong English translation "actual neurosis" is fundamentally unintelligible as the description of another *kind* of neurosis. The prefix "*aktual*" refers to the present moment and for Freud indicates a type of neurosis *without* a childhood etiology. In fact, Freud encouraged masturbation as a temporary solution, for women as well as men, yet always with that "real object" in mind, a real other existence in which to invest our love and desire. He hoped, on behalf of most people, for a "normal" and with that heterosexual relationship. "On Wild Analysis" (1910): SA *Ergb.* 137–9, SE11 223–5.

11 *Zur Gewinning des Feuers*, "The Conquest of Fire" (1932): SAIX 449–54, SE22 187–93

12 In *The Psychopathology*: GWIV 162, SE6 147. Examples he gives of such strategic forgetting include that of fourteen-year-old Matthilde, the patient who died of cancer shortly after he had diagnosed hysteria. See note 21 to Chapter 1.

13 Gay (p.281) writes of projection:

> Projection is the operation of expelling feelings or wishes the individual finds wholly unacceptable – too shameful, too obscene, too dangerous – by attributing them to another. It is a prominent mechanism for example in anti-Semites, who find it necessary to transfer feelings of their own that they consider low or dirty on to the Jew, and then "detect" those feelings in him. This is one of the most primitive among the defenses, and is easily observable in normal behavior, though far less prominent there than among neurotics and psychotics.

14 Quoted in Lieberman, *Acts of Will*, p.127. This letter to Zweig in 1937 was omitted from the collection edited by Ernst Freud.

15 *Freud Zweig Briefwechsel* (8.5.1932), p.51

16 SAVII 51, SE10 177

17 SAII 327, SE4 330. The Freudian dream of course routinely affects this transvaluation of "daytime" values.

18 Proust, *In Search of Lost Time*, Vol. II, p.457 (*Within a Budding Grove*, Part 2): "Inebriation brings about for an hour or two a state of subjective idealism, pure phenomenalism; everything is reduced to appearances and exists only as a function of our sublime self." Dream of Brücke asking him to prepare a cross-section of his own body, SAII 436–9, SE5 451–5; Lessing, *Nathan*, Act IV, Scene 4, quoted in SAIV 87, SE8 92.

19 *Briefwechsel* (13.6.1935), p.118. For Freud's fascination with the magic of numbers, which Fließ helped inspire, see Gay, pp.57–8. Freud's power obsession, and his refusal to have

psychoanalytic terms applied to himself, came out especially in the decline of his relations with Jung. It has been plausibly suggested that the four-to-five-year analysis also guaranteed Freud an income and that he felt proportionally hostile towards deserters who caused him financial insecurity; but the possibility of Freud having a business motive is hardly startling. More interesting is the possibility that the abstinence Freud recommended during analysis derived from the diminution of his own libido during self-analysis (*Briefe an Fließ* [31.10.1897] p.298). This sentence has been mistakenly read out of context as implying Freud had no further personal interest in sex after the age of forty.

20 Lieberman, *Acts of Will*, p.272

21 Letter to Ferenczi (6.10.1910), quoted in *Briefe* (1986), p.xiii. "Since the case of Fließ...this need in me [for the full revelation of my personality] has been extinguished. A portion of homosexual interest has been internalized and used to extend my own self. I have succeeded where paranoiacs fail.'

22 SAII 465, SE5 371. See also, SAII 436–7, 409–12, SE5 451–3, 421–5; and *Über Deckerinnerungen*, "Screen Memories" (1899): GWI, SE3.

23 Harold Bloom's *agon* theory in *The Western Canon* of how culture progresses as a contest with the previous generation evidently owes its origins to Freud. Freud sees Napoleon as having had a Joseph complex (*Freud Zweig Briefwechsel*, p.107 6.11.1934).

24 To Jung (*The Freud–Jung Letters*, 42F) "I have always felt that there is something about my personality, my ideas and manner of speaking that people find strange and repellent, whereas all hearts open to you. If a healthy man like you regards himself as a hysterical type, I can only claim for myself the obsessional type, each specimen of which vegetates in a sealed-off world of his own." Jones (*Freud*, Vol. I, p.117) noted that his subject was

not good at disguising his feelings, nor affecting charm. Having identified his shortcomings, however, Freud still minded when he proved unpopular, and it might be speculated that psychoanalysis as a technique was an attempt to invent a science of charm, using in particular the charm of words.

25 For metapsychology see, "The Unconscious": SAIII 140, SE14 181; and *The Psychopathology*: GWI V 288, SE6 259.

26 Francis Huxley, "Psychoanalysis and Anthropology," in *Freud and the Humanities*, p.146. The later thinker is of course Jacques Derrida.

27 SAI 45, SE15 19. In *Das Unheimliche*, translated as "The Uncanny," Freud spends a chapter demonstrating through etymology that *heimlich/unheimlich* mean both the opposite and the same (SAIV 248, SE17 224). Something can be both familiar and strange or mysterious at the same time. I apply this dual meaning to the notion of becoming strange from oneself. If Freud had not consulted English dictionaries and stuck to their literal offerings for *unheimlich*, Strachey might have chosen a different title, such as "Strangeness."

28 *The Gay Science*, tr. Walter Kaufmann (New York, 1974), pp.34–5 (Second Preface)

29 SAI 291, SE16 293. This revision of the possibility of rationality was Nietzsche's before it was Freud's. Rank, who in my view had great insight into Freud's character, acted significantly when he presented Freud with a collected works of Nietzsche before going abroad. But Freud was reluctant to have to recognize as a mentor a predecessor who only fortuitously shared his thoughts. My sympathy is with Freud here, the self-confessed monomane (*Briefe an Fließ*, p.67), who rightly believed in his own originality and the great significance of his discovering certain secrets of nature for the first time.

30 Goethe is quoted in SAII 158 and 438, SE4 142 and SE5 454. Freud calls both "Dora" and "Schreber" fragments.

31 Webster (p.219) observes that Marie Bonaparte, whose most important role in Freud's life was dually to save the letters to Fließ and arrange Freud's departure from Nazi-run Vienna, planted in Freud's mind the idea of standing on a par with Plato and Goethe. But it is more of a striving for self-understanding through reference to Goethe that comes out of Freud's lifetime writings.

32 GWIV 284, SE6 255. This paragraph, the English of which I have amended with Freud's German alongside, is translated into partial nonsense by Brill, and retains mystifications in Strachey. Brill's unique service to Freud was to use "faulty act" for *Fehlleistung*, the Freudian Slip, in place of Strachey's "parapraxis."

33 *Psychopathology*: GWIV 255, SE6 229

34 SAVII 189, SE12 66

35 *The Freud–Jung Letters*, 288F. Crews' correspondents rebut his attack on Freud, and defend the scientific quality of free association and the heuristic value of psychoanalytic theory (pp.142–6). The problem really is what to do with the degree of subjectivity and intuition Freud puts into his universal theory. For Crews subjectivity *per se* is a dirty word. His love of science reflects the puritanism of the righteous 1990s.

36 *Psychopathology*: GWIV 288, SE6 259

37 Envy is deeply engrained in Freud's system. Compare note 9 above. Because of the effort his work costs him, and because writers seem to get there and beyond him with far less effort, Freud also quite consciously envies writers, instead of simply admiring them as he once did. Cf. *Briefe*, letter to Arthur Schnitzler (8.5.1906), p.266. I suggest translating "pen envy" into German as *Dichterneid*, which oddly sounds like something worth having.

38 Jones, *Freud*, Vol. I, p.116

39 Webster (p.389) presents Freud as in flight from his religious rather than his artistic nature. He writes, "The more [Freud] denied the reality of his religious personality, and the more he tried to represent his own crypto-theological system as a purely scientific construct, the more discomfited he was to see his most prominent disciple [Jung] openly displaying the very religiosity he was suppressing." If Webster is right, then an almost exactly parallel process takes place with regard to the two aspects of himself which Freud rejects. In the case of his artistic nature, he first of all tries to psychoanalyze art out of existence (as he does with religious systems), then he denies the presence of art in himself and his work. His actual work is meanwhile often artistic in character, just as Webster contends it is religious. But elements of paranoiac imagination don't make a religion, unless one views such things the way Freud himself did. Another dissimilarity from Webster's religious scenario is that Freud didn't have any one writer in mind as outdoing psychoanalysis, but *Dichter* in general, whom he described as colleagues and rivals.

40 This fear is expressed repeatedly in the essay on *Gradiva* (SAX 19, 74, 75, SE9 14,81,82), and in the Postlude to the Second Edition (SAX 84, SE9 94) Freud seems to be hammering at the door of art, insisting on knowing where the writer got his material and how he made his story. See also "Dora" (SAVI 132, 139, SE7 59, 68) and "The Wolfman" (SAVIII 133–4, SE17 12–13). The value of the famous pronouncement in the essay on *Gradiva* (SAX 14, SE9 9) is the way it allows Freud to split himself off from art, as a scientist.

Writers are valuable colleagues and their testimony cannot be praised enough, for they know many things between heaven and earth of which our academic learning doesn't yet dream. In the knowledge of the human soul they are far ahead of us everyday folk, because they draw on sources which we have not yet opened up for science.

41 SAX 296, SE21 212. *Ein psychologisches Verhängnis* is literally "a psychological bad fate." Compare also *Totem and Taboo* (SAIX 340, SE13 49), where Freud also expounds his ambivalent attitude to great men.

42 *Briefe an Fließ* (23.3.1900) p.445

43 *Freud and the Twentieth Century* (1958), p.249

44 *Briefe an Fließ*, pp.260–2, 268

45 These destructive similarities which dominated Freud's earlier thinking notwithstanding, Freud's actual remarks on the October Revolution and Bolshevism, in the *New Series of Introductory Lectures in Psychoanalysis* (1933), are marked by the sobriety and wisdom of old age. His rational and skeptical personality coupled with many years of therapeutic experience give Freud great authority as a critical but affirmative spokesman for the society he lives in. What strikes him about Bolshevism is its similarity to religion, in its intolerance and its promise of a better world tomorrow. Its practitioners are men of action, insensitive to real human suffering and unsusceptible to doubt. Against this backdrop the very qualified optimism and scientific skepticism of psychoanalysis make it stand out as the beacon of humanism which it was taken to be in Britain and America in the 1950s. The insights of psychoanalysis also quickly see off the ideas of all conflict being class conflict, and offer a model for the sources of ideology which stresses how little of what we live now comes from the present.

46 Freud's attitude to the authority of science and the greatness of art, as institutions, is as ambivalent as any feeling he claimed to discover in empirical investigation of his own "tribe" or, through the reports of anthropologists, any other. He is conscious of it so far as art is concerned and tells us about it; it also comes out in his dreams. With science however we have to look deeper, for in his own parlance, he introjects the totem, he becomes the authority he has committed himself by his

professional life to respect. Hence his famous secrecy, designed to cover over any cracks which might appear in the professional surface, and even his readiness to lie to enforce a certain image in the public eye; but once again his dreams betray his fears. The authority of science is not to be envied but stands or falls with Freud's own judgement, and diligence, which he knows to be fallible. Examples of retreating into science are SAV 187, SE11 166; and SAI 400, SE16 415. Mahony, *Freud as a Writer* (p.49), considers the art/science duality the primary feature of Freud's style, which he describes as "bilateral, Janus-faced, amphibian..."

47 "On a Particular Type of Object Choice Made by Men": SAV 187, SE11 166

48 I take Buñuel's *The Discreet Charm of the Bourgeoisie* to be a tribute to Freud.

49 Sebastian Gardner, *Irrationality and the Philosophy of Psychoanalysis* (1993)

50 "Beyond the Pleasure Principle": SAIII 225, SE18 15–16

51 Derrida pursues the similarity between Freud and Rousseau in *Of Grammatology*, tr. Gayatri Chakrovorty Spivak (1976), Christopher Norris, *Derrida* (1987), Chapter V, "Rousseau: Writing as Necessary Evil," is a helpful starting-point.

52 *Psychopathology*: GWIV 55, SE6 47

53 *Psychopathology*: GWIV 171, SE6 154–5

54 *The Freud–Jung Letters*, 178J. "Between the Dionysian and the Apollonian... I really don't know which is the lesser evil... must we not love evil if we are to break away from the obsession with virtue that makes us sick and forbids us the joys of life?'

NOTES TO *Chapter 4* **Man of the Soul**

1 Lieberman, *Acts of Will*, pp.36 and 163. The novelist Arnold

Zweig was remorselessly enthusiastic about Freud's art three decades later. Havelock Ellis is quoted (SA *Ergb* 254, SE18 264) "On the Prehistory of Psychoanalytic Technique" (1920). Lieberman (p.l62) and Mahony (*Freud as a Writer*, p.12) pick up from Jones Freud's contention that Ellis was actually trying to undermine his science with this compliment. Otto Rank failed to see the struggle, but otherwise he had great insight into Freud's artistic nature and the place of his work. He realized that with Freud medicine began tunneling down under the domain of art to see what lay beneath it, and exploring the shadow world of the psyche in which all men and women, not just artists, share. Rank didn't see the personal struggle in Freud. He developed in practical terms Freud's vision of an artistically inspired therapy. Whatever it was that made the writer a successful human being as opposed to an unsuccessful neurotic could be taught by the therapist. Lieberman's unique biography traces this development at the centre of Rank's thought. He observes (p.xvi), "Rank wavered like many artists between creative work and wholehearted engagement in living. Finally he resolves the dilemma, saying that creating one's personality, one's life, becomes the artist's task in the post-Freudian world."

2   "On the Aphasias" (1891): SAIII 172, SE14 214. For the link with structuralist poetics, see Dosse, *A History of Structuralism*, Vol. I. More generally Dosse stresses the origins of structuralism in "Western self-hatred" and the consequent desire to destroy the traditional canon by bringing in all the subjects and subject matter which had previously been excluded from serious discourse. The psychology of this position has much in common with Freud's own as a sexually disturbed and sometimes infantile personality and one who has made great efforts to overcome being an outsider. On the stimulus Freud's thinking gave purely to the linguistics out of which structuralism in literary criticism and the social sciences would grow, George Steiner ('Linguistics and Literature," in *Linguistics*

at Large, ed. Noël Minnis, 1973, p.121) observes: "Though initially unaware of the fact, even resistant to it, the psychoanalytic movement was, fundamentally, an exploration of language habits, of the verbal gestures of consciousness; the raw material of the psychoanalytic process is inevitably linguistic. The insights of psychoanalysis into the neurophysiology of mental life remain conjectural; its disclosures in the realm of linguistic usage and taboo, of semantic ambivalence and pathology, are firmly established." Steiner speaks (p.115) of "significance as the exact, determined sum of all linguistic means employed and non-substitutability of any of these means by some unit brought in 'from outside'." This may serve as a comparison with a sentence of Freud's from *The Interpretation of Dreams* (SAII 336, SE5 341):

> The word, as the nexus of multiple representations, is so to speak a predestined multiplicity of meanings, and the neuroses (compulsive ideas, phobias) exploit the advantages which the word offers by way of compression and disguise, no less unabashedly than the dream.

Freud's fundamental interest in aphasia as the way to understanding how words link up with consciousness was taken up especially by Lacan.

3 *Psychopathology*: GWIV 222, SE6 199. This work, except in Brill's abbreviated translation, also contains many examples of plots and characters from literature that Freud has collected.

4 SAIX 27, SE9 198

5 Erich Heller, *The Ironic German*, London, 1958

6 SAX 46–7, SE9 48

7 SAII 160–1, SE4 144–6

8 SAI 379, SE16 391

9 Proust, *In Search of Lost Time*, Vol. I, p.202 (*Swann's Way*, Part 1), "I would still find it there, on one walk after another,

always in the same helpless state, suggesting certain victims of neurasthenia, among whom my grandfather would have included my aunt Léonie, who present year after year the unchanging spectacle of their odd and unaccountable habits, which they constantly imagine themselves to be on the point of shaking off but which they always retain to the end; caught in the treadmill of their own maladies and eccentricities, their futile endeavors to escape serve only to actuate its mechanism, to keep in motion the clockwork of their strange, ineluctable and baneful dietetics. Such as these was the water-lily, and reminiscent also of those wretches whose peculiar torments, repeated indefinitely throughout eternity, aroused the curiosity of Dante, who would have enquired about them at great length and in fuller detail from the victims themselves had not Virgil, striding on ahead, obliged him to hasten after him at full speed, as I must hasten after my parents."

10 SAI 273, SE16 273; SAVII 16, SE9 121

11 GWVIII 21, 52, SE11 24, 48 ('On Psychoanalysis')

12 SAI 277, SE16 277–8

13 GWVIII, SE 11 ('On Psychoanalysis')

14 SAI 52, 248–70, SE15 27–8, SE16 246–71

15 Freud uses nouns and adjectives prefixed by *über*– (meaning over– or super– or extra–). SAV 233 (*Übergüte, Übergewissen-haftigkeit*), SE12 307; SAII 462, 464 (*Überängstlichkeit*), SE5 479,482; SA *Ergb.* 130 (*Überzärtlichkeit*), SE11 148; SAI 261, SE16 260

16 SAIII 141, SE14 182

17 SAIII 142, SE14 183–4

18 SAIII 142–3, SE14 183–4; SAI 262, SE16 261; GWIV 180, SE6 163

19 GWIV 199, 192, SE6 180, 174. Brill's translation (*Psycho-*

pathology of Everyday Life, Harmondsworth, 1938, p.124), "a report... which gives some insight into the mechanism of damaging things," strikes the right note of generality, i.e. what happens psychologically when we damage things accidentally. Strachey speaks misleadingly of "the mechanism of *a case of material damage.*"

20 SAIII 142–3, SE14 183–4; SAI 259, SE16 258. For the limited degree to which something can be done about this lack of self-knowledge, see SAIII 151, SE14 192. This theme from the 1915 essay "The Unconscious" is taken up in "The Ego and the Id" (1923), SAIII 286–7, SE19 17–18.

21 GWIV 65,79,97–8, SE6 57, 70, 88–9. Brill (p.70) includes some good examples of his own, e.g., "While writing a prescription for a woman who was especially weighed down by the financial burden of the treatment, I was interested to hear her say suddenly: 'Please do not give me *big bills*, because I cannot swallow them.' Of course she meant to say *pills.*" The "it has come to my nose" slip is my retranslation of the *Vorschwein/Vorschein* slip which Strachey renders literally and Brill omits. Freud's examples are mostly amusing anecdotes which can be read as parables teaching us not to take ourselves and our good intentions too seriously. The ideal consequence of such advice would be a more loosely constituted psyche, more conducive to psychic health.

The scientific demolition of the *Fehlleistung*: Timpanaro argues in a fine, rich and provocative book that Freud universalizes situations which are specific to one class and one time. What Timpanaro fails to see, I think, is that the *Fehlleistung* is only one instance in time of the way repression can always affect behavior and speech. If one were to take an example of a very different society from bourgeois Vienna, Communist Central Europe, it would surely be possible to show that as a result of collective self-censorship and historical forgetfulness practiced on an individual basis as the means to survival in a repressive society, bizarre unintentional blunders were made. A continuous symptom was the way the citizens of those countries occupied by the Russians in the name of friendship rarely managed to remember the Russian language they learned for thirteen years in school. Timpanaro fails to read Freud as a writer interested above all in the irony of the human situation, and the way it is reflected in the use of language. Driven by "scientific" Marxism, he attacks Freud's wild use of etymology to show "scientifically" that the same words originally meant opposite things, and his fondness for unbounded linkages by association. Timpanaro's position has been rendered ironic today now that Marxism looks no more scientific than Freudism though the intelligence of his book survives. In particular Timpanaro was right to attack Freud's idea that the unconscious is polyglot. Quite the opposite seems to be the case.

22 SAI 259–60, SE16 258

23 GWIV 309, SE6 278. The translation using "surely" is mine. Strachey's English is correct, but the subjunctive in the German is unclear, as it so often must be in English translation.

24 *Mr. Men* series by Roger Hargreaves. Fairy tales were an older form of direct Freudian appeal to children's natural kinship with the subversive.
Fawlty Towers written by John Cleese and Connie Booth, BBC TV, 1975. Cleese is the hysteric given to slapstick visual humor: crying, stamping, spitting, pulling faces, gagging people. Much of the action consists in losing/finding, concealing/revealing, naming/renaming, and also on misunderstanding and mishearing. The verbal humor also exploits taboos such as class and racial prejudices, money and sex, though the latter seems contained to suit a mid-evening television audience. Mr. O'Reilly/Mr. Orally sneaks past in "The Builders" along with a number of other insertions and penetrations obscured by panic, rage, deviousness and blame. "When we were manacled oops! . . . married." "Zoom – that

was your life, mate. Back to the world of dreams." "For the first time in my life I'm ahead, I'm winning," cries a desperate Fawlty in "Mrs. Richards." His guests, like the oratund spoon salesman in "The Hotel Inspector," usually match him in peculiarity. "I have been given an erroneous dish." German-speaking fans should address themselves to Herr Fehler, spend a week at the Hotel Zum Irren, Lower Bewußtsein, and send a few unconsciously encoded *Absichtskarten* about the general atmosphere of *Gastfeindschaft* back to their analist, along with the discovery that Herr Fehlwirt started life in Darmdorf.

The quote from Freud is from *The Interpretation of Dreams*, SAII 160, SE4 144.

25 *Briefe an Fließ* (24.1.97), p.240. "The story of the devil, the common people's lexicon of curses, the songs and customs of the nursery are all acquiring a meaning for me." For Descartes's exposition of his position see his *Meditations on First Philosophy* (1641).

26 One would want to consider as a case of unconscious "splitting" the projected difference between the actor Woody Allen and the man. SAVII 154, SE12 26–7.

27 Brill omits the quote from *Faust II*, Act V, Scene 5.

28 Freud appeals to those who begin with a conscious sense that they are bad. Anaïs Nin is a real example from her diaries. She went on to be analyzed by Otto Rank. Italo Svevo's eponymous protagonist in *The Confessions of Zeno* (1924, tr. 1930) is an example from fiction, who believes he has found the way to transcend his weakness and indecision by mastering immoralism, or the Freud-inspired capacity for deviousness and mischief. Svevo's view is that Freud creates an excuse, and a set of symptoms which do not exist. See the final chapter headed "Psychoanalysis."

29 Sartre got Freud's view of character quite wrong when he read Freud as positing two minds, with the human person divided.

Gardner, *Irrationality*, is a specialist treatment. With the notion of skeins, familiar from Aristotle, or "discourses" I want to suggest how Freud's dynamic way of conceiving the personality as a living and unruly whole prompts the now familiar idea, especially in writing, of various versions of the same person. This is not, however, the Jekyll and Hyde problem of the same body, different man, or the multiple personality, where one "person" disclaims responsibility for or knowledge of what the others do. Mahony, *Freud as a Writer*, p.49. SAI 370, SE16 382.

30 SAI 364–5, SE16 374

31 SAX 157, SE11 136 ('A Childhood Memory of Leonardo da Vinci'). Compare also *Three Essays on Sexual Theory*, Preface to the Third Edition (1914): SAV 44, SE7 131.

32 SAI 262, SE15 153

33 SAI 418 and 365, SE16 435 and 375. I translate Freud's *Lust/Unlust* as pleasure and pain because Freud is clearly incorporating into his thinking the hedonist utilitarianism of Bentham which consistently figures in German in these terms. Cf. *Historisches Wörterbuch der Philosophie* (Stuttgart, 1980), Vol.5, p. 561: "...alles andere hat Wert nur so weit, als es dem Lustgewinn zuträglich ist." "Nur durch Motive der Lust und Unlust kann auf den Willen eingewirkt werden." And also *Uberwegs Grundriß der Geschichte der Philosophie* (Graz, 1953), Vol.5, p.93: "Jeder Mensch strebt nach Lust, jeder weiß was Schmerz ist. Lust und Unlust bestimmen sowohl was wir tun werden, als was wir tun sollen." As a student of philosophy and a translator of J.S. Mill, Freud would have known this terminology well. Strachey, by using "unpleasure" instead of "pain," fails to set up this reverberation.

34 *Briefe an Fließ* (25.5.95), p.130

35 *Briefe an Fließ* (15.9.95), pp.141–2, (not included in the 1950 edition)

36 Webster, *Why Freud was Wrong*, pp.172–3

37 Sarah Kofman (*Freud and Fiction*, pp.8–19) makes the complex case for Freud *acting* as a philosopher like the post-Socratic Aristotle, imposing new methodology on a science of philosophy which was in its infancy, and yet at the same time *being* like the Presocratics in a vision of the world that leads to the deconstruction of metaphysics and the tradition for which Aristotle laid the foundation. Surely the same could be said for/against Marx, currently under attack for his prosecution of "the Enlightenment project." Marx's dialectical materialism was inspired by one of those Presocratics, Democritus. For Brentano, see notes 12 & 13, Chapter 1, and especially McAlister, p.120. In the language of the medieval Scholastics, the intentionally inexistent object possesses only "imminent objectivity."

38 SAVII 149–50, 157, 199–200, SE12 20–1, 31, 77–9

39 Kant divided knowledge into scientific, moral and aesthetic. The limitations of the human mind meant knowledge of the world would always be imperfect, though Kant believed moral judgement could be absolute. Kant's *Critique of Pure Reason* and *Critique of Practical Reason* were fundamentally absorbed into the tradition of Anglo-American analytical philosophy. But it was Kant's *Critique of Judgement*, published in 1791, which most powerfully affected Continental thinking and continues to designate a separate tradition. Kant described as reflexive, rather than constitutive, judgements about the beauty, wholeness and purpose of the world which neither reason nor moral intuition can verify. Such judgements, which would include religious belief, seem to have both a moral and a factual content, but their unprovability excludes them from science and links them closer to art. But art itself occupies only a small part of the aesthetic realm as Kant defined it.

The German Romantics abandoned Kant's rigorous division of the forms of human judgement. For them philosophy and poetry offered equal access to the higher truth. They emancipated the unconscious and the non-rational as part of an overall quest for truth. In turn, the Romantic philosophical world was the polar opposite of the one into which Freud graduated almost a century later. Freud seems to have been split between a devotion to science, which predominated in an age of positivism, and exasperation with a discipline which marginalized poetry and passion as instruments of true understanding. Specifically the rise of "science" downgraded the unconscious to something of less value and quality than some putative full awareness. Freud thus had to return in spirit to an earlier, broader age for the foundation to carry his new contribution to science forward: to an age when philosophy, art, literature and science were perceived as illustrious close relations. They never ceased jostling with each other, with art supreme for the Schlegels, philosophy on top for Hegel, and the dubious science of dialectical materialism victorious for Marx. But no one ever suggested art and science and philosophy weren't related. Madame de Staël had the wit to realize that these thinkers, from Goethe and Schiller through to Schelling and Hegel, new on a European scene hitherto dominated by French rationalism, were essentially workers in imagination. The world she discovered in 1811 was essentially the world of learning Freud came from, give or take a little mid-century materialism, and it is perhaps the reason why Freud said (*Outline of Psychoanalysis*, GWXVII 129, SE 23 199) that psychoanalysis had "made in Germany written all over it." It is astonishing to read in a work published in London in 1985 (Horden, ed., *Freud and the Humanities*, p.28) that "Freud's indebtedness to nineteenth-century German philosophy is only now becoming apparent."

Another strand in the story concerns the way Kant's description of the nature and scope of the aesthetic judgement was taken up in Freud's day by Hans Vaihinger who recast it as *The Philosophy of As If*. Vaihinger's book achieved great popularity in the German-speaking world after the end of the First World War. Its thesis, that it is possible to live with ideas and beliefs of value, knowing that they are only fictions, Freud incorporated into his 1927 essay on the problem of belief, "The Future of an Illusion" (SAIX 162–3, SE21 28–9). Freud quoted Vaihinger (1922), "We let all that continue as a practical fiction, while as theoretical truth it dies out." But Freud thought the common man, as opposed to the philosopher, could never be content with Vaihinger's solution, and it fell rather to the psychologist to account for strong and persistent non-rational beliefs. The reader will see, however, that critical assessment has since moved Freud's own work to the non-rational realm, and that, as I suggested at the beginning of this book, we are right now being invited to view Freud and Marx as perpetrators of the kind of valuable fictions Vaihinger described. It seems we can do no better than make all our claims to knowledge of the world, including Freud's, subject to Kantian scrutiny. Certainly we should not assume we can get beyond the limitations he established.

40 SAI 86 SE15 67

41 The transmigration of desires helps us home in on the Romantic aspect of Freud's science, which Webster (pp.175–8, 180) treats as negative, while noting that this spiritualist view of nature is rooted in the Judaeo-Christian tradition. His portrait of Freud as "normally portrayed as a child of the Enlightenment, raised in a severely scientific and rationalistic intellectual regime...," but who turns out to be "the intellectual heir of Fechner, a man at once a religious mystic and a messiah," looks naïve and programmatic beside Kofman's careful dissection of Freud's complex position.

42 J. W. von Goethe, *Gedenkausgabe der Werke, Briefe und Gespräche* (Zurich, 1949), Vol. 16, pp.921–6. The translation is mine. *Naturphilosphie* effectively brought Plato and Kant into biology in the late eighteenth century, with the view that reality is entirely organized according to a few basic archetypes, with at its summit a vision of perfection, in which all the world is enjoined. The range of views compatible with this basic-blueprint outlook

ranges from Goethe's *Urpflanze* to Stephen Jay Gould's *Bauplane* (*Oxford Companion to Mind*, p.608).

Webster, attacking Freud's science, fails to grasp the bond, both elected by Freud and validated from without, between Freud and Goethe and to see in it a clue to Freud's peculiarity. His "maternal" reading (p.41 of "On Nature') seems to derive entirely from Ernest Jones. The scientists apart from Darwin who most impressed Freud were Goethe and Leonardo, which gives a clue to his ideal, if repressed, notion of science as straddling the border with art.

43 Freud, of course, stresses the need for disguise, charm and illusion to maintain civilization. His divergence from Goethe sets up the dialectical tension in his whole work.

44 SAII 424–6, also 324 and 433ff., SE5 439–41, SE4 327, SE5 449.The dream of Goethe's Attack was examined in connection with Fließ in Chapter 1.

45 Freud's fear of what Breuer would think is quoted SAV 13, SE3 261.

46 SAI 332, SE16 338

47 SAIX 360–2, SE13 70–2 (*Totem and Taboo*)

48 Mahony, *Cries of the Wolfman*, p.103. Freud shared a fascination with the descent or "katabasis" in literature with Jung (*The Freud–Jung Letters*, 114F, 300J).

49 SAI 154, SE15 142. Whether all human energy was characterized by libido and thus was linked, however broadly, with sexuality, was the bone of contention between Freud, who held this view, and Jung, who dissented (*The Freud–Jung Letters*, 355J). In *On Psychoanalysis* (1909), Freud defends his outlook with the notion that "I use the word sexuality in a far wider sense than you are used to" (GWVIII 48, SE11).

50 GWVIII24, SE11 26

51 Some of Freud's fiercest pronouncements about human nature begin with what dreams censor and end with what emerges in conscious life as crime and the brutality of war. The continuity suggests the human capacity for evil, and how it can be kept partly under control (SAI 153–8, SE15 141–7). But hell is also about perversion (SAI 301–2, SE16 304–5) and guilt. Freud seems to depict in his system the world he recognizes in Sophocles' *Oedipus Rex*. It is one of extreme violence in which human morality is powerless to intervene but where the gods punish men and women for their unconscious desires by burdening them with guilt and driving them to their own destruction. Freud observes that this is of course his thesis in *Totem and Taboo*, that morality and religion begin from the feeling of guilt. See also SAI 326, SE16 331.

The unconscious has no language. For what Lacan added to Freud and how he misrepresented Freud by insisting that the unconscious is structured like a language, see Malcolm Bowie, *Lacan* (1991), pp.47–53.

52 SAI 400, SE16 415

53 For Darwin, see Chapter 4 pp.121–2 and note 9 Chapter 2.

NOTES TO *Chapter 5* **Real Love**

I

1 *The Freud–Jung Letters*, 45J

2 *Anna Karenina* (1873), *Madame Bovary* (1886). The men, Karenin and Charles Bovary, are surely too easily set up as standards of the emotionally real.

3 "Three Essays on Sexual Theory" (1905): SAV, SE7. See also SAV 207–9, SE11 187–90, "On the general devaluation of the love life." The sense that all our loves are substitutes for the original, never-again-attainable parental love sets the Oedipus Complex in an unfamiliar and instructive light. The cultural

damage done to our sensuality through social taboos is always present in Freud, but emerges as a definite preoccupation in the later work, culminating with *Civilization and Its Discontents*.

4   SAVII 42, SE10 163

5   SAI 394, SE16 409; SAV 128, SE7 225. Webster (p.189) writes of what we have called the *Kräftespiel der Seele*: "Freud postulated . . . a whole series of entirely imaginary pathways, diversions, blockages and holes through which sexual excitation supposedly travelled around the body." But the emphasis on imaginary here is surely misleading when experience confirms that lack of any sexual outlet, not to mention lack of a sexual outlet in love, causes the average human being a great deal of psychological pain, and interferes with his or her general social performance and well-being, whether by fostering conscious fears of inferiority, exclusion and guilt, or by provoking an isolation which distorts subsequent social behavior, or by engendering such a strong need to repress all these potent, ever proliferating signs of trouble in order to survive that a degree of illness is reached. It may be that Freud's model is more Heath Robinson than Harvey, but the processes he is trying to map are new to systematic scrutiny. Popper is only one of Freud's scientific critics who didn't rule out that science might one day discover what Freud conjectured.

6   SAII 301, SE4 300. Freud never supposes a neurosis without sexual amnesia. His science or art of memory, however, links him broadly with Plato, for without right memory, and the reactivation in the present of what was once known but is now forgotten, truth cannot be reached. The link to Proust, for whom memory is no guide to truth but serves the emotional enrichment of "those for whom the process of development is purely internal," takes us in the direction of a more personal Freud, absorbed by his own childhood and self-analysis, and discovering the self-sustaining power of imagination in the process. Both these attachments to Freud's name stand out in

stark contrast to the Recovered Memory industry. Recovered Memory embraces the use of an adult patient's therapy-assisted "memories" to incriminate a parent for sexual molestation in the patient's childhood. Crews was right to lash it with his pen, but quite wrong to lay the blame at Freud's door, whether by citing the discarded Seduction Theory or any other passage in Freud.

7 SAV 59, SE7 148

8 SAI 437, SE16 455

9 Nietzsche, *Human All Too Human* (1986), p.319 (Part 2, "The Wanderer and His Shadow," para.37). Freud makes clear his disapproval of contemporary sexual morality, which causes more harm than it is worth (SAI 418, SE16 435).

10 SAV 109, SE7 204. Freud was perhaps building on Brentano's perception of similarities between correct/incorrect intellectual judgement and the emotional sphere of loving and hating. (See Roderick M. Chisholm, "Brentano's Theory of Correct and Incorrect Emotion," in *The Philosophy of Franz Brentano*, ed. McAlister, pp.160ff.) The question is what it is to relate positively to a real or purely mental object, knowing that it exists. Brentano is interested in the moral goodness of this position, whereas Freud concentrates on the question of psychic and physical intensity. He observes that intellectual work brings with it a kind of sexual excitement, and that overwork can be a legitimate cause of mental disturbance in this connection. Presumably disturbance would follow because there is no real outlet for the "noxae" or toxins which Freud believes form in the body with abnormal sexual activity or abstention. One doesn't have to accept this superstitious neurophysiology to appreciate that Freud here alights on a fascinating subject, that of intellectual pleasure, which both delights and frustrates the body which is its carrier. In *The Freud–Jung Letters*, however, he is less than sympathetic to Jung's claim (295J) that "I am not giving out any libido, it is all going into my work," retorting 298F, "You hide behind your religious–libidinal cloud."

11 "Preface to the Fourth Edition" (1920): SAV 46, SE7 134

12 Freud himself is not reductive, but many readings of him are, as they are also psychoanalytically unself-conscious, like the recovered memory practitioners, who seek a way of assuaging a whole society's guilt towards its sexually exposed children, and lovers of science, who pursue a self-deceiving quest for purity. Specifically to counter one line of reductive criticism pursued by Webster (pp.315ff.) and Gellner, Freud was not a spokesman for Original Sin. He begins from the general abnormal condition of man and works towards the more normal, but this abnormality is caused by man's condition in society, not by his possession of a divided self. For Freud, man is not ontologically divided against himself, but given to the unbounded pursuit of pleasure which society must repress. Freud's specific quest, far from being a reprise of Christian self-torment, is a post-Nietzschean quest to lessen the unnecessary burden of loneliness and guilt which a sexually repressive society imposes. It seems more relevant to remember Rousseau and Tolstoy than Swift and Wesley, as Webster does. Webster (p.323) goes on to suggest it is untenable to ask human beings rationally to accept a picture of themselves as degraded and abhorrent beings, but Freud never pushes his terms this far. He asks that we accept an unconscious which supplies us with other motives, less supportive of our rationalistic pride from those which we consciously suppose ourselves to have. To allege, by contrast, that the human being is abhorrent just because his deepest wishes emanate from his unconscious, is to inflict the genetic fallacy on Freud which says we are what we come from. Donald Levy (*Freud among the Philosophers* (1996), p.33) makes clear that to do so is to misunderstand Freud, for his psychoanalytic interpretations are not of this reductive nature. There is a strong moral message in Freud, but it does not reveal itself in condemnation of a human nature which *ought* to be better.

13 With the compassion of a Dickens, Freud attacks Victorian large families and the psychology of the nursery, including

mistreatment by nurses and siblings, and by parents through cruelty and absence and their own psychological shortcomings. SAII 211, SE4 200 depicts a child of a family of six, desperate for love. This line of thought leads to enquiries into "the politics of the family" (R.D. Laing) and "surviving the family" (John Cleese and Robin Skinner), and also to the work of Anna Freud and Melanie Klein. For many it also sexualizes family relationships to a stifling degree, and they would willingly hark back to a world where fathers could passionately love their sons and daughters, as they do in the prelapsarian world of Verdi. Freud's interest in childhood was of his time (*Briefe an Fließ*, 5.11.1897, p.299), as he realized. Others were also working on revealing the world of the child. Meanwhile, anthropology was beginning to work on the childhood of the world, which gave it a great weapon against a society too ready to believe in its own perfection. A.E. Housman observed of Frazer's *Golden Bough*, which gave Freud his anthropological method, "There you have gathered together, for the admonition of a proud and oblivious race, the scattered and fading relics of its foolish childhood, whether withdrawn from our view amid savage folk, or lying unnoticed at our doors" (quoted in Horden, ed., *Freud and the Humanities*, p.131). Freud also revealed an obvious writer's desire to master his childhood through writing.

14 Webster (pp.323–4) admires Freud's "generosity and considerable moral courage" in defending homosexuality and other "perversions" against the bullying of self-righteous moralists and quotes a famous letter in which Freud advises a mother not to worry about her son's homosexuality (*Briefe* (9.4.1935), p.438). But he sees him succumbing to "a harshly demanding moral vision of his own," culminating in the admission to Lou Andreas-Salomé (*Briefe*, 28.7.1929) that (in the translation Webster uses) "In the depths of my heart I can't help being convinced that my dear fellow men, with a few exceptions, are worthless." Against Webster's *bien pensant* position it must be clear that Freud based his life's work on helping human beings.

Nor, *pace* Webster, is it immoral not to admire the human race, only alien to the socialist mentality and not very fashionable. What Freud actually wrote, in a witty, slightly self-deprecatory letter to a highly valued fellow mind from whom he held nothing back, on the same day as he finished *Civilization and Its Discontents*, was that his work could have been far better, and that it must bear the imprint of his stubborn courage in pursuing the truth as well as his feeling that his fellow men were "rabble" (*Gesindel*). The letter does not have the misanthropic bite Webster would like it to have; it is only honest and private. Webster is concerned that Freud sorts the sheep from the goats. What he does insist (SAI 421, 422, SE16 437–8) is that a measure of intelligence makes the process of psychoanalysis easier.

15 "Civilized Sexual Morality and Modern Unease": SAIX 27, SE9 198. This essay contains quoted material on the non-sexual causes of modern nervosity which would seem to lead directly to Thomas Mann's inversion of the *Bildungsroman* in *Buddenbrooks* (1902) with its subtitle "*Verfall einer Familie*." Sarah Kofman sees Freud as nevertheless having written "analytic novels" which *force* the diversity and heterogeneity of the material Freud uncovers into a new dominant form which inflicts on to it an overriding meaning. This, of course, would be normal procedure *if* Freud were a novelist. But the element of force repels the historian of philosophy and psychology, so that once again Freud's reputation as a thinker suffers from his not having chosen the writing way. For his interest in people's family stories, see *Briefe an Fließ* 15.10.97 and 20.6.98.

16 The hysterical pursuit of pedophiles in British newspapers is a ritual acknowledgement of this guilt. I share Freud's dislike for hypocrisy, and Arthur Miller's for witch-hunts.

17 GW 165–6, SE6 149–50. "I thought of the excellent figure of the poor bookkeeper in Alphonse Daudet's *Nabab*...I remembered clearly one of the fantasies, which this man – I

called him Mr. Jocelyn – hatched on his walks along the streets of Paris, and I began to reproduce it in my memory. I remembered that Mr. Jocelyn threw himself bravely against a runaway horse in the street and brought it to a halt. The door of the carriage opened and a distinguished person got out. He shook Mr. Jocelyn's hand and said to him, 'You are my saviour, I owe my life to you. What can I do for you?'" When Freud checks this memory against the text, he finds he has changed the name of the character, whom Daudet called Mr. Joyeuse. Realizing that the masculine form of this adjective for "joyful" perfectly translates his own surname into French (*die Freude* = joy), Freud sees behind the mistake to a possible daydream of his own when he was in Paris. He was lonely and needed a protector during his study year in France with Charcot. A paragraph which Freud withdrew from the text of *The Psychopathology* from 1924 continues by examining Freud's converse conscious wish never to be the protegé, but rather "the strong man." Nor had he ever wanted to be the protected (this is Brill's translation, superior to Strachey's "favorite') child. "The incident is a good illustration of the way in which the relation to one's own self, which is normally kept back but which emerges victoriously in paranoia, disturbs and confuses us in our objective view of things." (This is Strachey's sentence. Brill's is this time barely intelligible.)

The interest of this dream is great for Freud's character – great enough for him to withdraw it once he was under attack for what Webster (p.304) describes as the merging of his messianic personality with the fate of the psychoanalytic movement, in order to strengthen it. Yet he probably was wrong to withdraw it, for it shows feelings of uncertainty beside certainty and the temptation to be recognized as a saviour, which humanize Freud. The strong man was also once the dependent child. The complex of feelings surrounding being a child, and saving a life/being saved, Freud dealt with elsewhere as an unconscious response to a child's being told that his parents gave him life. As the child grows older, in order to be his own person, he must give that life back, or become the lifegiver himself, and even sacrifice himself for a parent or cause (SAV 193–4, SE11 172–3). There remains that part of the dream untouched on by Freud, and which he surely would not have neglected in anyone else's dream, the pairing of Joyeuse/Joyeux. The feminine form was given to a masculine character in the book. Freud's false memory made that man and his name (Freud uses "Mr" for Monsieur) wholly masculine (Mr/Herr Jocelyn), but the reality was he was half-feminine, and a translation of Freud. Freud may have believed in and feared his underlying bisexuality, after discussing the theory at length with Fließ and seeing it published by Weininger. As we know (see above pp.25–27), he had other dreams about the brilliance of the theory. Only this dream is much more personal. He appears to be walking the streets of Paris dreaming of sexual satisfaction for himself both as a man and a woman. This would finally compensate for the loneliness and insecurity of his childhood.

18 At Freud's birth, and until they moved to Leipzig three years later, and thence to Vienna, Freud's parents lived in one room in Freiberg, Moravia. Seeing his mother naked in a hotel room was a conjecture on Freud's part, *Briefe an Fließ* (3.10.1897), p.288. He set his age at two or two and a half, but the journey in question from Leipzig to Vienna happened when Freud was four. According to this letter it left Freud with a permanent fear of travelling.

19 *Briefe an Fließ* (15.10.97), "I found that I too was a case of being in love with my mother and being jealous of my father and consider it now a general occurrence of early childhood, though not always so earlier [*sic*] as with hysterically constituted children... If that is the case then one understands the gripping power of King Oedipus..." (Mahony, *Cries of The Wolfman*, especially pp.103–5 and p.110). Mahony (p.32) makes clear that although Freud was under pressure to refute Adler and Jung and prove the development of an infantile pathology in this case, his attempts to do so in "The Wolfman" were contradictory and

confused, even at one point (p.87) pushing him into using the very theory of Jung's, of retrospective fantasy, that he sought to disprove.

20 For society creating perversions, see, for example, SAI 306, 317, SE16 309, 322. Nabokov, though an avowed enemy of the white-coated [sic] man from Vienna, tackled many of the same problems, not least sexual perversity and human evil. "We are well aware of the fact that Nabokov was in the habit of borrowing mostly from those very writers he publicly ridiculed and denounced in his polemics; he simply called these borrowings a parody." Zinovy Zinik, "Letter from Middletown," *Times Literary Supplement*, 25.6.1999, p.17.

21 The Ratman lacks success in life (SAVII 38, SE10 158). Freud, was not a model of tolerance (cf.SAI 304, SE16 307–8, Webster, p.4 and *passim*, and note 14 above). All a mixture psychologically... (SAV 123, SE7 220).

22 Webster (p.29) contends: "We do not understand Freud. In the entire complex body of psychoanalysis he left us no theoretical means by which we might unravel his own deepest motives or analyze his development and his evident sense of mission."

23 Freud's dream theory rose in popularity after the Great War, and his work generally, because it seemed he could treat battle trauma, which was something good. Rebecca West's *The Return of the Soldier* reflects the literary attraction of the new standpoint. Freud's unpopularity has something to do consciously with fear of losing privacy (a response Virginia Woolf inscribed in *Mrs. Dalloway*) and unconsciously with the taboo of self-indulgence. Since this taboo was well-nigh exhausted in the 1980s and 1990s, resistance to Freud took shelter in the argument that he was useless because unscientific and wicked because his theories led with Recovered Memory to the persecution of the innocent. Protestations of the sacredness of childhood, against molesters, perverts and Freud himself, seem to mark the banality of the last decade of the twentieth century.

24 SAV 188–95, 222, SE11 166–75, 202-3

25 SAV 209, SE11 190

26 SAI 415–16, SE16 431–2. The first sentence here lacks a main verb in Freud's original, hence my emendations to make it read. Webster (pp.212–3) prefers to follow Masson in alleging that Freud wasn't sympathetic to "the actual world of sadness, misery and cruelty."

II

27 SAI 359, SE16 368

28 These remarks are based on "Introduction to Narcissism" (1914) and the Twenty-Sixth of the *Introductory Lectures* (1915–17), "Libido Theory and Narcissism." They take "ego" in this context and at this stage of Freud's thinking to mean "the self," possibly including the body. SAIII 278, SE19 7 traces the changes this term undergoes when Freud uses it to designate a dynamic aspect of the psyche in the 1923 essay "The Ego and the Id."

29 SAIII 17, SE12 218

30 SAI 430, SE16 447. In *TLS*, 29. 10. 1999, Simon Blackburn cites Antonio Damasio in *Descartes' Error* (1995) as reminding us "that patients who cannot attach positive and negative emotions to the representation of courses of action go altogether off the rails … we need things to matter to us before we have any motivation to go one way or the other, and it is our emotions that determine how things matter." In 1915, in "The Unconscious," and again in 1917, in the Twenty-Sixth Introductory Lecture, Freud considered "the detachment of the libido from the object as the source of a pathological condition." Surveying the various ways this impaired psychic functioning can come about, he concludes that in the most severe cases, of dementia praecox (modern schizophrenia), the patient's libido makes a real self-healing effort to link up with

the object, i.e. socially given reality, but ends up only grabbing at shadows, in the form of words without anything real attached to them. Freud's mode of expression has evidently had its day, but his deep concern with how a healthy person makes a continuous emotional investment in reality ensures his continuing relevance.

31 SAIII 23, SE12 224. Apart from Freud's evident hysteria on the subject, one might feel instinctively reluctant to agree with a scheme that regards masturbation as a stage the individual passes through the same way that Hegelian antitheses eventually negate themselves, and Hegelian nations and cultures pass through stages on the way to greater self-development.

32 "The Dynamics of Transference" (1912): SA *Ergb*. 159–60, SE12 99–100

33 GWIV 255, SE6 229

34 Feelings of not being loved, "Introduction to Narcissism": SAIII 64–5, SE14 97–8

35 Arthur Schnitzler, *Gesammelte Werke* (1912), *Die Theaterstücke*, Bd 2, *Paracelsus* (1892). Freud wrote to Schnitzler that he envied him his insight (*Briefe* (8.5.1906) p.266; SAI 273, 371, SE16 273, 382–3). "There are cases in which even the doctor must admit that the outcome of a conflict in neurosis presents the most harmless and socially bearable solution."

36 SAV 134–5, SE7 231–2. On this naturally perverted state, see note 47 below.

37 Jones, *Freud*, Vol. II. p.322. In *Totem and Taboo* (SAIX 377–8, SE13 88–9) Freud gives an excellent one-paragraph résumé of his thoughts on narcissism as coinciding with the animism of primitive peoples. Freud, bound up with his concept of "intellectual narcissism," made clear that many people never progress from believing in the omnipotence of their own thoughts, and project themselves into all their relationships. This

sounds partly true of Freud himself, and in the first instance must be the case with writers of fiction. To get beyond *all* narcissism would be perhaps to get beyond subjectivity, which is impossible.

38 SAIII 41, SE14 73

39 SAI 402–3, SE16 417

40 SAIII 42–3, SE14 74–5. I am reminded of the divorce judge who told Sir Terence Conran he had "a very healthy ego" and therefore could afford an expensive separation; and of those modern British legends Robert Maxwell and James Goldsmith, whose narcissism in both cases was surely enhanced by their original outsider status. Clearly narcissistic relations to the world can become paranoid, with dreams of the world's end.

41 SAIII 61, SE14 94. For the section on idealism, see SAIII 60–2, SE14 93–5.

42 SAI 430, SE16 447. At SAIII 52, SE14 85 Freud can only give a poetic reason why the Ego-dominated position should give way to love-of-the-Other. For "the narcissism of small differences," see SAIX 243, 538, SE21 114, SE23 91. See also Erich Fromm, *The Art of Loving* (1956).

43 Aristotle, *Ethics*, VI, 2, quoted in McAlister, p.160 (Roderick M. Chisholm, "Brentano's Theory of Correct and Incorrect Emotion'); Brentano quoted, ibid. p.184 (Gabriel Franks, "Was G.E. Moore Mistaken About Brentano?'). To adapt one of Chisholm's examples (p.172): If I love Smith because he is pleased that there are flowers in the world, my love is good; if I cease to love Smith because he is pleased, etc., or love him because he is displeased there are flowers in the world then already there is some contamination of love. Perhaps I am jealous that Smith is paying more attention to flowers than to me; or envious that Smith is a far greater connoisseur of such things than I am, which only reminds me that he enjoys more love from others and a higher social status; or I want confirmation, by seeing their duplication in Smith, of my own negative and destructive feelings

about a world others find good. Psychoanalysis would hope to trace the impediments to my loving the real Smith back to an unresolved problem in my childhood.

44 Freud is so deeply embedded in Western culture that many seem not to realize his presence. Thomas Nagel, responding to Crews, *The Memory Wars*, p.218, emphasizes that common sense has expanded to include parts of Freudian theory. He speaks of "the pervasive Freudian transformation of our modern working conception of the self." Crews' response is trivial.

45 Freud was notoriously unable to appreciate the "oceanic" feeling which many people associate with religious sentiment. Anthony Storr's *Solitude* takes up the problem of Freud's lack of appreciation of this way of being which is often conducive to creativity and genius. The book does not succeed, because the case is a difficult one for a therapist to prosecute without attacking the institution of psychotherapy in which he plays an exceptional part.

46 SAI 301–3, 359, SE16 304–7, 368

III

47 SAV 223, SE11 203. "The husband is so to speak always only a substitute, never the real thing." I have taken a slight liberty by translating *der Richtige* ('the right one') as "the real thing." The sense that all our loves are substitutes for a lost original sets the Oedipus Complex in an unfamiliar and instructive light, at the same time as it confirms Webster's conviction that Freud's outlook is deeply embedded in the Judaeo-Christian metaphysical tradition. However, I don't read it as confirming "Absolute Sin."

48 See the concluding pages of Plato's *Meno*.

49 "Freud and Literature," in *The Liberal Imagination* (1951), p.44

50 The French response to Freud through Sartre, Lacan, Barthes, Foucault and Derrida has of course been quite different, giving

rise to a parallel post-structuralist tradition in America which hardly recognizes its theories as being in part traceable back to Freud. Jacques Derrida, "Freud's Legacy," in *The Postcard*, 1980 (tr. Alan Bass, 1987), p.305, asks the key question about the coming into being of psychoanalysis: "How can autobiographical writing, in the abyss of an unterminated self-analysis, give to a worldwide institution *its* birth?" Horden, "Thoughts of Freud," in *Freud and the Humanities*, gives an overview of the way the two Freud traditions diverge.

51 eg., SAIX 363, SE13 73

52 SAV 61, SE7 151

53 SAVI 94, SE7 15

54 SA *Ergb*. 160, SE2 266

55 "It is called transference because, where it is neurotic, it is characterized by the blurring of an adult relationship through the transfer upon it of infantile loves and hates, dependencies and impotent rages. Transference thus also implies a partial regression to childish attitudes" (Erik H. Erikson, "The First Psychoanalyst," in *Freud and The Twentieth Century*, p.92). In love and in transference we seem to become aware of some other part of our personality which we are suppressing, which gives in turn the feeling that "he/she changed my life." The temptation in love is surely to take the change at face value, and imagine that progress has been made without an effort at self-understanding concomitant with Freud's self-analysis. Wollheim (pp.151ff.) on the transference writes very much from within the orthodox psychoanalytic tradition, without exposing the boldness, the waywardness and the poetry of this aspect of Freud. Lieberman (*Acts of Will*, p.116) is amongst many more moderate commentators on aspects of psychoanalysis to have found the manipulation of love as a therapeutic technique very harsh. Crews (*The Memory Wars*, p.119) is at his *most* subtle when he writes, "Transference as Freud understood it is the patient's

reliving of infantile cravings and disappointments through an unconscious casting of the therapist as a substitute parent.'

56 Webster rehearses the sexual accusations on p.276 and p.357, and on p.333 stresses that transference creates psychological dependency. Crews (p.14, p.120) suggests that the real function of the transference is to ensure that the patient can't complain about the analyst's irritating present behavior or accuse him of being wrong. He concludes (p.121) by underscoring "the cognitive dubiety of psychoanalytic formulations in general and of the analyst's surmises in particular." "All in all this pivotal notion has proved itself to be not only scientifically vacuous but also considerably worse than useless as a guide to the rational addressing of patients' initial complaints.'

Crews is right that transference is a difficult concept on which to found a school of treatment. But that is not to deny what Freud has uncovered for all time about the delicate mechanisms of sympathy and indeed "love"; about the transformations and substitutions which lie at the heart of our unconscious creative and restorative thought processes; and it is significant that Crews does not once honor Freud's original intention by glossing transference just once, simply and directly as "love." Crews may find analysts irritating as a breed, but many patients have fallen in love with them genuinely, and vice versa. Scott Fitzgerald's *Tender is the Night* is a fine example of how the healer loves way beyond his powers, or even the patient's needs. Tom Kempinski's play *Duet for One* (1980), later made into a film, is a fine study of the analyst and patient changing places in the course of her treatment. We love those we can help and teach. We are attracted to those who help and teach us. The erotic-didactic relationship familiar to Plato is not out of place in Freud's original conception, and in the philosophy expressed in his texts, however much even he abused it in practice by yielding to his own vanity.

David D. Olds, an associate clinical professor of psychiatry, replies to Crews (*The Memory Wars*, pp.91–2): "Critics of psychoanalysis seldom see that it is a process of dealing with a wildly moving target from a slightly less wildly moving platform . . . The phenomenon of erotic transference, in fact of any transference, took the early analysts by surprise . . . It may well be that Freud was somewhat corrupted by the power that was thrust upon him, and which he no doubt enjoyed. But he did not sleep with his patients, nor found a lucrative ashram. His heart went mostly in a scientific direction, despite the peculiar nature of the instrument."

57 But Freud's first specific paper, "On the Dynamics of Transference" (1912), intended as technical, remains theoretical, and "Observations on Transference Love" (1915) only goes further in warning of the practical danger to analysts who should realize they are dealing with highly explosive substances. Lieberman (*Acts of Will*, p.119) quotes Freud as saying in 1910 of the analyst overcoming counter-transference, or the personal feelings with which the analyst responds to the patient, "It makes him the perfectly cool object whom the other person must lovingly woo.'

58 "Observations on Transference Love": SA *Ergb.* 229, SE12 170. This dire warning to colleagues replaces the ingenious bragging of five years earlier. Still, that in that same essay (SA *Ergb.* 222, SE12 162) he can accuse women patients of deliberately falling in love to subvert the cure suggests he still has a lot of work to do on the problem of counter-transference.

59 Lieberman, *Acts of Will*, p.374. Lyndall Gordon, *A Private Life of Henry James*, London 1998. Derrida sees the *fort/da* game also as the fundamental structure of Freud's writing. "To Speculate – On 'Freud'," in *The Postcard*, especially pp.261–2, and "Freud's Legacy," ibid., pp.295ff. See also, "Freud and the Scene of Writing," in *Writing and Difference* (tr. Alan Bass, 1978). Freud responding to criticism of evasiveness might however say that you just can't win, for his school also has a legacy of coldness and non-responsiveness. In the film comedy *A Couch in New York* (1995), the analyst played by William Hurt has developed such

a remote and dry style that all the patients are worse. When the untrained but sympathetic and beautiful Juliet Binoche takes his place they all get better. Hurt becomes a patient and also gets cured by love in this sanitized version of psychoanalysis which contains a grain of truth.

In general, this point of the presence or absence of the emotional subjectivity of the analyst, and the subjectivity of the first analyst *qua* writer, in any psychoanalytic engagement with "the other" feeds both Freud traditions. It emerges as part of literary/linguistic/structuralist enquiry in France, and therapeutic concern for the emancipation of the patient into normal social relations in America.

60 Jung had a love affair with fellow analyst Sabine Spielrein. For his *ménage à trois* and other involvements, see Frank McGlynn, *Carl Gustav Jung* (1996). Jung in his turn (*The Freud–Jung Letters*, 46J) admired another Freudian disciple Max Eitingon's "uninhibited capacity to abreact the polygamous instinct." Jones's strongly erotic personality led him also into many affairs. These were not with analytic patients, though his sexual character was not entirely blameless, since he had earlier been dismissed from his post at a London children's hospital for sexual misbehavior with children he was examining (Gay, *Freud*, p.184) Elisabeth Roudinesco (*Jacques Lacan*, 1994, tr. Barbara Bray, 1997) acknowledges that Lacan had affairs with patients. However, all of this is gossip and circumstance beside the extraordinary theory of sexual release that was developed out of Freud's work by Wilhelm Reich and taken to America, where it found a few adherents for therapy by orgone box.

61 *The Freud–Jung Letters*, 42F: "I have always felt that there is something about my personality, my ideas and manner of speaking, that people find strange and repellent, whereas all hearts open to you. If a healthy man like you regards himself as a hysterical type, I can only claim for myself the 'obsessional' type, each specimen of which vegetates in a sealed-off world of his own." Jung later put about the rumor of Freud's sexual

involvement with his sister-in-law Minna surely out of malice. Gay (*Freud*, p.752) decides on the available evidence that Freud did not have this affair, but notes that a correspondence with Minna remains suppressed in the Freud archive, fuelling continuing speculation.

Freud generally lacked diplomatic skills, Jones (Vol. II, p.117) noted. He especially didn't rate his charm alongside artists, as we have seen from his fears about rival suitors for Martha's hand.

For Freud simultaneously on Rank's exceptional *charm*, see Lieberman, *Acts of Will*, p.134.

Beauty doesn't need beauty. See Plato's early dialogue *The Lysis*.

62 SAX 25, SE9 22

63 Brecht wanted the process of returning to reality through alienation effects, ending the tradition of bourgeois "identification," to be at the core of his theatre of political awareness. But Freud was stuck with "identification." We are reminded of the fundamental link between psychoanalysis and dramatic performance, and the difference: that there is no way to bring the analytic play to an end, except by calling "time."

64 SAI 423, SE16 440. Freud's tone over these paragraphs begins by being remarkably sensible but is subverted by the prospect of the workings of charm and love, which in turn make him suspicious.

65 SA *Ergb.* 227, SE12 167 Freud insists this *is* a real love until the last moment. Still one feels the patient is sacrificed to the concept of transference. The counter-evaluation begins with the heuristic value of Freud's inventions. "The value of such a 'fiction' depends on how much one can carry out with it." "The Question of Lay Analysis" (SA *Ergb.* 286, SE20 194). This passage also contains a reference to Vaihinger's *Philosophy of As If* (see note 39, Chapter 4, above).

66 Frances Huxley in *Freud and the Humanities*, p.146; SAIX 363,

SE13 73 *Totem and Taboo*. Crews may be right that Freud had problems with "reality-testing," but then so did Descartes. What we are interested in is finding out what that weakness or strength means for the emergence of Freud as an artist. For the way the upper layer of the personality is modified by the social, see SA *Ergb*. 287, SE20 195.

67 That neurotic symptoms work by imitation of the ways of the body is one of the most disturbing ideas in Freud, because it seems we can't trust that body to be identical with itself. The same happens with language, where in Freud's view, because of the unconscious, words and even parts of words, and their sounds, have unlimited supplementary meanings. Derrida speaks of the "logic of supplementarity" and its unsettling effects. Christopher Norris (*Derrida*, 1987, pp.107–8) elucidates this point as Derrida applies it to Rousseau. "What is in question is a powerful mythology of human nature which can only be asserted (as Rousseau asserts it) by forgetting or effacing the signs of its cultural production. To acknowledge these signs would be to set in train a series of disruptive shifts and reversals whose effect would reach back to the putative origins of man, language and society. And Rousseau cannot help but acknowledge them... Always there is a moment of *différance* at the source, a falling-away from nature, identity and origins which makes it impossible for Rousseau to say what he evidently means to say..." Derrida brings us effectively back to Freud's world, and perhaps the beginning in reading Freud of his key theory of *différance*, when he observes that for Rousseau supplementarity begins with the child's turning to substitutes for the real object of desire, the mother. The child's fantasy is stimulated, but also his autoeroticism. Both Freud and Rousseau are plagued by their masturbatory habits, and derive terrible consequences from this temptation to fall away from nature.

68 Frank Cioffi, quoted in Crews, *The Memory Wars*, p.11; Mahony, *Cries of the Wolfman*, p.4

69 "The Artist and Creative Imagination": SAX 179, SE9 153

70 "Treatment of the Psyche" (1890): SA *Ergb.* 17, SE7 283

71 SAX 179, SE9 153

72 Dixon, *Rhetoric* (1971), p.35. Freud talks in "The Artist and Creative Imagination" of the comparable *Lustgewinn*, the pleasure gain, when children play. Children have more of this freedom than adults and are not ashamed to fantasize. Primitive peoples had more freedom to play according to Freud (and Schiller) compared with modern self-conscious man. Once again the parallel with Rousseau comes to mind, on which Gay comments (pp.325–6), and with Schiller, who said we were most free when as adults we were able to play. The inspiration from this understanding of childhood fed directly into the art movements of Dadaism and Futurism. Schiller's concept of play was to give mankind a holiday from moral and physical necessity, to be able to avoid judgement, and to hold opposites in balance. "The Joke and Its Relation to the Unconscious" contains Freud's remarks on the secret freedom jokes afford.

73 Disguise has an obvious connection with Freud's later theory of sublimation as essential to civilization.

74 "Three Essays on Sexual Theory": SAV 106–11, SE7 201–6; "The Ratman": SAVII 99–101, SE10 243–6

75 The death instinct seems to be a generalization from Freud's own experience of bereavement. It is not aggressive.

76 The breakdown of a comfortable view of love marks the *fin de siècle*. The young Freud, who referred to Amor-Luzifer (*Briefe an Fließ*, p.463) was fascinated by the way the Viennese public was both morally damning and emotionally fascinated by French works featuring crimes of passion and adultery; fascinated too by the way poetry could make "immoral" love, like that of Tristan and Isolde, acceptable and understandable. Without naming it as such, Freud is captivated by the tension between Amor and Eros,

between love as charm and love as blind, heedless wanting. Eros beneath the mask of civilized flirtation is a howling sickness at the extent of the unobtainable. The temptation of giving way to Eros is one of Thomas Mann's recurring themes, fostered by reading Schopenhauer, Nietzsche and Freud. *Death in Venice* features art as the Apollonian ideal, a creation of civilization and self-control, gradually giving way to the Dionysian or the repressed homoerotic passions of Gustav von Aschenbach. The mask of civilization is undone by illness and sexual passion, which lead in turn to death. Of the many rich themes running through *The Magic Mountain*, a German bourgeois version of medieval courtliness also gives way to a desperate metaphysics of love and death, as the idea of illness seduces Hans Castorp.

77 SAI 365, SE16 365

78 See the passage quoted on pages 159–160 (SA *Ergb.* 17, SE7 283). Freud wrote to Jung (*The Freud–Jung Letters*, 139F), "I confront the despiritualized furniture as the poet confronted undeified Nature after the gods of Greece had passed away," but my contention was that Freud rather more followed, like Nietzsche with his "superabundant substitutes," the lure of fantasy, than that he stuck to a scientific confrontation of the unadorned truth. This is evident in the way he was unable to adhere to the strict terms of his own theory of metapsychology. In his letter, the poet is Schiller and the poem *Die Götter Griechenlands* ('The Gods of Greece'). The notion of modern German culture succeeding the Greek but forever falling short of its perfection is a fixed and recurrent idea, shared by many writers and poets.

NOTES TO *Chapter 6* **Reality Reconsidered**

1 SAII 339, SE5 344. "The dreamwork spares itself no effort first to remould an unwieldly thought in another linguistic form if that makes its presentation possible and so brings an end to the psychological pressure of blocked thoughts."

2 *Pace* Lacan, the unconscious is not structured like a language in Freud's view (Bowie, *Lacan*, pp.49ff.). The crucial explanation of Freud's position comes in the essay "The Unconscious" (1915): SAIII 159–60, SE14 200–1. Freud uses the word *Sachbesetzung* to assert that the mind contains a certain energy charge on behalf of the object it perceives; it is ready to know it; it intends to know it (*Sache* = thing, *Besetzung* = interest, occupying force, energy charge). This was the word Strachey translated as "cathexis." Freud's unconscious then contains this stored intentional energy. It also has "mental dispositions" – *Sachvorstellungen* – from a previous experience which mean it will call up a similar idea under similar mental circumstances in the future. *Vorstellung* = representation, and comes to mean what we represent to ourselves, that is, ideas. The *Sachvorstellung* is what is present to the mind as an object, but the object does not necessarily exist at that moment. The *Sachvorstellung* comes to consciousness when it links up with the *Wortvorstellung*, the appropriate word to name the experience. Perhaps we can keep the link in the German terms by calling it the pre-disposed word, though "word representation" and "thing representation" are the literal translations.

   Brentano taught this theory of perception by association: "Any idea leaves behind a disposition towards the appearance of a similar idea under similar mental circumstances" (McAlister, *Brentano*, p.37). Associationism was endorsed by Freud's reading of J.S. Mill's *An Examination of Sir William Hamilton's Philosophy*. Mill gave Freud the sense of an enormous and highly inventive freedom of thought lurking beneath the point where words linked up with mental impressions. "The mental disposition – *Sachvorstellung* – therefore appears to us not as a *closed* notion, and hardly as *closable*, while the pre-disposed word – the *Wortvorstellung* – seems to us something *closed*, although susceptible of amplification." I have italicized a term which seems to have passed directly into post-structuralist theory as "closure."

   A further difficulty with translation in this last sentence from

Appendix C to "The Unconscious" comes with Freud's sudden use of *Objektvorstellung* in place of *Sachvorstellung* used in the main essay. For guidance on these points, and also an excellent diagram provided by Freud, the German *Studienausgabe* of Freud's works is invaluable. The diagram shows one reason why Lacan, who forged his system by merging Saussure's linguistics and Freud's psychoanalysis, proceeded as he did. Saussure's signifier/signified seems to bear *some* relation to Freud's *Sachvorstellung/Wortvorstellung*, and it certainly does once it has become Lacan's S/s. Bowie brings this out when he observes that for Lacan the great anti-creative limitation occurs when signifier (acoustic realm) and signified (thought realm) are irreversibly joined in the sign. He writes (p.65) that "[Lacan] needed a way of describing conjointly two features of language that mattered equally to psychoanalysis but that had not until then been brought into alignment. The first was its obdurate and impersonal systemic force, and the second its fecundity, the pluralizing semantic power that is enjoyed in the speech of individual persons." What we see is Lacan picking up on a neglected corner of the philosophical underpinning of Freud's unconscious. Freud for his part suggests that each of us beneath the surface of our logical speech and our capacity for mimetic representation tends towards a more obscure, possibly creative and certainly less stable form of processing reality, which gets more conventionally ordered by the necessary encounter with words if we are to communicate successfully. But he only deals with this creative power *within the confines of the creativity of symptoms and dreams.* "With regression the network of dream thoughts is resolved into its raw materials" SAII 519, SE5 543 gives the nature and extent of Freud's idea here, which is essentially about releasing creativity.

Besides the theory, however, Freud is helped to talk about the unconscious by his empirical experience of the *breakdown* of language. For his studies of aphasia, see "The Unconscious" and also "On the Aphasias" (1891). *The Oxford Companion to Mind* (p.32) has a helpful article on this phenomenon. The link between aphasia and the Freudian unconscious underscores the wrongness of interpreting Freud as if he were attributing to the human being two minds in conflict. It points rather to Freud's dynamic system of the unconscious through which ideas and energy *pass through*. See note 12 below.

3   SAI 215–6, SE15 211–12. For how dreams are made the notion of residues is important. Strachey sometimes translates inconsistently across the related terms, so that we have "day residues" but "memory traces." Freud's terminology – *Tagesreste, Erinnerungsreste, Wortreste, Wahrnehmungsreste* (residues from the day, from memory, from words and from perception respectively) – evidently comes from Mill's Theory of Residues (*System of Logic*, Book III), *die Methode der Reste* in German, which says that when all other causes have been accounted for, what is left over is the explanation being sought. Alan Ryan (*The Philosophy of J.S. Mill*, 2nd edition, London, 1987, p.47) quotes Mill, "Its principle is very simple." But (p.139), "This theory only works when we know the causal links between all the other phenomena involved and are waiting only to solve the last causal clue." Freud says of residues that they are like the grains of sand in the mind which grow into pearls (SAI 379, SE16 391). They grow through chains of association. Reversing this process in order to understand the formation of dreams, he can speak of the Wolfman's dream as having been *restlos aufgeklärt* (SAVIII 161, SE17 42). "Exhaustively explained," the obvious translation, would miss the allusion to Mill.

From the point of view of stored, i.e. unconscious, emotional energy or intensity, the residues offer a choice of guise in which to surface into consciousness. Freud (SAI 229, SE15 226) uses the metaphor of capitalist enterprise. Psychic energy is the capitalist who provides the means/fuel/money, while the residue is the entrepreneur who has the idea and carries it out.

4   SAII 519, SE5 543. Regression, the same word in German, should be carefully distinguished in English from repression = *die Verdrängung*. Regression is what happens in artistic

inspiration, dreams and mental disturbance. It represents a simpler, earlier, more childlike order, not logical, not accountable, not consequential. To requote from note 3, "With regression the network of dream thoughts is resolved into its raw materials" (SAII 519, SE5 543).

5   Ernst Gombrich, "Psychoanalysis and the History of Art," in *Freud and the Twentieth Century*, pp.182–201 (pp.198–201), reprinted in *Meditations on a Hobby Horse* (1963)

6   SAI 377, SE16 389. "The teaching structure of psychoanalysis which we have created is in reality a superstructure [*ein Überbau*] which at some time should be set on its organic foundation: but we don't know this foundation yet." The terminology is the same as that of Marx. Freud and Marx were both materialist philosophical descendants of Hegel and Feuerbach. What we see in Freud is how the norms of society, and especially often its inequalities, are absorbed *into* the unconscious and come out in dreams and other manifestations of the unconscious, which may also be manifestations of mental disturbance. Freud explicitly rejects social revolution to change the circumstances which create the contents of the unconscious. Marx takes the opposite view, having had his own perception of deformities and missing fulfillments in the individual. SAII 314, SE4 316; SAII 158 and 454, SE4 142, SE5 471–2 are particularly personal statements of bad faith. Freud has to affect a polite disguise of his contempt where the other person has superior social status and *power*.

Freud always insisted the unconscious was real and was disappointed when Pierre Janet, whose work he admired, finally called the unconscious only "a manner of speaking." "Something not real, from which proceed such really graspable effects as a compulsive action!" (SAI 277, SE16 277). Wittgenstein in his turn could only accept Freud's unconscious as a "norm of expression." See Jacques Bouveresse, *Wittegenstein Reads Freud* (1995), p.54.

Webster (p.242) concedes that the unconscious was Freud's most successful and plausible strategy but (p.250) quickly demotes it to a fantasy: "It is the fact that we so frequently deceive ourselves about our own motives . . . that makes psychoanalysis both so plausible and so attractive. One of the central objections to Freud's methodology, however, is that by positing the existence of an unconscious he effectively deepens the very mysteries which he claims to unravel. For the unconscious is not simply an occult entity for whose real existence there is no palpable evidence. It is an illusion produced by language – a kind of intellectual hallucination."

7 Freud attempts to explain something which gets very little philosophical attention, though many of us feel we know what is being described, and that is the shadow that falls from the past on the present and from the present back on the past. It seems to be a matter of the way one association clouds another, without our realizing it. Such shadows are cast by our individual experience; and also by our language. This is one way of understanding the primary dynamic unconscious, which because Freud has passed through the intentional school of Brentano, the Freudian shadow is seen actively to *cause* the present, not just to lurk. (This is what makes Freud's unconscious different from the Looking-Glass World of Alice, which does not *cause* the normal room she has left behind.)

An immediate therapeutic interpretation of this relation of conscious to unconscious suggests itself. We can learn to let this unconscious, this mental factory, this in-body entertainment centre, amuse us and keep us company. The "Dreamwork" section of *The Interpretation of Dreams* which focuses on this playground is a telling two hundred pages long. There is a positive interpretation of the self-sufficiency of the mind here. It also suggests a link between the shadows in our minds and some other philosophical shadows, namely fictional characters. It may help us to get to know our own fictions. Winston Churchill called the shadow which threatened to blight his life Black Dog.

However, there is also evidently a link between this causal

Freudian shadow and what Henri Ellenberger (quoted in Ronald C. Clarke, *Freud*, p.103) lists as the great "negative diseases" of the early nineteenth century, including somnambulism, deep lethargy and catalepsy. These would normally speaking be states not to befriend, but to get out of. They were the kinds of disturbances the medical doctor in Freud was trying to explain with his unconscious, and they led him to uncover a vast underbelly to the conscious spiritual life. He pitched his professional camp in the shadows cast by art, by health, and by the outward appearance of society and its institutions. A deformed realm of not-quite-being came into his sights. Freud here picked up on something which characterized the St Petersburg stories of Gogol and Dostoevsky and shared their insight. Lives effectively divorced from first-hand ideas and direct human contact would fail to furnish their owners with a sense of a shared reality and end in profound *alienation*. Freud in his own way is as much a student of alienation as Marx. For him the dream is the shadow equivalent of art, which is *successful* communication; it is art by default. Similar neurosis exists in the shadow, and by default, of love.

Freud variously describes the Unconscious as systematic, dynamic and descriptive. We have touched on the first two here. The dynamic unconscious is causal and has primary urgency whereas the unconscious as system (SAIII 160, SE14 201) features various urges to self-realization imprisoned in an unrealized state.

It is interesting that like all Freud touched, the concept of the unconscious also split in his hands, seemingly confirming our suspicion that the doctor and the artist in Freud pulled his work in opposite directions.

8   The key concept is *wirksame unbewußte Ideen*, which would explain how an idea held in the unconscious can precipitate a physical action or state. Freud derives it in the first instance from hypnosis, see "Some Remarks on the Concept of the

Unconscious in Psychoanalysis" (1912): SAIII 30, SE12 261. Roughly it seems to have been this point in Freud which was reworked into Alfred Hitchcock's compelling, if misleading, film *Spellbound* (1946). This American interpretation of Freud was typically geared to rehabilitating the individual in society. But what the unconscious as causal shadow and limitation meant in an intellectually more refined world was a staggering new richness available to art and critical theory.

9   For the key to understanding this passage, see note 2 above. The representational theory of perception, the equivalent of perceiving the world from a television screen in one's head, is Locke's, whose ideas Brentano taught. In the sentence "the grass is green" the greenness is in my head. If I didn't have the capacity to perceive green, I couldn't know what the grass was like. The cumbersome nature of this theory is important to bear in mind when we consider the technical intricacy of Freud's own scheme of things. Freud's machinery is compared to a Heath Robinson machine, though Locke is spared that calumny.

10 SAIII 160, SE14 201

11 SAII 287, SE4 285

12 SAIII 162, SE14 204

13 Here is another attraction of Freud's for structuralism. On fluidity in the system, see SAIII 137–8, SE14 178–9. Nietzsche's old battle with the too-rational, anti-Dionysian Socrates is rejoined here with Freud's campaign to make rational procedures only part of the mind.

14 SAII 400, SE5 411. German *eine Weiche*, French *les aiguillages*. Synonyms used by Freud include *Assoziationsbrücke*, *Wortbrücke*, *Mittleres Gemeinsames* and *Mittelbildung*.

15 SAII 227, SE4 219. See also E.H. Gombrich, "The Symbol of the Veil: Psychological Reflections on Schiller's poetry," in *Freud*

and the Humanities (1985). Mahony suggests in *Cries of The Wolfman* that the German for "tearing off" a veil is also the popular German for "to masturbate" but my German-speaking husband cannot corroborate this.

16 SAII 285, SE4 282

17 SAII 296, SE4 295

18 SAII 280–1, SE4 277–8. The italics are mine to draw attention to Freud's ever-present artistic interest. I have used the English "tale" for *Dichterspruch*, though the German is much richer, relating to *Das Buch der Sprüche*, The Book of Proverbs, also called *Die Sprüche Solomons*. I had "rabbinical tale" in mind and also Freud's identification of his gifts with Solomon's in *The Psychopathology*.

19 SAII 486, SE5 507

20 SAII 450, SE5 467

21 For Mr. Jocelyn, see Chapter 5. Leaps of association, e.g. at SAII 390 and 207, SE5 399 and SE4 196. For the gradual unfolding of psychoanalytic meaning as in a play, see SAII 266, SE4 262.

22 SAII 403–4, SE5 414–16

23 SAII 337–8, SE5 342–3

24 SAII 244–5, 252–3, SE4 238–40, 247–8

25 SAII 214–18, SE4 204–8. Here surely is a fine example of the dream picture as rabbinical tale, once the meaning has been deciphered.

26 Many references bring out how strong is the dreamwork's desire to create a unified story, SAII 192, 235, 242, 310–11, 337, and to manufacture symbols, 321 (SE4 179, 228, 236, 311–12, 324, SE5 342).

27 The polyglot unconscious is so named by Timpanaro but shown to be, as most of us intuit, the ability of the *conscious* mind to

savor the plural meanings of sounds. As with any writer, the invention reflects Freud's multilingualism (German, French, English, Spanish, Latin, Greek and Hebrew). It is a creative tool and a facet of imagination which can be assessed on its merits beyond Freud's theory. In his case-studies it makes for some risky transitions as from the English malaria to the quasi-Italian *mal aria*, which is outlandishly taken to mean "heavy breathing" in "The Wolfman" (SAVIII 165, 183, SE17 47, 67). On the other hand, Freud has inspired several generations of writers and critics to follow him, and to include in the evidence of the clever unconscious, but rather more the writer's imagination, typographical errors and mishearings in the list of entertainments. Bizarre interpretations by critics who would out-freudize Freud from within his work include reading across from the Russian *noch'yu* (at night) to "not you," from Gruzya, the Russian for Georgia (but misleadingly transliterated as Grouja), to Grusha, the name of the Wolfman's Russian nanny, from *vdrug* (Russian for suddenly) to the English "truth" and from *samo soboi* (Russian for the reflexive "it of itself") to the English "somewhat as a boy" (Mahony, *Cries of The Wolfman*, pp.54 and 64–5). This verbal playing in the space between English and Russian is invited by the Wolfman's multilingual upbringing. It is often said that Modernist writing is a game for *cognoscenti*, and perhaps that habit draws strength from Freud's puns. Nabokov's Russian-English puns are splendid examples, for which, for once, Nabokov acknowledged Freud's influence (*The Nabakov–Wilson Letters*, ed. Karlinsky, 1979, p.88, 24.11.1942). Joyce is the great master of the multiple pun, for which see Anthony Burgess, *Here Comes Everybody* (1965) and *Joysprick* (1973). Freud admits all kinds of wordplay to his "unconscious" armory perhaps *because* it gets his imagination going. *Unconsciously* Freud the would-be scientist needs to classify *somehow* the extraordinary imagination he has discovered in himself.

28 See notes 2 and 13 above.

29 Frances Huxley, *Freud and the Humanities*, p.146. It is tempting to see Freud's Binary Touch as generating his extraordinarily bifurcated following across the Western world, which can be roughly characterized as the American therapeutic and the French fantastic/linguistic Freud.

30 This is Freud's fundamental definition and the title of a whole section of *The Interpretation of Dreams*: "The dream is the fulfillment of a wish" (SAII 141, SE4 122).

31 For "made-up" German compare Freud's dream including the words *auf Geseres* (SAII 426–9, SE5 441–4).

32 The hallucination indictment is Webster's, p.250.

NOTES TO *Chapter* 7 **Freud as a Writer: Studying the Case**

1 Clarke (*Freud*, p.229) quotes Freud as saying that "Dora" was really a continuation of his Dreambook, and also that the case histories if they were not worked over would be completely indigestible.

2 Mahony pictures it as the history of the early twentieth century, including the break-up of the Austro-Hungarian Empire and the Russian Revolution, beginning in a bedroom one hot afternoon in Odessa. This superbly cinematic vision only confirms my view that Freud's case-studies need rewriting, and to be given, as here, a wider explicit context, such as would have been known to Freud but was not relevant to the case, to bring out their richness.

3 SAVIII 135, SE17 13

4 Webster, self-elected spokesman for Anglo-Saxon common-sense, calls this etiological pass-the-parcel. Freud insists on finding the causes for the Wolfman's illness in childhood to prove his case against Jung and Adler.

5 SAVIII 146–7, SE17 27

6 Compare the title of Jung's *Wandlungen und Symbole der Libido*, translated into English as *The Psychology of the Unconscious!*

7 SAX 47, SE9 49

8 *wie Blumenfestons über Drahtgewinde*, SAVI 153, "like festoons of flowers over wire mesh" (SE7 84). The German term *Leitmotiv* was coined around 1880 by the editor of the *Bayreuther Blätter* to describe themes with specific associations in the music of Wagner. "They provided a concentrated and economical method of cross-reference and dramatic comparison" (*Oxford Companion to German Literature*, ed. Garland, p.520). Freud touches on related ideas when he sets the scene for repeating memories with *Erinnerungsumfang*, and then suggests how associated memories will repeatedly trigger each other off with the notion of related groups of ideas of *Vorstellungsgruppen* (SAII 296, SE4 295). Thomas Mann adapted the Wagnerian Leitmotiv for use in literature.

9 This is Freud's belief, that ontogeny repeats phylogeny. Scientifically discredited, it nevertheless lays the basis for the creation of mythical characters like Oedipus and his kind.

10 *Totem and Taboo*: SAIX 439, SE13 156

11 SAI 360, SE16 369

12 SAVIII 194, SE17 79

13 SAVIII 193, SE17 78. "We turn away because we are always inclined to treat unconscious processes in the soul as we do conscious ones, and to forget the deep-seated differences between the two psychic systems." This goes for the general understanding of Freud, that we must somehow be *aware* of lusting after one parent and wanting to kill the other, and for critics too. We are not. Webster (p.29) seems to treat the Oedipus Complex as if it were conscious.

14 SAVI 146–7, SE7 76–7

15 Donald Levy, *Freud Among the Philosophers*, makes this clear with his attack on the genetic fallacy. See Chapter 5, note 12.

16 The principle involved in this approach is mimesis. As art in its creations imitates nature, so psychoanalysis produces a narrative which imitates the inner life of the patient. The process is related to the mimicry of physical symptoms (cf. *Briefe an Fließ*, 20.6.98) to which repressed ideas resort to express themselves. Dreams also mimic thoughts (SAII 420, SE5 434). In this neurotic mimesis there is both a sense of a congruence and of a new creation. Thus Freud can write that "symptoms are the sexual activity of the sick" (SAV 72, SE7 163) and exclaim to Jung in wonder at what the psyche creates to help itself (*The Freud–Jung Letters*, 149F), "How bungled our reproductions are, how wretchedly we dissect the great art works of psychic nature!" The element of new creation comes to the fore with the view that paranoiacs reconstruct the world in order to survive (SAVII 193, SE12). The element of mimesis has more to do with the provisional nature of the constructions, the intermediate realm in which they exist, a kind of skating-rink of possibilities. Freud sees our minds as well as our psyches as too much given to this *Vorstellungsmimik* (*Jokes and Their Relation to the Unconscious*: SAIV 179, SE8 192) to buy ourselves a provisional freedom.

Mimesis becomes, by imitation of nature, an important part of psychoanalytic treatment. In nature, repressed ideas find some external correspondence with themselves which, however distorted, allows them to come out and exist in their own right. A similar result obtains for the patient, whom psychoanalysis provides with a provisional story. Having a story is important, for it gives us something to work on. This principle from creative-writing classes is also fundamental to the psycho-analytic process, in which transference means a kind of new story in the patient's life coming into being. This story, which is of course a living experience of a new relationship, imitates the psychic structure of whatever neurotic illness the patient suffers from. The advantage to the analyst is that the story exists in a domain he can get at. Freud writes (SA *Ergb.* 214, SE12 154), "[The new condition] has adopted all the characteristics of the illness, but presents an *artificial* illness, which is accessible to our enquiries at every point. It is *simultaneously* a piece of real experience, but made possible through particularly favorable conditions, *and* of a *provisional* nature.'

I have italicized key terms here, because it is vital to realize that the psychoanalytically encouraged story or the random memories produced on the couch are only *provisional*. They serve the doctor as a kind of text to work on. Freud brings this out in "The Wolfman" (SAVIII 168–70, SE17 50–52) in reply to accusations that the analyst forces untruth upon the patient. (Mahony approves in *Cries of The Wolfman*, p.11: "Truly one of the great contributions of psychoanalysis is that it gives us tools to doubt some of its proposed findings.') Provisionality and artificiality remind us at once of the limitations of psychoanalysis in pinning down facts, as opposed to psychic facts, and at the same time its proximity to an artistic transaction. With the phenomenon of mimesis in literature, art, *really* experienced but only *provisionally* existing, imitates nature. Psychoanalysis imitates this process, and encourages the patient to copy it too, as it were to make a mirror image of the portion of nature which is himself. For once he can do that, once any of us can see ourselves as if we were someone else, we are already on the route to better psychic health. Yet in so far as the analyst is pursuing a kind of knowledge, and acknowledgement, as the route to health, the idea of *congruence* seems to me to be an important supplement to the role of imitation. Memories bring up material, the structure of which repeats or imitates the fundamental illness. This structural congruence is what the analyst is looking out for and what he wants to call *right*. Freud argues at the beginning of "Dora" that there *is* a right story, which the patient only can't produce because she is consciously or unconsciously holding something back. "Part of her anamnestic knowledge, which the patient usually has at her disposal, doesn't come into play during the relating of this story" (SAVI 95–6, SE7 16–17).

To understand *how* Freud would claim a story to be right is vital for any critic who would face up to the abundant accusations that Freud is carried away by his own stories (Webster, p.134; Crews, p.58–9) and simply invents things. I understand him as helping the patient to create a story of her own, in order to make a provisional sense of her life and find new well-being. Once health has been rejoined the story doesn't matter. It can be discarded like the ladder to knowledge, which most recently Wittgenstein and Derrida have encouraged us to pull up behind us. Like Freud, Plato uses myth and love as ladders. There is also in Plato the sense of a possible congruence test for truth which I would like to highlight, from *The Meno*. Socrates draws a simple geometric diagram in the sand. When it is recognized/understood by the slave boy we are led to believe not only that in principle all truth *can* be recollected and thus all men are capable of the highest knowledge, but that the means to knowing this higher truth will be by analogy: the simple structure we now understand is somehow congruent with a complex figure we shall come to know, in a higher sphere. The ultimate truth Plato has in mind for us to "remember," the world of The Forms, is almost certainly geometric. We approach it in the interim with simplified but congruent examples, which are a kind of guaranteed imitation.

To return then to the psychoanalytical story, and to take an example of near-congruence which fascinated Freud, namely Galton's montages of members of the same family as nature follows patterns of duplication and variety: Freud puts up stories to see if they can be recognized by the patient as congruent. Even though he did supply patients with elements of his own life, his fallibility was not ill-intent, but a misplaced faith in his powers of divination. After all, his and Schreber's paranoid symptoms did seem strikingly to coincide. As I have stressed, Freud's thinking has spawned two legacies which have developed in surprisingly parallel and yet barely recognizable ways. In one respect, on the intellectual and literary side, Freud sets up a model for intextual reading. The patient's initial story, the material story, presents a twisted view of the world through twisted thoughts and irrational actions. The doctor responds with his interpretation. The psychic story sets the disorienting warps and bends alongside what the doctor supposes to be their causes. The patient takes stock of the distance between the two versions of himself, and a new round of telling and retelling proceeds. This fundamental dualism, between the material and the psychic, sets up a ping-pong rhythm and a double-lens perspective in an attempt to discern a provisional truth.

But in the real world of therapy the overlapping dualism can easily become an actual duel between two competing subjectivities. This is what Freud's Anglo-American critics have brought out in view of the sad fate of the actual Wolfman, Serge Pankeyeff, as he is usually known in the French transliteration of his Russian name, and to a lesser extent of Ida Bauer who was Dora.

Interestingly the therapeutic tradition approaches the concerns of the literary tradition when, instead of real fates, another question is raised as to the status of Freud's assisted autobiographies on behalf of his patients. Are they real or fantastic, and who owns them? Is it my story you invented, or your story you only pinned on me, or is it simply my story because it is my story, in which you functioned as a ghostwriter or a Socratic editor?

The problem seems to hark back to the insufficiency Freud saw in hypnotism, namely that the patient played no active role. He wanted input and he wanted to be guided by it. But this does not clear up the question of possession, nor secure the gap between the patient's memory or invention and the doctor's interpretation or invention, once the story is written down. Who is the author, can it be proved, and does it matter, once the text exists? This is the original lapse of writing, as Derrida would see it, away from the reliability of the oral hand-me-down. To it palely correspond the worries of Crews and his allies, that Freud's is "a totalizing worldview."

In a footnote to "The Ratman" (SAVII 54, SE10 181), Freud defends his fundamental therapeutic practice:

> It is never the intention with such discussions to evoke conviction. Their job is only to usher repressed complexes into consciousness, to encourage a quarrel over them on the level of conscious spiritual activity and to facilitate the appearance of new material out of the unconscious. Conviction only comes about after the patient has worked through the material that has been won back, and, as long as it vacillates, one is entitled to regard the material as not yet exhausted.

I am convinced Freud wants a congruence of two perspectives which will give liberating insight and then allow patient and doctor to move on. There is no question of possession, or a life story suddenly set in stone. The patient suddenly sees that the doctor *is* talking about her life. Like one lens fitting over another to give better sight, she fits the analyst's version over hers and suddenly focuses on why she suffers, and the suffering stops. This functional transience recalls the yearning in certain strands of Modernist art to sanctify the ephemeral and make it the key to the new canon. But it is clearly at odds with the writing down and publishing of psychoanalytic interpretations as scientific or biographical texts, and here was a difficulty which Freud, in so far as he was not consciously an artist, could hardly solve.

In Freud the psychological goal of health supplants Plato's philosophical goal of truth, but a sizeable trace of the old Idealist structure for reaching the goal remains in these metaphysically tinged stories. Wittgenstein quite rightly smelled a metaphysical rat. He called it the problem of assent. We have no way of knowing whether mental proceedings are the same as our description of them, which ought to be enough to stop us claiming the status of scientific knowledge for our speculations. Wittgenstein was the first to see that Freud's claims to science were misfounded. Freud's stories, in so far as they comprise a mixture of metaphysics, magic and faith, do not offer their descriptive-truth value as their most important claim on our attention.

17 "The Question of Lay Analysis": SA *Ergb.* 293, SE20 202

18 "Dora" (SAVI 115–17, SE7 39–41), and "The Ratman" (SAVII 100, SE10 245) both convey a sense of inner pressure seeking a physical escape.

19 Walter Hamilton, Introduction to Plato's *Symposium* (Harmondsworth 1951) p.21

20 Mahony (*Cries of The Wolfman,* p.75ff.) points out how inadequately *Nachträglichkeit,* a "lexically Janus-faced" term, "in which prospective and retrospective directions are reflected and condensed," is translated by Strachey as "deferral." Mahony echoes Derrida's insight that Freud's relation with his text is one of alternating separation and *rapprochement,* or *fort/da.*

21 Exemplifying this psychic duplication, over Dora's relations with women, for instance, stands the threat of repeated betrayal (SAV 133–5, SE7 60). SAII 295, SE4 183 refers to Galton's pictures.

22 A matter of shared content with Dostoevsky, eg., in *The Ratman* (SAVII 93, SE10 235). The greatest overlapping theme between the two is the *Doppelgänger* or "double." Freud also rehearses Tolstoy's preoccupations in *Family Happiness* (SAI 210, SE15 206) and *The Death of Ivan Ilych* (SAII 261, SE4 256).

23 SAVIII 196–8, SE17 81–4

24 SAVI 168–171, SE7 101–5

25 SAIX 363, SE13 74

26 GWIV 30–1, SE6 24–5. The music of Freud's passage is destroyed by Strachey's wordy and clumsy English. Brill is surprisingly better, but the German is best of all: *Ein beständiger Strom von Eigenbeziehung geht so durch mein Denken, von dem ich für gewöhnlich keine Kunde erhalte, der sich mir aber durch solches Namenvergessen*

verrät. Est ist, also wäre ich genötigt, alles, was ich über fremde Personen höre, mit der eigenen Person zu vergleichen, als ob meine persönlichen Komplexe bei jeder Kenntnisnahme von anderen rege würden. Dies kann unmöglich eine inviduelle Eigenschaft meiner Person sein; es muß vielmehr einen Hinweis uf die Art, wie wir überhaupt "Anderes" verstehen, enthalten. Ich habe Gründe anzunehmen, daß es bei anderen Individuen ganz ähnlich zugeht wie bei mir.

NOTES TO *Chapter 8* **Music, Painting and Comedy of the Night**

1   A fundamental process of dream-making is *Verdichtung*, which literally means condensation or thickening (*dicht* = thick). But because of its relation to the word *Dichtung*, "poetry" or "poetic truth," *Verdichtung* also means to turn into art. SAII 335–6, SE5 339–41.

2   SAV 107, SE7 30

3   SAVII 36, SE10 156

4   SAV 193–4, SE11 172–3

5   SAVII 186–7, SE12 63. This is just one illustration of how Freud's interest in language links up with that of the later Prague Linguistic Circle, linked to Husserl's phenomenology. Husserl, like Freud, was a pupil of Brentano. See Dosse, *A History of Structuralism*, Vol.1.

6   SAVIII 154–5, SE17 34–5

7   SAVII 183, SE12 58

8   SAV 194, SE11 172

9   SAVII 174, SE17 12, 48–9. Bowie (*Lacan*, p.89–90) praises what seem to be the literary consequences of this paranoid tendency in Freud himself: "The extraordinary last chapter of 'The Ego and the Id'...teems with stage characters...Freud's intricate mental dynamics are simplified...by the idea of *a person in whom there are persons...*"

10 SAVI 109–10, 114, SE7 33, 38. On "The Double" in literature, see *The Freud–Jung Letters*, 274F, and Mahony, *Freud as a Writer*, p.120.

11 GWIV 38; SE6 32

12 Here we take up again the themes of imitation necessarily in the form of mimicry and caricature, and of Derrida's *différance*. It is interesting to compare the splitting of concepts that appears in Schiller, derived from Aristotle's golden mean, to quite different effect.

13 SAVIII 183, SE17 67. Exegesis of the word "*dukh*." Freud's sense of an unconscious which plays havoc with conscious sounds and allusions, familiar intonation and meaning, gives him a natural affinity with nonsense genres. Dream-language could be Lewis Carroll's Jabberwocky, or "Professor Stanley Unwin's" nonsense language in *Carry On Regardless*. It could be the nonsense verse of Ivor Cutler, surely invented as a parody with Freud in mind, and it could find a home in the tradition of English nonsense verse, which, as Noël Malcolm (*The Origins of English Nonsense*, 1997, pp.14–16) says, "presents the form of meaning while denying us the substance... it makes funny noises... to achieve any other affect it must dilute itself with words (or at least recognizable vestiges of words) which are not nonsense." Nonsense includes parodies of logical method and formal explication, such as the cabbalist tradition of analysis of Hebrew scriptures. It is organized in rigid rhetorical patterns, and it constitutes a large measure of rebellion. The limits of the comparison seem to fall where Malcolm suggests (p.30) that "to write nonsense was not to express the strangeness of unconscious thought but to engage in a highly self-conscious stylistic game." Yet much of the inventiveness Freud attributes to an unconscious seems to come from his own conscious mind.

14 Ernst Gombrich, "Psychoanalysis and Art," in *Freud and The Twentieth Century*, p.199–201

15 Freud's name is more often connected to Surrealism, but the connection is not a rich one. "Freud, the analysts and the Surrealists each went their own way. They did not share a starting-point, nor did they intend to reach the same destination. But this did not prevent their paths crossing from the very beginning." (S. Dresden, "Psychoanalysis and Surrealism," in *Freud and the Humanities*, p.118). Gombrich (in "Verbal Wit as a Paradigm of Art: The Aesthetic Theories of Sigmund Freud," 1981, reprinted in *The Essential Gombrich*, London, 1996) details Freud's dislike of modern painting generally, and Expressionism in particular. Dresden takes up André Breton's disappointment at meeting Freud and attempting a conversation, apparently hampered by their lack of an adequate common language (though surely Freud's French was good). But both essays stress how impressed the aged Freud was with the person of Salvador Dali, and how, though Freud had reservations about how art could arise without a significant element of (pre-)conscious elaboration, Dali's painting related to the unconscious. What strikes the reader of *The Interpretation of Dreams* and the viewer of Dali's work is perhaps the notion that Dali seems to paint the *manifest* dream, whereas Freud's artistry goes into the interpretation which produces out of this brief vision a life history embedded in the *latent* dream. Because of the element of confronting the psychic puzzle which is the individual and his mind, I prefer to see Freud as a Cubist of the word. Of course, Freud had in common with the Surrealists a great interest in what happens when the mind is freed from conscious constraints, as in their concept of automatic writing. But this ideally passive, receptive state of the mind was not what Freud thought conducive to *art*. Yet Freud's therapeutic pursuit of some facility close to art which would help restore psychic health to the personality comes to depend so much on the impersonal Storifier in all of us that his insistence on art as a conscious formative process is undermined in his own legacy.

16 *Freud–Zweig Breifwechsel*, (6.11.1934), p.107

17 Harold Bloom, *The Western Canon* (1994)

18 "On the Acquisition of Fire" (1932): SAIX 452, SE22 191

19 See note 15 above for Freud's relationship to Surrealism.Virginia Woolf's comment in *Mrs. Dalloway* about wanting to preserve privacy shows the vast simplification which accompanied Freud's early intellectual reception.The stream-of-consciousness novel is a kind of bogus relation of psychoanalysis, appearing to follow the same ideal of "free association."

20 The idea that dreams present reality as if distorted by water is an idea which goes back to Aristotle, and is cited by Freud in *Dreams.*

21 Lionel Trilling, *The Liberal Imagination* (1951), pp.52–3

22 Richard Ellman, *James Joyce* (1954)

23 Anthony Burgess's *Here Comes Everybody* (1965) and *Joysprick: An Introduction to the Language of James Joyce* (1973) forge the link between Freud and Joyce, Joyce and Burgess, and thus Freud and Burgess, via the subject of wordplay and dream invention. Though the name of Freud appears only twice in *Joysprick* and not at all in the earlier volume any reader interested in the implications for poetic imagination opened up by *The Interpretation of Dreams* could do no better than to read Burgess. Freud as a character also features in Burgess's *The End of the World News.*

24 *In Search of Lost Time* Vol 2 "Within a Budding Grove."

25 Franz Kafka, *The Castle* (London, 1930, reprinted 1992), p.13. Recurring metaphors insist that K cannot trust his senses, and especially not his sight in this world which is designed to trick him and undermine him. Here is another fictional realization of Descartes's *malin génie.*

26 SAII 584–5, SE5 617–18

NOTES TO *Chapter 9* **Poetry, Truth and Freedom**

1   *On the Aesthetic Education of Man* (1795). Schiller's correspondence with Goethe is not only the obvious companion volume but offers a parallel with *The Freud–Jung Letters*. In both cases a new way of thinking arises out of the almost daily collaboration and rivalry of two great minds.

2   Not "instincts" but drives. Brown, *Freud and the Post-Freudians*, pp.10–11 spells out the confusion Strachey's mistranslation caused.

3   Erich Fromm, *The Crisis of Psychoanalysis* (1970). Amongst other points of attack, Fromm represents the "success" theme in Freud as part of bourgeois ideology.

4   *Human All Too Human*, p.326 ('The Wanderer and His Shadow,' para 67)

5   Freud's desire to free the creative imagination and the soul had political implications which were later brought out by ingenious Marxist readings of Freud. The result was a new split: a Left and a Right Freud. The richness and ambivalence of Freud's thought, with this split roughly corresponding to his revolutionary dreams and his wakeful conservatism, landed him in the same dual position in the history of thought as Hegel and Nietzsche. The Right Freud was a political liberal concerned only to modify certain conditions of capitalist society; a firm believer in individualism and the individual; and a thinker who, despite his forays into anthropology, had as fixed a view of "man" and "society" as did Kant in the eighteenth century. The Left Freud was by contrast not Freud at all, but a kind of thinker called a Left Freudian, whose concepts were apt to criticize a society which too often thwarted the full development of the individual. Capitalist society was seen to push back into a state of repression unconscious desires which, had they been fulfilled, would have complemented the humanity of the individual, not marred it. Fromm (p.18) asked, seeing the great dual potential in Freud:

Would [his followers] follow the Freud who continued the work of Copernicus, Darwin and Marx, or would they be content with the Freud whose thought and feelings were restricted to the categories of bourgeois ideology and experience? Would they develop Freud's *special* theory of the unconscious, which was related to sexuality, into a *general* theory that would take as its object the whole range of repressed psychic experiences? Would they develop Freud's special form of sexual liberation into a general form of liberation through the widening of consciousness? To put it in another and more general way: would they develop Freud's most potent and revolutionary ideas, or would they emphasize those theories that could most easily be co-opted by the consumer society?

Freud and Marx had a common heritage in the aesthetic idealism of Schiller. Freud was Marxized, in some ways compellingly, by Fromm, and most corruptly by Ludwig Marcuse. As a Marxist he lost his pessimism and secret belief in the self-sufficiency of fantasy. Only the therapist and social improver remained.

In Freud, the unconscious remains very much the individual's possession, and is her unique manufacture, based upon the psychic conditions pertaining to humanity which reach back to primitive times. Fundamentally this is the attitude to father and mother. However, in the Marxist view the unconscious contains the seeds of a fuller humanity which the present socio-political reality makes impossible to realize; thus any improvement in the human condition must begin not with private therapy but public change.

Fromm (pp.46–7) pushes against the private origins of Freud's unconscious by pointing out that Freud's concept of repressed wishes – his libido theory – exactly mirrors his position as a liberal in a capitalist society because it is based on a notion of scarcity.

It is based on the concept of scarcity, assuming that all

human strivings for lust [sic] result from the need to rid oneself from unpleasureful [sic] tensions, rather than that lust [sic] is a phenomenon of abundance aiming at a greater intensity and depth of human experience. This principle of scarcity is characteristic of middle-class thought, recalling Malthus, Benjamin Franklin, or an average businessman of the nineteenth century. There are many ramifications of this principle of scarcity and the virtue of saving, but essentially it means that the quantity of all commodities is necessarily limited, and hence that equal satisfaction for all is impossible because true abundance is impossible; in such a framework scarcity becomes a most important stimulus for human activity.

One possible answer to this is that this pattern of behavior which presupposes shortage and need is the most successful for the perpetuation of the species; that it offers the best adaptation to human circumstances which require an ideology or rationalization of voluntary restraint. Freud himself would say that the neurotic, who does not survive in spirit, is the necessary price that civilized society pays to flourish; neurosis is the real price we pay. The other answer is intuitive: love and happiness are scarce, and we recognize this from the first moment of deprivation in infancy.

But both Marx and the therapeutic Freud would say that the human being does not live happily in the unreal, deprived of a sense of connection to her environment. The therapeutic Freud rightly concentrated on love as the key to most people's sense of social reality and their fulfilled place within it; while at the same time he wisely kept open an alternative route to fulfillment, via the sublimation of pre-genital urges, for a more unusual type of person. Fromm is fond of calling Freudian man *homme machine* and seeing him as exploiting society for his needs. But this does less than justice to what we have seen is the rich but unstarry notion of love in Freud. For Freud love, but not necessarily sexual love, is our unique and active engagement with the world. Though this statement could have been made by the young Marx, in an irony I cannot explore here, to hold this view of love seems to be the opposite of believing that one's consciousness is the creation of historical forces.

Freud is also enough of a psychologist to realize that a theory which holds the present state of society responsible for individual happiness will readily be seized upon by repressed desires, and its propounding become itself a neurotic symptom. In fact, his theory of unconscious motivation nicely undoes any ideology, while his libido theory begins to explain human nature very satisfyingly by looking at what can go wrong with it under pressure from both within and without (J.A.C. Brown, *Freud and the Post-Freudians*, pp.12–13, and chapter on Fromm, especially pp.150–1). The more radical attack on Freud is based on his limited concept of human nature, open to Marxist charges that "human nature" is just an ideological construct. The experience of societies such as those which called themselves Communist last century suggests that efforts to produce "a new man" tend to lead to a decline of the human, which cannot be stated as an ideal theory, only worked with on the basis of honest, unstarry-eyed practice. In that part of Europe which was Freud's original constituency as a soul doctor, a type of "liberating" society grew up classless but full of unfair privileges; and so repressive, secretive and fearfully hypocritical that it deformed human nature far more than it enabled it to flourish. Collective neuroses were generated because many unpleasant facts about society had to be "forgotten" in order for the individual to survive. This is not conclusive evidence that no change in society can affect the general psychic health of individuals; but it certainly shows by negative example how much damage can be done when society becomes more false and unreal than any capitalist society ever managed to be, when it closes its eyes to the daily experience of human nature as it is.

6   SAII 439–42, SE5 455

7   "Dostoevsky and Parricide": SAX 272, SE21 178

8   SAI 157–8, SE15 146–7. This paragraph of the Ninth
    Introductory Lecture was written during World War I, to which
    Freud had previously referred.

9   Italo Svevo, *The Confessions of Zeno*. Compare SAI 399. The
    question arises, and is particularly well addressed in Svevo, as to
    whether self-making is black or white magic. There is after all
    an ambiguity built into the nature of regression. Regression is
    at once a form of breakdown and a chance for renewal and new
    freedom. To touch the depths of life in confronting one's origins
    and one's end are part of self-discovery and self-renewal. When
    the psyche is freed from the constraints of consciousness there
    is a chance for creation. The theory of the necessity of
    regression, especially in art and dreams, is what mitigates the
    horror of human descent. But what if the personality just
    disintegrates? The therapeutic Freud encourages a strength-
    ening return to reality. *The Interpretation of Dreams* in this respect
    establishes the foundation for a comprehensive therapy. Analysis
    has as its goal to follow the patient's way of regression and to see
    her out the other side, into health. And yet as a kind of counter-
    project, the other positive outcome of regression may be health
    through art. The disturbed patient may remain disturbed, but
    will have released her talent to write or paint or make music.
    Now *this* notion of creativity, especially where the journey
    backwards produces nothing but more confusion and a greater
    distance from life and its real tasks, may amount to a dangerous
    dabbling with shadows.

10 SAX 15, SE9 9

11 Lacan draws attention to the drama of Freud's thinking played
    out against the background of Descartes, which amounts to a
    thinning of the concept of self. Cf. Bowie, *Lacan*, pp.75–7. See
    also Chapter 5, p.157, where I spell out the milkskin theory.

12 *Briefe an Fließ* (12.12.1897), p.311

13 SAVII 89, SE10 230

14 SAVII 93, SE10 235

15 SAI 43, SE15 17; SA *Ergb.* 17, SA7 283

16 SAVII 169, SE12 43; SAX 173, SE9 146

17 SAIII 162, SE14 204

18 SAI 246, SE16 243

19 It is surely embedded in the idealism to which Freud, the would-be materialist, often turns, or in the view of Timpanaro (Chapter 2, note 9), regresses.

20 Among the phenomena testifying to this shift in value are media and editorial emphasis on "the creative process" instead of the finished work. Thus more than half the latest Pléiade edition of Proust is devoted to the *raw* material which would be transformed into his great novel. This approach helps to open up art for the leisure industries of tourism and lifestyle.

21 SAX 296, SE21 212. Richard Ellmann ('Freud and Biography," in *Freud and the Humanities*) pins down Freud's dual view of art and looks at its implication for biography, alongside the psychological approach he provides.

22 On envy as a prominent motif in Freud, see Forrester, "Justice, Envy and Psychoanalysis," in *Dispatches from the Freud Wars*. In one way this view of envy is just a general theory of progress, what Harold Bloom calls the *agon* driving one generation to supersede the next. Nietzsche also saw envy as holding the bourgeois world together.

23 Mahony, *Freud as a Writer*, p.12

24 SAVI 163, SE7 95

25 Erik Erikson, "The First Psychoanalyst," in *Freud and the Twentieth Century*, p.92. The "project" was his self-analysis. The reason why Freud's oeuvre is so problematic is that it may be the form sublimation of his own problems took, and as such a

description of reality, or it may be only about himself. Here the relationship Freud understood to obtain between narcissism and sublimation is of the highest interest. Both make use of the energy that comes from unfulfilled wishes, but only one relates to a reality outside the self. One may feel one is talking about an object outside the self, that is, the real world, whereas the object may only be a continuation of oneself. The most one can do is bear in mind Freud's father complex and his propensity to envy and to see if something remains as a description of a wider human reality than his own; to continue to ask whether there is an unconscious, and where the usefulness of this hypothesis might continue to lie.

26 SAVI 88, SE7 8

27 Webster, pp. 166–7

28 SAII 285, SE4 282

29 The dream of being Mr. Joyeuse who saves a life. See Chapter 5. For the feeling that his readers won't believe him see Chapter 3, note 40.

30 Alfred de Vigny, *Servitude et grandeur militaires* (1835). I think of this book when Freud expresses incredulity about talk of his Oedipus Complex being banned on the Austrian war front. He failed to see where his ideas put into practice as extreme personal libertarianism would lead.

SELECT BIBLIOGRAPHY

Freud's relevance stretches immensely wide. The books listed here reflect where he has led me. The list is not intended as a scholarly bibliography in what is itself an almost immeasurable field.

Aristotle, *The "Art" of Rhetoric*, tr. J. H. Freese, London, 1926

Bettelheim, Bruno, *Freud and Man's Soul*, Harmondsworth, 1983

Bloom, Harold, *The Western Canon*, London, 1994

Bowie, Malcolm, *Lacan*, London, 1991

Brown, J.A.C., *Freud and the Post-Freudians*, Harmondsworth, 1964

Bouveresse, Jacques, *Wittgenstein Reads Freud*, Princeton, 1995

Burgess, Anthony, *Joysprick: An Introduction to the Language of James Joyce*, London, 1973

— *Here Comes Everybody*, London, 1965

Cesarani, David, *Arthur Koestler: The Homeless Mind*, London, 1998

Clark, Ronald C., *Freud: The Man and The Cause*, London, 1982

Crews, Frederick, *et al.*, *The Memory Wars*, London, 1997

Derrida, Jacques, *Writing and Difference*, tr. Alan Bass, London, 1978

— *The Postcard: From Socrates to Freud and Beyond*, tr. Alan Bass, London, 1987

Dixon, Peter, *Rhetoric*, London, 1971

Dosse, François, *A History of Structuralism*, 2 vols, tr. Deborah Gassman, Minneapolis, 1997

Ellmann, Richard, *James Joyce*, London, 1954

Empson, William, *Seven Types of Ambiguity*, 1930

Forrester, John, *Dispatches from the Freud Wars*, London, 1997

Fromm, Erich, *The Crisis of Psychoanalysis*, 1970, reprinted New York, 1991

— *The Art of Loving*, 1956

Gardner, S., *Irrationality and the Philosophy of Psychoanalysis*, Cambridge, 1993

Gay, Peter, *Freud: A Life for Our Times*, London, 1988

Goethe, Johann Wolfgang von, *Gedenkausgabe der Werke, Briefe und Gespräche*, Zurich, 1949

Gombrich, Ernst, *The Essential Gombrich*, London, 1996

Gregory, Richard L. (ed.), *The Oxford Companion to Mind*, Oxford, 1987

Gunn, Daniel, *Psychoanalysis and Fiction*, Cambridge, 1988

Habermas, Jürgen, *Knowledge and Human Interests*, tr. Jeremy J. Shapiro, London, 1978

Hoffman, Frederick J., *Freudianism and the Literary Mind*, Baton Rouge, 1957

Horden, Peregrine (ed.), *Freud and the Humanities*, London, 1985

Jones, Ernest, *The Life and Work of Sigmund Freud*, 3 vols, London, 1953–7

Joyce, James, *Finnegans Wake*, 1939

Kenny, Anthony (ed.), *The Wittgenstein Reader*, Oxford, 1994

Kofman, Sarah, *Freud and Fiction*, tr. Sarah Wykes, London, 1991

Körner, Stephen, *Kant*, Harmondsworth, 1955

Lawrence, D.H., *Fantasia of the Unconscious* and *Psychoanalysis and the Unconscious*, Harmondsworth, 1971

Levy, Donald, *Freud among the Philosophers: The Psychoanalytic Unconscious and its Philosophical Critics*, London, 1996

Lieberman, E. James, *Acts of Will: The Life and Work of Otto Rank*, New York, 1985

Mahony, Patrick J., *Freud as a Writer*, New York, 1982

— *Cries of The Wolfman*, New York, 1984

McAlister, Linda L. (ed.), *The Philosophy of Brentano*, London, 1976

Nelson, Benjamin (ed.), *Freud and the Twentieth Century*, London, 1958

Nietzsche, Friedrich, *Human All Too Human*, tr. R.J. Hollingdale, Cambridge, 1986

Norris, Christopher, *Derrida*, London, 1987

Phillips, Adam, *On Flirtation*, London, 1994

—— *Terrors and Experts*, London, 1995

Proust, Marcel, *In Search of Lost Time*, tr. Scott Moncrieff and Terence Kilmartin, 6 vols, London, 1992

Schiller, Friedrich, *On the Aesthetic Education of Man*, ed. Elizabeth M. Wilkinson and L.A. Willoughby, Oxford, 1967

Arthur Schnitzler, *Gesammelte Werke*, Berlin, 1912

Steiner, George, "Linguistics and Literature," in *Linguistics at Large*, ed. Noël Minnis, 1973

Storr, Anthony, *Solitude* (aka *The School of Genius*), London, 1988

Svevo, Italo, *The Confessions of Zeno*, London, 1930

Timpanaro, Sebastiano, *The Freudian Slip*, tr. Kate Soper, London, 1976

Trilling, Lionel, *The Liberal Imagination*, London, 1951

—— *Freud and the Crisis in Our Culture*, Boston, 1955

Webster, Richard, *Why Freud was Wrong: Sin, Science and Psychoanalysis*, London, 1995

Wimsatt, William K., Jr, and Brooks, Cleanth, *Literary Criticism: A Short History*, first edition, New York, 1957

Wittgenstein, Ludwig, *see* Kenny

Wollheim, Richard, *Freud*, second edition, London, 1991

Index

Index

Index